Fables of Development

Contemporary Hispanic and Lusophone Cultures

Series Editors
L. Elena Delgado, University of Illinois at Urbana-Champaign
Niamh Thornton, University of Liverpool

Series Editorial Board
Jo Labanyi, New York University
Chris Perriam, University of Manchester
Paul Julian Smith, CUNY Graduate Center

This series aims to provide a forum for new research on modern and contemporary hispanic and lusophone cultures and writing. The volumes published in Contemporary Hispanic and Lusophone Cultures reflect a wide variety of critical practices and theoretical approaches, in harmony with the intellectual, cultural and social developments that have taken place over the past few decades. All manifestations of contemporary hispanic and lusophone culture and expression are considered, including literature, cinema, popular culture, theory. The volumes in the series will participate in the wider debate on key aspects of contemporary culture.

14 Paul Julian Smith, *Dramatized Societies: Quality Television in Spain and Mexico*

15 Joan Ramon Resina, *The Ghost in the Constitution: Historical Memory and Denial in Spanish Society*

16 José Colmeiro, *Peripheral Visions/Global Sounds: From Galicia to the World*

17 Regina Galasso, *Translating New York: The City's Languages in Iberian Literatures*

18 Daniel F. Silva, *Anti-Empire: Decolonial Interventions in Lusophone Literatures*

19 Luis I. Prádanos, *Postgrowth Imaginaries: New Ecologies and Counterhegemonic Culture in Post-2008 Spain*

20 Liz Harvey-Kattou, *Contested Identities in Costa Rica: Constructions of the Tico in Literature and Film*

21 Cecilia Enjuto-Rangel, Sebastiaan Faber, Pedro García-Caro, and Robert Patrick Newcomb, eds, *Transatlantic Studies: Latin America, Iberia, and Africa*

22 Ana Paula Ferreira, *Women Writing Portuguese Colonialism in Africa*

23 Esther Gimeno Ugalde, Marta Pacheco Pinto and Ângela Fernandes, eds, *Iberian and Translation Studies: Literary Contact Zones*

24 Ben Bollig, *Moving Voices: Poetry on Screen in Argentine Cinema*

25 Daniel F. Silva, *Empire Found: Racial Identities and Coloniality in Twenty-First-Century Portuguese Popular Cultures*

26 Dean Allbritton, *Feeling Sick: The Early Years of AIDS in Spain*

27 María Chouza-Calo, Esther Fernández and Jonathan Thacker, eds, *Daring Adaptations, Creative Failures, and Experimental Perfomances in Iberian Theatre*

Fables of Development

Capitalism and Social Imaginaries in Spain (1950–1967)

ANA FERNÁNDEZ-CEBRIÁN

Translated by Luis de Juan Hatchard

LIVERPOOL UNIVERSITY PRESS

For my parents

"—Porque es un poco así, el tiempo transcurre a hurtadillas, disimulando, no le vemos andar. Pero de pronto volvemos la cabeza y encontramos imágenes que se han desplazado a nuestras espaldas, fotos fijas, sin referencia de fecha, como las figuras de los niños del escondite inglés, a los que nunca se pillaba en movimiento. Por eso es tan difícil luego ordenar la memoria, entender lo que estaba antes y lo que estaba después."

[—Because that's more or less how it is, time steals by so furtively that we don't even notice it, we don't see it passing. But all of a sudden we turn around and find images that have moved behind our backs, frozen photographs that bear no dates, like the figures of the children in the game of Red Light, who could never be caught moving. That's why it's so difficult later on to put the things we remember in order, to be sure of what happened before and what happened later.]

Carmen Martín Gaite, *El cuarto de atrás* (1978)

"Qualsevol nit pot sortir el sol"

Jaume Sisa (1975)

First published 2023 by
Liverpool University Press
4 Cambridge Street
Liverpool
L69 7ZU

Copyright © 2023 Ana Fernández-Cebrián

Ana Fernández-Cebrián has asserted her rights to be identified as
the author of this book in accordance with the Copyright,
Designs and Patents Act 1988.

All rights reserved. No part of this book may be reproduced,
stored in a retrieval system, or transmitted, in any form or by any means,
electronic, mechanical, photocopying, recording, or otherwise,
without the prior written permission of the publisher.

British Library Cataloguing-in-Publication data
A British Library CIP record is available

ISBN 978-1-80207-805-3 cased

Typeset in Borges by
Carnegie Book Production, Lancaster
Printed and bound by CPI Group (UK) Ltd, Croydon CR0 4YY

Contents

Acknowledgements	ix
Introduction	1

I. Dreamworlds of Development: Cold War Imaginaries in Franco's Spain

1. Fables of Intervention	31
2. Fables of Outer Space	71

II. Providential Capitalism

3. Fables of Chance	115
4. Fables of Grace	149
Afterword	179
Works Cited	187
Index	205

Acknowledgements

In order for someone to write a book, many people contribute their knowledge, their work or their affection. For this reason, I would especially like to thank all the workers at the Sidney Kimmel Cancer Center at Jefferson Hospital in Philadelphia and the Public Health workers in Spain. They all worked hard so that we patients could receive our cancer treatments and they accompanied us in the hospitals when no one could do so because there was still no vaccine. We will never forget their efforts in such a difficult time.

I feel very fortunate for the conversations and support provided by both colleagues and friends who helped me during these years in the Latin American and Iberian Cultures Department at Columbia University: Carlos Alonso, Orlando Bentancor, Bruno Bosteels, Ronald Briggs, Hernán Díaz, Jerónimo Duarte-Riascos, Patricia Grieve, Tianna Hewitt, Maja Horn, Ana Paulina Lee, Seth Kimmel, Alfred MacAdam, Alberto Medina, Graciela Montaldo, Kosmas Pissakos, Wadda Rios Font, Eunice Rodríguez-Ferguson and Alessandra Russo. I am also grateful to the students who offered valuable comments and questions in different courses and seminars. My gratitude goes to Columbia University in general for facilitating the development of this book through a Lenfest Junior Faculty Development Grant that funded both the translation of the manuscript and the reproduction of images. For their guidance and intellectual engagement, I would also like to thank the members of the dissertation committee that is at the origin of this book, written at Princeton University: Germán Labrador, Ángel Loureiro, Rachel Price, Arcadio Díaz-Quiñones and Rubén Gallo. Thanks to Fernando Acosta for helping me get some of the images reproduced from the Princeton University Library and to Martí Sales for granting me permission to reproduce the photograph of Pepe Sales that appears on the cover. I am particularly grateful to Chloé Johnson for being such a kind and helpful commissioning editor and to Liverpool University Press for believing in this project.

It gives me great joy to express my gratitude to so many friends, colleagues and interlocutors for having been able to share conversations about some topics related to the content of the book as well as about the writing process: Yasmina Aidi, Iria Ameixeiras and Pablo García Martínez, Juan Andrade, Eduardo Bravo, Jennifer Calles, Cristina Catalina, Antonio Córdoba, Juan Escourido, Marta Fernández and Javier Alonso, Rodrigo Fernández, Felisa Ferraz and José Calvo, Marta Ferrer, Elena Fraj and Miguel Ángel Ramos, Belén Gopegui, Liz Hochberg and Francisco Robles, Daniel Hübner, Vega López, Luis López Carrasco, Almudena Marín-Cobos, Andrea Toribio, Gonzalo Torné, Carlos Varón and Juan Manuel Zaragoza. Many thanks also to my wonderful gang of friends: las Anas, Noelia, Fanana, Esther, Lorena, Carmen and my virtual friends. Miguel Caballero has been an exceptional interlocutor and friend for the past decade, and I very much appreciate his valuable comments and that he has been the "custodian" of the manuscript every time I went under the knife. I am deeply grateful for the beautiful translation of the text into English by the team formed by Luis de Juan Hatchard and Twister, his bilingual Border Collie; their attentive reading and suggestions, as well as their sense of humour were of great help in the final stretch of writing.

Although he is no longer able to read it, this book is dedicated to my father, Antonio, who always supported me with affection in my decisions; he also helped me get many of the files that are part of this study, an attempt to understand what it was like in the country where our parents —and all those who were born or grew up in the 50s and 60s— lived. It is also dedicated to my mother, Ana, a person whose generosity improves the lives of so many people, and to the rest of my wonderful family, Víctor, Patricia, Elena and Guille. The whole process of writing this book has been possible thanks to Víctor Pueyo, who has accompanied me and enlightened me on this journey with his kindness, his joy, and his wisdom so that life and writing can go on.

Introduction

"Llaman milagro al desarrollo,
pero el milagro está en el reparto"

[They call development a miracle,
but the miracle is in the distribution]
  Anonymous poster placed on the door of the church of Sástago (Zaragoza) (1973)
(Fernández Clemente and Forcadell 7)

"Development is the new name for peace"
  Populorum Progressio. Encyclical letter of Pope Paul VI (1967)

In a speech delivered in Murcia on April 28, 1946, General Francisco Franco described his role as the person primarily responsible for the nation's economic policy in these terms: "Nadie nos ha de regalar nada: hemos de deberlo todo a nuestro esfuerzo; y tened presente que yo no soy el Rey Mago que os traiga las cosas de regalo, sino el Jefe de un Estado que vengo a deciros: 'Hay que luchar, hay que trabajar'" [No one has to give us anything as a gift: we must owe everything to our efforts; and keep in mind that I am not the Magician King who brings you things as a gift, but the Head of State who has come to tell you: "We must fight, we must work"] ("Pensamiento" 937). In this speech, made weeks after the Spanish government was condemned through a United Nations General Assembly resolution, the Caudillo evoked the figure of the Magi, providential donor agents in the Catholic tradition, to warn his compatriots of the limits of his management at the head of an autarchic regime relegated to isolation. Seven years later, in 1953, the same comparison that Franco had presented to describe his role was used by the *ABC* newspaper in an article celebrating the policy proposals of the newly elected president of the United States, Dwight Eisenhower. For the Madrilenian newspaper, following the termination of the Marshall Plan aid to European countries, Eisenhower would cease to play the role of "Rey Mago y el prestamista del mundo" [Magician King and the world's moneylender]

("La administración" 57). The new American administration was praised for its intention to put an end to "la era de economía dirigida de los presidentes Roosevelt y Truman" [the era of command economy of Presidents Roosevelt and Truman] and to inaugurate what the newspaper described as "el comienzo de un nuevo ensayo político de individualismo capitalista" [the beginning of a new political trial of capitalist individualism], which would operate as the main "factor de cohesión mundial del que depende hoy en gran parte todo el sistema de occidente" [factor of world cohesion on which the whole system of the West depends to a great extent today] (57).

That same year, in September 1953, the Franco government sealed its alliance with the United States in the Pact of Madrid, bilateral agreements on economic aid, technical assistance and mutual defence. Although the country had not benefited from the Marshall Plan aid, the Pact was a continuation of the financial support to Franco's regime that the US government had initiated in 1950 with the authorization of an initial loan of 62.5 million dollars from the Export-Import Bank (Lieberman 39), following General Franco's announcement of his cooperation in the war with Korea.[1] After the evidence of the failure of autarchic policies that had led the country to the brink of bankruptcy, General Franco reorganized his cabinet in 1957, incorporating into the executive a group of technocrats who willingly obeyed the dictates of the institutions into which the country integrated from 1958: the International Monetary Fund, the World Bank and the Organization for European Economic Co-operation.[2] The government technocrats, in many cases linked to the Opus Dei lay Catholic order, were in charge of carrying out the reforms that materialized in the 1959 Stabilization and Liberalization Plan, and in the subsequent indicative planning of the three Economic and Social Development Plans (1964–1967, 1968–1971 and 1972–1975).

Developmentalism in Franco's Spain was forged in this complex dialectic between the sovereign power of the dictator, understood as a theologico-political power, and the emergence of an authoritarian technocratic regime in which new modes of governance promoted and ordered emerging forms of life. The collective fictions that I have called "fables of development" mediate at the crossroads between National–Catholic ideology, economic liberalism and

---

1 This international financing continued into the 1960s, a decade in which "more than a billion dollars in additional funding was made available from foreign sources through various loan and credit devices" (Payne, "The Franco Regime" 474).

2 Alberto Ullastres and Mariano Navarro Rubio were appointed Ministers of Commerce and Finance, and Laureano López Rodó, head of the Government Secretariat and the Office of Economic Coordination and Programming. In 1962, López Rodó became the commissioner of the Development Plan, and a new member of Opus Dei, Gregorio López Bravo, joined the government as Secretary of Industry.

Introduction 3

the political theology of Franco's dictatorship, and originate from a reflection by Jacques Derrida in which he demands a careful analysis of the social fantasies that sustain capitalism: "No capital without an accredited fable" (39). According to his reflections, the fabulous "also engages act, gesture, action . . . in organizing, disposing discourse in such a way as to recount, to put living beings on stage, to accredit the interpretation of a narrative, to *faire savoir*, to make knowledge" (35–36). On the basis of this proposal, this book examines the imaginaries that shape fictions, political discourses and social practices that revolve around the staging of "fables" about capital in which the historical "know-how" is publicly administered, as well as the political and moral lessons that can be drawn from them. In this regard, the notion of "social imaginaries" is taken in the sense proposed by Cornelius Castoriadis in *The Imaginary Institution of Society* (1975) when referring to the imaginary social meanings that are part of the collective generative activity that shapes the self-understanding of communities, and that are embodied in institutions which they animate and transform. Following these approaches, the analysis I propose of the transition from autarchy to technocratic capitalism is based on the exposition of this process as a socially instituted problematic at the imaginary level and fictitiously portrayed in a set of providential narratives. The study of social imaginaries in literary texts, cinema, newsreels, comics and journalistic sources, among other cultural artifacts, will lead us to understand why General Franco alluded to the figure of the Magi to talk about his economic responsibility (as pointed out at the beginning of this introduction), why visions of strange airships proliferated in the Spanish skies, or why charity and games of chance became devices for the redistribution of wealth or resources in the 50s and 60s.

The "fables of development" examined in this book are characterized by the recreation of a providential content that modernity often ostensibly denies; thus, in the wake of recent debates about the theological and "enchanting" implications of capitalism, I focus on a basic paradox: Why was the so-called "Spanish economic miracle", supposedly a secular, rational and technocratic process, portrayed through narratives in which providential, supernatural or extraordinary elements were often involved?[3] To answer this question, I examine the cultural fictions and collective social life of the 1950s and 1960s, when Spain moved from autarchy to the project of industrial and tourist development. Beyond the narratives about progress, modernity and consumer satisfaction on a global and national level, the cultural archives

---

3 On the processes of "capitalist enchantment" and the "deification" of the market, see Lears (1994), McCarraher (2019), Bennett (2001), Federici and Linebaugh (2019).

of the period offer intellectual findings about the expectations of a social majority who lived in precariousness and who did not have sufficient income to acquire the consumer goods that were advertised. Through the scrutiny of interdisciplinary archives, each chapter of this book offers an analysis of the social imaginaries about the circulation and distribution of capitals in the period from 1950, when Franco's government began to integrate into international markets and institutions following its agreements with the United States, to 1967, when the implementation of the First Development Plan (1964–1967) was completed.

The philosopher Louis Althusser spoke of "uneven development" (177) to describe the process by which, in any social formation, the *décalage* between the economic, political and ideological instances not only does not pose a threat but is completely necessary for the underpinning of its coherence as a historical totality. In the case of Spain in the 1950s and 60s, this *décalage* was expressed through a series of social imaginaries that mediated the contradictions between economic liberalism and theologico-political ideology. These contradictions, which represent the contradictions inherent in the immanent uneven development in any social formation, characterized the very possibility of Francoist developmentalism. In this sense, the notion of uneven development helps us to explain the proliferation of providential narratives in the literature, audiovisual arts, media, and political discourses in the transition from autarchy to technocratic capitalism. In the essay "The Experiments of Time: Providence and Realism", Fredric Jameson described providential narratives as forms that articulate notions of destiny and providence in a historical time that was beginning to be experienced in modernity as a secular time. The "providential" is examined as an overcoming of the antinomy between free will and predestination, between voluntarism and fatalism, that unfolds in narrative structures in which the notions of salvation, miracle or resurrection are re-signified in a secular key. At a moment marked by the growing pressure of the monetary economy, Jameson highlights the "synchronic role of money" (223) as the "nexus" of individual and collective destinies, making the financial essence of the notion of "providence", understood in both a sacred and secular sense, key to analysing the fictions of a historical conjuncture.

The social imaginaries that are articulated at transitional junctures such as the one analysed in these pages are precisely those that help us to understand the contradictions between the economic, political and ideological instances of a social formation in the space of historical change.[4] The miraculous, prodigious

---

4 On the specificity of periods of transition see Balibar (1990) and Toscano (2014).

Introduction

or supernatural elements that populated the "fables of development" used by the Francoist regime and creators sympathetic to the dictatorship to celebrate the achievements of economic growth and the flow of capital were endowed with new meanings in the aesthetic and political resistance practices of anti-Francoist creators. Their cultural productions made possible not only the interruption, displacement or symbolic destruction of the narratives enunciated by the ideological apparatuses of the Francoist state, but also the creation of spaces of communication in which alternative imaginaries promoted reflection on the possibility of new forms of common life that challenged those narratives. On the basis of both the experiences of the people who lived through the Francoist dictatorship and of their imagination of a future that includes us, it is possible to elaborate new historical sequences that contain proposals for the transformation of the current economic, political and social model— a model that harbours historical and cultural continuities and discontinuities that shape our own experience of the present and our imagination of other possible futures.

The first part of this book, entitled "Dreamworlds of Development: Cold War Imaginaries in Franco's Spain", adds a new dimension to the existing scholarship in Spain's positioning within the Cold War global order. By examining an unexplored corpus of cultural objects and social practices, the chapters in this section propose an analysis about alleged or fantasized sightings of unidentified aerospace phenomena, and their representation in space science fiction. In the Spanish context, the presence of UFOs and aerospace technologies was commonly interpreted as a providential sign that permeated and shaped new social and political imaginaries about US intervention, the role of Catholicism and the economic liberalization policies implemented in Spain after its incorporation into the Western capitalist bloc. The second part, "Providential Capitalism", studies social and cultural institutions that the mass media controlled by the state presented as Smithian "invisible hands" of wealth and resource distribution: national lotteries, games of chance, raffles, contests, charitable policies and practices, and the functioning of state capitalism itself. In this complex relationship between the proliferation of gambling opportunities, the emerging consumer culture and the management of social inequality, the chapters in this section describe how the liberal notion of "chance" and the Catholic idea of "providence" overlapped in fictions, social practices and institutional discourses. Such ideological overlapping, I contend, is particularly significant inasmuch as it functions as the symbolic matrix of social imaginaries of circulation and distribution of capital in this period.

Fables of Development establishes a dialogue with other works that have examined this period, such as *The Mobile Nation: Spain Changes Skin (1954-1964)*

(2011) by Tatjana Pavlović, a book on the so-called "hinge decade" conceived as a "socio-cultural history of consumerism" (3).[5] Following this line of research, my goal is to emphasize the materiality of social imaginaries about capital, with the hope that this research can serve as a companion to Patricia Keller's (2016) and Jo Labanyi's (2000) work on aesthetic and political practices in post-war Spain. Reflections on the political characteristics of the Francoist regime have also been informed by books such as Tatjana Gajić's *Paradoxes of Stasis: Literature, Politics, and Thought in Francoist Spain* (2019), which examines the regime's concern over its capacity to guarantee its reform, continuity and survival, and William Viestenz's *By the Grace of God: Francoist Spain and the Sacred Roots of Political Imagination* (2014), which studies the literary productions of authors that echoed the omnipresent Francoist sacred and deconstructed the dictatorship's categories of political imagination. This book engages in conversation with these works and other studies on cinematic fictions of the period, such as Steven Marsh's *Popular Spanish Film Under Franco: Comedy and the Weakening of the State* (2006) —a pioneering analysis of comedy during Francoism that makes us better understand the role of resistance played by popular culture and how the cultural agenda of the regime was weakened by the very same popular practices it sought to foster— and both Jorge Pérez's *Confessional Cinema: Religion, Film, and Modernity in Spain's Development Years, 1960–1975* (2017) and Elizabeth Scarlett's *Religion and Spanish Film: Luis Buñuel, the Franco Era, and Contemporary Directors* (2014), both of which explore the cultural and sociopolitical understanding of religion and the Catholic Church as driving forces in the national modernization process.[6]

---

5 Tatjana Pavlović asserts that in the so-called "hinge decade" (1954–1964) "Franco's regime ceased to be providential and became technocratic. Spaniards would no longer be preparing for the heavenly paradise, but enjoying an earthly one" (1). Along with the recognition of this secularization process that occurred during the development years, I argue that economic and social transformations in the transition from autarchy to technocratic capitalism were portrayed through providential narratives filled with supernatural and extraordinary elements.

6 Noël Valis has looked into the important but largely overlooked connections between religious faith and modern realism in *Sacred Realism: Religion and the Imagination in Modern Spanish Narrative* (2010). This same approach is explored by Daniel García-Donoso in *Escrituras postseculares: sedimentos de la religión en la narrativa española (1950–2010)* (2018).

"The Spanish Miracle": Development and Re-enchantment of the Market in the Era of the Economic Miracles

The 1959 Stabilization and Liberalization Plan was a project that Franco initially welcomed with reluctance, and which included a series of reforms related to the liberalization of trade and imports, greater facilities for foreign capital investment, new controls on the fiscal deficit and inflation, and the homologation of exchange rates with the dollar (López and Rodríguez 138; Núñez and Tortella 562–567; Prados de la Escosura 111–168). After a year of recession, between 1961 and 1964 the Gross Domestic Product grew at an annual rate of 8.7% and per capita income surpassed that of Ireland, Greece, Portugal and the countries of Eastern Europe (González González 394; Gallo 343). The agricultural working population, which in 1950 still represented 50% of the total, fell to 28% in 1968, and between five and six million inhabitants left their rural communities to seek work in the cities or abroad. In this sense, foreign currency, both in the form of remittances sent by emigrant workers and money flowing in through tourism —which grew from 7.5 million tourists in 1961 to more than 17 million in 1966— were decisive for the country's economic growth (Longhurst 17–19). Using these macroeconomic data, the technocrats began to propagate the political myth of Spain's "economic miracle" as a roadmap for what in the 1960s they envisioned as "an administered post-ideological society" (Pavlović 10), whose legitimacy rested not on democratic popular will but on "efficiency" in guaranteeing development and access to consumption.

As early as 1949, Alberto Ullastres, Minister of Commerce from 1957 to 1965 and a member of Opus Dei, extended an invitation to economists such as Friedrich von Hayek, Walter Eucken, Joseph Schumpeter and Wilhelm Röpke.[7] Hayek gave a series of lectures accompanied by his disciple at the London School of Economics Lucas Beltrán, the only Spaniard present at the annual sessions of the Mont Pèlerin Society, and by Joan Sardá, future architect of the 1959 Stabilization and Liberalization Plan. Since the 1950s, members of Opus Dei —in the role of economists, executives, educators, legislators and opinion makers— became agents of the neoliberal realignment in Spain as well as throughout the Spanish-speaking countries.[8] The "Navarra School

---

7 Ullastres was a disciple of economist Heinrich von Stackelberg, a former member of the Nazi Party, a leading figure of ordoliberalism and a tenured lecturer at the Complutense University of Madrid (Ban 102–115).

8 The Spanish technocratic economists worked together with their fellow ideologues who were close to Opus Dei, such as Rafael Calvo Serer, Gonzalo Fernández de la Mora and Florentino Pérez Embid —epigones of the radical right-wing organization Acción Española (1931–1937) and its founder Ramiro de Maeztu. These

8   *Fables of Development*

of Catholic Neoliberalism" (Moreton 88) operated as a project of economic theology that can be added to the network of neoliberal schools, although with its own characteristics based on its National-Catholic roots.[9] According to Bethany Moreton, where Chicago School economists "quietly outsourced the chore of discipline, the subsidy of care labor, and the function of private wealth capture to the New Christian Right", the Navarra School "forthrightly evangelized the gospel of the free market's dependence on sacred, intimate forms of unfreedom" (137). Its project thus joined other economic currents gathered in the Mont Pèlerin Society, such as "the Austrian-inflected Hayekian legal theory, the Chicago School of neoclassical economics, and the German Ordoliberals" (Mirowski 42). The uniqueness of the Navarra School would lie in the expansion of a "spiritualized" capitalism, because while other economic schools advertised their products as positive science, Opus Dei technocrats, instead, explicitly "justified business theology and embraced the intimate task of transforming souls for markets" (Moreton 91). In this way, the technocratic authoritarianism of Opus Dei could appear as a mediator between the ideological code of National-Catholicism and that of technocratic developmentalism. Opus Dei acted as a vanishing mediator that was able to overcome and suture the contradictions between economic development and ideological "backwardness" that were restructured at the political level with the implementation of recurring technocratic policies that remained embedded in a neo-feudal ideological matrix.

With the emergence of the European welfare states, the neoliberal schools reinforced a model that rejected the idea that distributive justice could be part of the attributions of the state, whose only effective social policy should be to guarantee the legal and juridical order for society to develop as a business. It was a patriarchal and authoritarian vision of wealth distribution, anchored in a patrimonial model of social stratification; a vision in which individual responsibility and charity in its different forms were considered the only remedies to solve the problems of structural poverty. The Opus Dei technocrats thus continued the National-Catholic project that the proto-fascist ideologue Ramiro de Maeztu had imagined for Spain (Villacañas 413–480; Botti 160–176; Arbaiza 154–186). As a project it aimed to consolidate a Catholic capitalism sustained by a depoliticized

---

ideologists formed part of the founding group of the magazine *Arbor*, of the CSIC and of the publishing house Rialp, spaces from which they disseminated the work of the ordoliberal and neoliberal economists (González Cuevas 30).

9 The name "Navarra School" is taken by Moreton from the flagship university from which members of the elite ultra-conservative movement disseminated their proposals for economic policy, business training and religious practice to the Hispanic arena.

Introduction

middle-class society that could be integrated into the international economic circuits. Florentino Pérez Embid, Opus Dei member and Secretary of Censorship, summarized this ambivalent attitude towards this integration in the formula "Hispanization in the ends, Europeanization in the means" (quoted in Casanova 29).[10] By 1971, in the presence of General Vernon Walters, Richard Nixon's envoy, General Franco affirmed categorically that the developmentalist project had successfully completed the consolidation of this social model in Spain with the statement: "Mi verdadero monumento no es aquella Cruz del Valle [de los Caídos], sino la clase media española" [My true monument is not that Cross in the Valley [of the Fallen], but the Spanish middle class] (quoted in García Escudero 254). In this sense, authors such as Emmanuel Rodríguez (2022) and José Luis Villacañas (2022) have recently considered Spanish developmentalism as a "passive revolution". According to this Gramscian-inspired interpretation, the authoritarian state would have undertaken the economic modernization of the country without carrying out the Fordist social pact.

During the 1950s and 1960s, Spanish capitalism was inscribed in what institutions such as the Banco Hispano-Americano called in 1962 the "Mística del Desarrollo" [Mystique of Development] (21), a paradigm that presented economic development and economic freedom as a source of legitimacy for the creation of organizations that shaped a new political but also moral order. Shortly before the entry of the technocrats into government in 1957, the Opus Dei intellectual Rafael Calvo Serer had published *La aproximación de los neoliberales a la actitud tradicional* (1956), an essay in which he conversed with some of the economists of the Mont Pèlerin Society to highlight the existence in Spain of a strong state that, sponsored by the National-Catholic sector of the Francoist regime, could allow the development of the economy under the umbrella of the new neoliberal rationalities. In his attempt to envision the integration of Spain at the international level, Calvo Serer adhered to the discourses of the intellectual architects of the global neoliberal movement, who since their founding meeting at Mont Pèlerin in Easter 1947 had focused on Christian theology and its relationship with the economy (Moreton 88–90).

The principles of economic liberalism that informed the post-war economies of the capitalist bloc during the Cold War were heirs to the providentialist theodicy that thinkers such as Adam Smith had articulated

---

10 In February 1962, Spain submitted its first application for membership in the European Economic Community and, despite a political veto, the government managed to ensure that the Spanish economy benefited from the European economic boom of the 1960s.

10   *Fables of Development*

in a metaphysical and moral vision that explained the workings of the market. In his famous allegory of the invisible hand, the *manus gubernationis* of scholastic philosophy returned as a theological metaphor of divine providence expressed in an order produced by a contingent play of immanent effects (Graeber 44; Oslington 429–38). In this vision, the invisible hand of the market worked to turn human commerce and the desires circulating around it into a structure that decades later economist Milton Friedman would describe as "the miracle of the free market" (Vogl 28). In this sense, the numerous economists of the second half of the twentieth century were explicit about the need to promote a "gospel of business efficiency" (Carr and Fusi 81) to justify not only an idea of the subject as "entrepreneur of himself" (Foucault 214), but also to promote competition in markets as the ultimate actualization and expression of human freedom. As Giorgio Agamben (2011) pointed out more recently, in the modern economy there would be a secular transfer of the Christian conception of history and Trinitarian providence, which emerged under the sign of the economic paradigm of *oikonomia*, understood as the divine activity of self-revelation, government and care of the world. According to Jorge Pérez, it is precisely in the transition from Francoist autarchy to developmentalism that "the shift from political theology, which pivoted on the figure of the sovereign invested with divine power (Franco), to economic theology, a managerial paradigm of governance in which the administration of the law matches the divine *oikonomia*" (142–3) took place.

These connections between theology and modern economy had already been examined in the interwar period by Walter Benjamin in his text *Capitalism as Religion* (1921), where he postulated that not only would capitalism have religious origins, but that it would itself be an essentially religious phenomenon. In his opinion, politics and daily life had been subjugated by economic power, which had completely hijacked faith, the future, the sense of time and hope. Benjamin thus explored the theological and supernatural dimension of capitalism and analysed, among other issues, the mythical dimension of money by comparing "the images of the saints of the various religions" with "the spirit that speaks from the ornamentation of banknotes" (290). It is especially significant to recall how in Spain from 1947 every coin was stamped with the motto "Francisco Franco, Caudillo de España por la Gracia de Dios" [Francisco Franco, Leader of Spain by the Grace of God] around the face of the Generalissimo —a motto with which Franco was consecrated after the Te-Deum of 1939 (Box 93) and which continued to be present on the coins that remained in circulation in the daily life of Spaniards until 1997.

The continuity of Franco's dictatorship after the defeat of European fascisms was possible thanks to US political intervention, which accompanied its strategy of expanding market capitalism with the deployment of bases and military technology in Spanish territory, including the presence of atomic weapons (Vilarós 45). It was a geopolitical strategy articulated around the idea of "development", a key concept used in the "Point Four Program" presented by Harry Truman at his swearing-in as president on January 20, 1949.[11] The notion of "development" became the political signifier around which the United States' proposal for intervention in the new global order pivoted, with which the country affirmed its hegemony by presenting itself as an ideal of modernity and progress. Development based on economic growth was presented as the only effective and feasible solution to solve humanity's problems within a new paradigm, according to which the prosperity of nations was associated with a new value indicator in which the United States occupied a position of superiority: the Gross Domestic Product. In his speech, President Truman offered financial and technical aid and advice for "underdeveloped" or "developing" countries. To this end, he encouraged other nations to be able to overcome their situation of "underdevelopment", considered as a shortcoming and not as the result of historical circumstances (Rist 75–79). As historian Victoria de Grazia states, the American development model associated with the Fordist mode of production and the corresponding "social consumption norm" (Aglietta 130) —which included consumer goods such as housing, automobiles and household equipment— was quickly adopted also among European countries:

> Western European states were more firmly joined to the White Atlantic, and more inclined to the appropriate vocation of a second order power, namely to guarantee the material improvement of their own citizens. Henceforth competition among them was no longer measured in terms of the power of arms, size of colonial territories, or wealth of empire, but within the framework of comparative data on gross national product, inflation rates, index figures for expenditure on health and leisure, and diffusion curves for indoor plumbing, automobiles, washing machines and television sets. (356)

The profound optimism regarding the consumer society offered citizens a "re-enchantment" of the market as a place that could satisfy their demands and desires. This "re-enchantment" grew parallel to the so-called "disenchantment of the world", the famous expression with

---

11 On modernization theory and the development paradigm, see Gilman (2003), Latham (2011), Ekbladh (2010), Escobar (1995), Furtado (1974) and Rist (2002).

which Max Weber had described the loss of magical expectations and spiritual explanations of reality as a consequence of the modern processes of rationalization and secularization ("From Max Weber" 55). Philosophers such as Theodor Adorno and Karl Löwith also analysed the implications that the theological paradigm would have had on Western thinking about progress and development, considering that it would be heir to the legacy of the tradition of patristic philosophy, in which the teleology of history was conceived as a salvation narrative (Löwith 9; Adorno 143–160). Thus, speeches such as President Truman's on development were not only addressed to his countrymen, but also appealed to a vision shared worldwide "by everyone who belonged to a salvationist religion" (Rist 77).

General Franco's vision of the Civil War as a crusade that divine providence endorsed also extended to his speeches on economic matters, in which the general had been announcing a "miracle" since the beginning of the war in statements such as: "Puedo anunciar que España se bastará a sí misma completamente en orden a las industrias de guerra; y que eso que podríamos llamar un milagro se producirá en un plazo de años muy corto" [I can announce that Spain will be completely self-sufficient in terms of war industries; and that what we could call a miracle will take place in a very short period of years] ("Pequeño libro" 16). Following a tradition that went back to St Isidoro of Sevilla's *Laudes Hispaniae* narrative, according to which Spain was imagined as a privileged land full of abundance, the Caudillo promoted a sort of "cornucopianism" that permeated the imaginary of the post-war economy, and which took the form of statements proclaiming the country's self-sufficiency as a consequence of its wealth in natural resources: "España posee en sus yacimientos oro en cantidades enormes y pizarras bituminosas y lignitos en cantidad fabulosa, aptos para la destilación, que puede asegurar nuestro consumo de combustibles líquidos" [Spain possesses in its deposits gold in enormous quantities and bituminous shales and lignite in fabulous quantity, suitable for distillation, which can assure our consumption of liquid fuels] ("Pequeño libro" 141).

In 1961, two years after the implementation of the Stabilization and Liberalization Plan, Francisco Franco addressed the Spanish people in his end-of-year speech, summarizing the achievements of his government up to that moment, in a stocktaking that he condensed in the following statement: "La sangre de los héroes y de los mártires produjo sus frutos en esto que los profanos llaman el milagro español" [The blood of heroes and martyrs produced its fruits in what the profane call the Spanish miracle] ("Discursos" 360). With this statement, the general laid the discursive foundations for the production of a new historical narrative in which the theological imaginary of martyrdom —the backbone of the imagination of

Introduction 13

the New State in the immediate post-war period— was redefined to justify national success in economic matters.[12] According to this new account of the Caudillo, the "economic miracle" in Spain would not only embody the culmination of the success of the new policies since the 1950s, but would also be an objective already inscribed in the providential mission of the regime since its foundational origin: "El Desarrollo económico no es cosa nueva, viene practicándose desde la Cruzada" [Economic development is not something new, it has been practised since the Crusade] ("Discursos" 480). In this dialectical turn, the dictator justified the new economic policies by arguing that these were already present in his plans since the so-called "war of liberation", which would have a political and theological but also an economic meaning: "La liberación que con la Victoria habría de conseguir para nuestro pueblo no sería verdaderamente efectiva mientras no hubiéramos conquistado la libertad económica que España había venido perdiendo al correr de medio siglo de abandono" [The liberation that the Victory would achieve for our people would not be truly effective as long as we had not conquered the economic freedom that Spain had been losing through half a century of neglect] ("Discursos" 112). As Raymond Carr pointed out, "the 'dictatorship of Victory' thus became in the 1960s the 'dictatorship of development'" ("España" 223).

Autarchy, Economic Liberalization and Development

The autarchy of the first years of the dictatorship responded to General Franco's limited and peculiar sense of economy and was coherent as an alternative to the liberal economic model; it was also coherent with the tradition of a protectionism consolidated since the times of Antonio Cánovas del Castillo, and which had been reinforced during the dictatorship of Primo de Rivera (1923–1930). Following the end of the Civil War, the army not only assumed the policies of justice, but also directed the industrial policy through the Instituto Nacional de Industria (National Institute of Industry, INI), an organization inspired by the model of the Istituto per la Ricostruzione Industriale created by the Italian Fascist government in 1933. The new Francoist state set itself up as the collective representative of productive and social capital through direct control of the means of production, the labour force and the exchange of goods in the market. As Carlos Barciela pointed

---

12 The continuity of blood ties between those dead in the "Crusade" and the survivors of New Spain, as well as the recovery of suffering as an element of collective "redemption" had served after the Civil War as a unifying and mobilizing force for the different political groups that had won the war. See Maria A. Thomas (2016).

out, it was a matter of state dirigisme of the economy impregnated with a military style that was imposed in institutional practices and discourses: "La confianza del Régimen en que la autoridad ... podía conseguir un orden económico más eficiente que el del mercado se consagró, incluso, como ley fundamental del Nuevo Estado. El Fuero del Trabajo de 1938 proclamaba, en uno de sus puntos, de manera rotunda y castrense: 'Se disciplinarán los precios'" ("Los años") [The Regime's confidence that authority, exercised without hesitation, could achieve a more efficient economic order than that of the market was even enshrined as a fundamental law of the New State. Its 1938 Labour Law proclaimed, in one of its points, in a resounding and military manner: 'Prices will be disciplined'].

Together with the proposals of the emerging liberalism, whose success was based on market and consumer freedom, some economists who designed the Development Plans for the 1960s were also inspired by the French model known as "indicative planning", based on the combination of Keynesian macroeconomics and government-corporate coordination (López Rodó, "Memorias" 307–313; Estape and Amado 206–214). However, as Bethany Moreton points out, this model formulated policy projections that "were mandatory for the public sector but only 'indicative' for the private sector", so that in this sense planning was "non-coercive", simply aimed at eliminating "the entrepreneur's worst enemy, risk" (116). State interventionism did not cease with the end of the autarchy but continued during the 1960s through various procedures such as the ex-gratia provision of subsidies, the existence of privileged credit circuits and the continued tutelary role of the state in labour relations —in which there was no autonomy of the parties since there was no right to strike, and unofficial unions were illegal. To help the implementation of the new economic model, a Public Order Law appeared in June 1959, constituting the last legal link in the repressive chain that would leave technocrats free hands for the implementation of the Stabilization Plan (Naredo 56). In this way, repression was prolonged in parallel to the progression of economic growth as part of the binomial that historians Michael Richards (1995; 2013) and Antonio Cazorla (2016) have called "fear and progress", the two elements of biopolitical control on which the modernizing project of Franco's developmentalism was based.

Autarchy had allowed those social groups that had won the war to carry out a process of wealth concentration that consolidated them as part of the ruling class that continues to own and manage a large part of the wealth in Spain today.[13] The main beneficiaries of this process were the financial sector and the social groups that had supported the military coup, which would

---

13 See Sánchez Recio and Tascón, Sánchez-Soler, Juste, and González and Ramiro.

Introduction   15

be joined by the so-called *nouveau riche*, favoured by their corrupt relations
with the state bureaucracy and by the economic activities carried out in the
black market during the rationing period.[14] There was a transfer of income
to these benefited sectors from the working classes, whose living conditions
were severely affected, not only by the decrease in wages but also by the
exploitation of the labour force (Sánchez-Mazas 3–5). Beyond the debate
as to whether economic policy decisions during the autarchic period were
voluntarily or forcibly applied by Franco's government as a consequence of
the isolation of the nation after the defeat of the Rome–Berlin axis, what is
certain is that the cycle of capital accumulation had reached the limit of its
profit expansion by the end of the 1950s.[15]

According to Luis Ángel Rojo, one of the economists behind the 1959
Plan, the regime was forced to recognize that the possibilities of economic
growth were exhausted and "opened the doors to a phase of incorporation
of new forms of production and life, the result of which would be an
accelerated social change in the following years" (quoted in Estefanía, 1998).
The economist and writer José Luis Sampedro, who had also participated in
the elaboration of the Plan, described it in 1967 as "a political instrument
with conservative ends" that benefited "a privileged minority" that "publicly
thanked God for the goodness of the results achieved" (1035). Beyond the
publicity regarding the "economic miracle" by which Spain would have
become the country with the second highest growth rate in the world
after Japan, Sampedro analysed other social changes that liberalization
would have brought about, stressing that the real change was "the growing
dynamism of an entire population" (1040) that was no longer resigned
to its traditional situation. The regime took advantage of these changes
in lifestyles to promote an image of "openness" that also translated into
economic benefits in the form of remittances from migrant workers as well
as new laws on freedom of expression and association that allowed for a new
type of social control, all within the regime's balancing act.

From the late 1950s, the press no longer portrayed Franco as a saviour
hero touched by divinity but as an effective and intelligent manager who
paved the way for economic liberalization. The new legitimacy granted to
the regime and its Caudillo by the ideologues of the technocratic period
would no longer be a charismatic or traditional legitimacy, following Max

---

14 In 1952, food rationing had ended and freedom of prices and circulation of
consumer goods was reestablished, although inequality and economic hardship
continued in a system conditioned by the budget deficit and the strangulation of
foreign means of payment (Guirao 175–180).

15 See Catalán (1995), Viñas (1999), and Barciela (2003).

16   *Fables of Development*

Weber's terminology, but a rational-functional legitimacy that considered the Francoist state as an instrument for the modernization of Spanish society, more effective than the socialist or the demoliberal. Thus, after the implementation of the 1959 Plan, General Francisco Franco began to refer in his speeches to "aquellos pueblos subdesarrollados" [those underdeveloped countries] that needed "acción sistemática de asistencia y ayuda" [systematic action of assistance and aid] ("Discursos" 122) in their take-off stage. According to his account, this was a stage that Spain had already left behind, stating in his 1960 New Year's message that "nunca nuestra economía ha sido tan fuerte y nunca como ahora podemos contemplar con tanta seguridad y esperanza el futuro" (never has our economy been so strong and never as now can we contemplate the future with so much security and hope) (114).[16] However, it is essential to remember that the so-called Spanish economic miracle, which triggered the growth of domestic consumption, was marked by deepening economic inequalities "among regions, professional groups, and social classes, as well as by continuing disparities in the well-being of urban and rural populations" (Afinoguénova 419). As for the reception of the regime's discourses, the writer Francisco Candel in his book *Ser obrero no es ninguna ganga* (1968 [Being a Worker Is No Bargain]) showed the other side of economic policies, gathering the testimony of Catalan workers who denounced the social costs derived from the new consumption practices:

> Esa chorrada de que antes se iba con alpargatas y ahora con zapatos ha calado incluso en las clases humildes, en ellos, que son víctimas de ese sofisma. Y todos están contentos porque ahora se ha pasado de la miseria a la pobreza, una pobreza llena de oropeles disimuladores. El fenómeno del neocapitalismo europeo ha deslumbrado. Ya tenemos la panacea ... Estamos ante un neocapitalismo ridículo porque el capitalismo y la burguesía española fueron y son mezquinos. No obstante, el pobre más pobre puede comprar un televisor aunque sea en 50 plazos, cinco años pagando letras. . . . Cada individuo que firma esas 60 letras es uno más perdido para la protesta social. (42)

---

16 During the 1960s, the Caudillo insistently mentioned in his speeches the causes of a national "secular backwardness" which, in his opinion, had its origin in the loss of the colonies in 1898 and was subsequently aggravated by successive cycles of "red depredations" ("Discursos" 260). Among the causes that would have prevented a "normalized" development of the Spanish economy, the Francoist regime appealed to narratives such as the loss of the "Moscow Gold" (the operation of transferring the gold reserves of the Bank of Spain to the USSR in 1936), the "pertinaz sequía" [persistent drought] or the intervention of foreign powers that condemned the national economy to isolation.

Introduction

[This nonsense about how people used to wear espadrilles and now they wear shoes has even caught on in the humble classes, in them, who are victims of this sophistry. And they are all happy because now they have gone from misery to poverty, a poverty full of disguising tinsel. The phenomenon of European neo-capitalism has dazzled. We already have the panacea ... We are facing ridiculous neocapitalism because capitalism and the Spanish bourgeoisie were and are mean. Nevertheless, the poorest of the poor can buy a television set even if it is in 60 instalments, five years paying bills. ... Each individual who signs those 60 instalments is one more lost to social protest.]

The arrival of technocrats in institutions brought about a change in rhetoric that was imposed in everyday language with terms such as "rationalization", "efficiency" or "competition", which had been popularized by one of the champions of modernization theory, Walter Whitman Rostow. In his *The Stages of Economic Growth: A Non-Communist Manifesto* (1960), Rostow synthesized his ideas on development as a uniform historical pattern occurring in five basic stages of varying duration. According to his proposal, the so-called "traditional societies" could overcome their lag with respect to "modern societies" through a period of counselling and financing that would lay the foundations for a take-off, after which they would enter a stage of "technological maturity" that would culminate in a phase of "high mass consumption". At the end of the so-called "decade of development", the writer Manuel Vázquez Montalbán described ironically in his *Crónica sentimental de España* the popularization that these discourses had had in the previous years in Spanish society:

La revolución cultural que realizaron los tecnócratas a partir de 1958 ya ha influido en la conciencia social. Las aceleraciones y los frenazos han magullado a los viajeros de metro o autobús, pero se les ha inculcado la sabiduría convencional de Rostow o Galbraith, y se intercambian miradas de inteligencia antes de musitar: Ya se sabe, pasamos una fugaz etapa de recesión . . . Hay que esperar de nuevo el despegue reactivador. (177)

[The cultural revolution wrought by technocrats after 1958 has already influenced social consciousness. Accelerations and slowdowns have bruised subway or bus commuters, but they have been inculcated with the conventional wisdom of Rostow or Galbraith, and they exchange glances of intelligence before muttering: You know, we passed a fleeting stage of recession. ... We have to wait again for the reactivating takeoff.]

Fables of Development

It was not by chance that Rostow's essay concluded with the allusion to a "creed" in which he unfolded the promise that the Western capitalist bloc would contribute to the full development of other nations, no longer in the name of civilizing values as in the old colonial logic, but under the belief that the principles of administrative rationality and increased productivity would lead to a new era of peace and prosperity. Following this scheme proposed by Rostow, Laureano López Rodó, Commissioner of the Development Plan since 1962, stated in 1971 that the country's development had been carried out precisely thanks to the providential intervention of General Franco:

> Rostow, en su conocida obra sobre *Las etapas del crecimiento económico*, señala como factor decisivo para el despegue de una economía la presencia de un hombre excepcional que sepa canalizar las energías latentes de un pueblo y darle confianza en sí mismo. El Caudillo ha conseguido que los españoles hayamos recobrado nuestra propia confianza. El cerco de la pobreza había que romperlo por un doble frente: el de la justicia social y el de la industrialización, motor principal de la expansión económica. ("Política" 53)

> [Rostow, in his well-known work on *The Stages of Economic Growth*, points out that the decisive factor for the take-off of an economy is the presence of an exceptional man who knows how to channel the latent energies of a people and give them self-confidence. The Caudillo has succeeded in making us Spaniards regain our self-confidence. The siege of poverty had to be broken on two fronts: that of social justice and that of industrialization, the main engine of economic expansion.]

López Rodó synthesized in this way the narrative that the Francoist state had constructed since the late 1950s about its role as the agent responsible for the process of national modernization. A story in which the "gospel of business efficiency" (Carr and Fusi 81) designed by the technocratic elites was thus presented as the ideal formula to lend a new legitimacy to a dictatorship that promoted itself as the guarantor of progress. The "mystique of development" appeared in this context to merge with the messianic rhetoric that had contributed to the construction of the charismatic image that had presented the general as a "providential man", anointed by God to rule the destiny of Spain as a nation "chosen" to lead the fight against communism in his role as "Sentinel of the West".[17] Thus, the story of

---

17 On the construction of the figure of General Franco from a mythical and messianic dimension and its propagandistic promotion, see Moradiellos (2017), Preston (1995), Reig Tapia (2005), Zenobi (2011), Cazorla (2013), Casanova (2015) and

economic growth became central to the dictator's narrative of recent history, a sign of his new secular faith in free market principles. With the change of decade, the regime called for "estabilidad, apariencia de crecimiento y bienestar del pueblo con la figura del General en lo alto como benefactor" (González González 299) [stability, appearance of growth and welfare of the people with the figure of the General at the top as benefactor], and this is the image that successive technocratic governments sold for a system without an electorate. The very idea of development not only served to promote a new image of the nation, but General Franco was able to capitalize on it politically to perpetuate in power one of the "families" of the regime: the group of technocrats linked to Opus Dei who carried out the economic reforms and, through it, the sovereignty of the regime.

The Navarra School of Catholic Neoliberalism: The Case of Opus Dei as a Vanishing Mediator

One of the specific characteristics of Spanish developmentalism resided in the fact that many of the members of Franco's administration who implemented the new economic policies belonged to the Opus Dei lay Catholic order. This secular institute, founded by the priest José María Escrivá de Balaguer in 1928, included among its members many of the protagonists of the professional and political elite that would transform the country, imbuing the world of business and economics with spiritualization. The organization introduced the typically Protestant notion of sanctification in the secular world through professional vocation. It was a vision of work as a form of apostolate that promoted inner-worldly asceticism and the rationalization of conduct as a means of attaining sanctity, which made the distinction between religious and lay vocations unnecessary. If from the Calvinist ethic the capitalist businessman saw in the accumulation of goods the sign of divine election, the member of Opus Dei is rather a professional expert who, chosen by God himself to carry out his task, sees the sign of election in the success of his company or organization.[18]

On the basis of his particular Catholic interpretation of Max Weber's work, Ramiro de Maeztu had advocated in the first third of the twentieth century the construction of a capitalism that should be placed at the service of sacralized ends. With the aim of ensuring a type of political power

---

Box (2010). On the providential account of the history of Spain elaborated by the historiography of the regime, see Herzberger (1995), Labanyi (1989), Medina (2001) and Alares (2017).

18 See Casanova and Estruch.

that under an authoritarian form could promote a process of bourgeois modernization, Maeztu proposed a Catholic version of the inner-worldly asceticism proper to the Protestant ethic, of that rationalized lifestyle which, according to Weber, presented elective affinities with modern rational capitalism. This connection between economic activity and the salvation of the soul was transferred in Maeztu's project to the nations of Catholic culture, in which a new sense of saving, investment and the production of wealth would be able to unite the people around values that would supposedly moderate the class struggle (Villacañas 413–480; Botti 160–176; Arbaiza 154–186). After his transatlantic experience, the model that the Basque thinker considered for this project was the United States, a nation that, in his opinion, occupied a superior position because it had managed to successfully connect religion with economic activity. Maeztu's project for the creation of a Hispanic form of capitalism based on admiration for the United States became important again in Spain at a time when General Franco required new elites, mentalities and styles for his government after the negotiations of the Pact of Madrid (1953). As part of that superior elite that Maeztu had imagined, the intellectuals and technicians of Opus Dei aspired to become the directing agents of this project as a "third way" between Falangists and Christian democrats, capable of mediating the contradictions implicit in the ideological production of Spanish developmentalism.

If the Protestant Reformation brought Christian asceticism and methodical life out of the monasteries and introduced them in professional life, four centuries later a secular institute such as Opus Dei sanctioned the same process within Catholicism (Estruch 424). In this sense, the technocratic authoritarianism of Opus Dei in Spain can be analysed on the basis of the dialectical figure that Fredric Jameson called the "vanishing mediator" ("The Vanishing" 52–89). Jameson described this figure as the element between two historical periods that would allow us to structurally formalize the narrative of a transitional juncture, translating the vagueness of flux and historical change into phenomena relatively anchored to two synchronic moments.[19]

---

19 Slavoj Žižek analysed the emergence of fascism in Europe following this explanation of the figure of the evanescent mediator, in a historical conjuncture in which the liberal democracies of the West faced the threat of a possibility of change in the form of communism. According to his analysis, there was a transformation of the political instance into the internal nemesis of these democracies, in order to produce a new antagonism (fascism/communism) that allowed them to survive: "Fascism, to take a worn-out example, is not an external opposite to liberal democracy but has its roots in liberal democracy's inner antagonisms . . . This is why negativity must be counted twice: effectively to negate the starting point, we must negate its own "inner negation" in which its content comes to its "truth". Fascism, although

Introduction 21

This concept was first used in Jameson's analysis of Weber's work, in which he described Protestantism as a necessary "vanishing mediator" in the transition between feudalism and capitalism, between medieval corporatism and capitalist individualism. With its universalization of Christianity, Protestantism became an indispensable element for the expansion of the affirmation of secular economic activity, which crystallized in a "work ethic" that promoted the accumulation of wealth and inner-worldly asceticism as an end in itself. Paradoxically, this universalization of Protestantism prepared the ground for the withdrawal of religion to the intimacy of the private sphere, separated from state and public affairs. Once this historical process concluded, Jameson explains, Protestantism became superfluous, it could disappear as a mediator between two historical trends at the moment when the reality of civil society itself became structured as a world of atomized individuals, defined by "the paradox of 'acquisitive asceticism' (the more you possess, the more you must renounce consumption)", that is to say, "the structure of the Protestant content without its positive religious form" (Žižek, "For They Know" 184–185).

According to this dialectic, the passage from one social formation to another occurs through a "vanishing mediator" that reverses the relationship between the base and the superstructure in such a way that, by emancipating itself from its base, the old superstructure prepares the ground for infrastructural transformation. In the elaboration of a Catholic business praxis in the post-Bretton Woods scenario, Spanish economists linked to Opus Dei thus joined the enthusiasm for neo-scholastic corporatism and the explicit recognition of the need for a strong state as a tool for establishing a competitive market order. In this nostalgic yearning for an imagined medieval order, Catholic neoliberalism reformulated the Church's social doctrine as "business ethics" and turned it into an intellectual product. In this way, Spanish technocrats understood themselves as market engineers operating on the basis of an ideology spiritualized as Catholic orthodoxy that promoted a supposedly "depoliticized" vision of the business world.[20]

---

opposed to liberal capitalism, is not its effective negation but only its "inner" negation: effectively to negate liberal capitalism, we must therefore negate its very negation" ("For They Know" 180).

20 The spiritualization and idealization that technocrats imbibed in the world of business and economy during this period were harshly criticised by Manuel Fraga, Minister of Information and Tourism who was dismissed from his post in 1969, following his confrontation with members of Opus Dei in government during the corruption scandal known as 'Caso Matesa', in which they were involved. In his essay *El desarrollo político* (1971), Fraga criticised what he called the "nuevo despotismo ilustrado de tecnócratas" [enlightened despotism of technocrats]

22   *Fables of Development*

The technocratic turn reached its extreme formulation with the essay *El crepúsculo de las ideologías* (1965 [The Twilight of Ideologies]) by Gonzalo Fernández de la Mora, an Opus Dei sympathizer. His proposal revolved around an ideal techno-authoritarian state run by elite experts whose legitimacy rested not on popular will or religion, but on the effectiveness of their technical management. In his view, political ideologies in the public sphere generated unnecessary social tensions leading to class struggles and should therefore be replaced by technical and economic planning culminating in an ideal society in which general political "apathy" on the part of the satisfied population was presented as a positive and successful model. As Jorge Pérez recalls, "ironically enough, the Opus Dei ministers' worst intellectual nightmare might have come out of their own camp" (25). *El crepúsculo de las ideologías* focused exclusively on the economic instance, proposing a system of government that deviated from the notion of development linked to the National-Catholic project. As Pérez points out, Fernández de la Mora fully assumed "a secularized notion of history in which 'progress' was associated with the rationalization of the public sphere" (26). Following this interpretation, the National-Catholicism of Opus Dei as an element of transition or vanishing mediator would disappear from the collective imaginary scenario once the technocratic code had been consolidated as a symbolic norm. Fernández de la Mora's essay was, in short, a model of anti-democratic social utopia that was proposed in parallel to the transformations in Spain in the mid-1960s, in which a progressive process of secularization of society was taking place, a process of "immanentization

---

(30), which he disqualified as "mandarines" [mandarins] or "maravillos señores feudales sin soberano" [wonderful feudal lords without sovereignty] (61). In his book, the former minister clearly exposed the contradictions of an organization such as Opus Dei, which strove to cultivate an image closely linked to Catholic orthodoxy in order to curb possible criticisms of the heterodoxy of a project whose roots were clearly Protestant. Fraga referred to Opus Dei as one of those secular institutes "que han ido mucho más allá que aquellos buenos calvinistas que tanto influjo tuvieron en el nacimiento de la sociedad industrial" [that have gone much further than those good Calvinists who had such an influence on the birth of the industrial society], affirming that they had come to "bendecir y canonizar el neocapitalismo y la subsiguiente sociedad de consumo" [bless and canonise neo-capitalism and the subsequent consumer society] (77). The Galician politician cited Max Weber's essay "Politics as a Vocation" to vindicate the work of professional politicians who acted under "una ética de la responsabilidad social" [an ethic of social responsibility] (46), as opposed to those who held their political posts shielded under "la técnica de la organización, de la empresa, del manejo de las personas" [the technique of organization, of business, of managing people] and the "activismo de cifras y estadísticas" [activism of figures and statistics] (46).

Introduction 23

of reality with the following closure to the transcendent order" (González de Cardedal 52–53).

After the dictator's death in 1975, the dialectic between reconciliation, normalization and development that characterizes some historiographic accounts of national democratization has continued to legitimize the Spanish economic model based on the tourism and real estate sectors to the present day. After the financial collapse of 2008 and the social movements of the 2011–2014 political cycle, this narrative has been widely questioned by some social sectors and there has been a critical distancing from the long-lasting effects of developmentalism and economic liberalism on Spanish democracy, characterized by a consensual logic that displaces expressions of dissent.[21] In a context of economic, social and ecological crisis such as the current one, the analysis that I propose about the cultural logics that organized the circulation and distribution of capital during the Francoist dictatorship invites us to continue questioning the impact of the "fables of development" on the construction of the collective fantasies that shape the Spanish model. As the inhabitants of Sástago (Zaragoza) stated in 1973 in a poster hung in the church of their town with the message "Llaman milagro al desarrollo, pero el milagro está en el reparto" [They call development a miracle, but the miracle is in the distribution] (Fernández Clemente y Forcadell 7), other alternatives regarding the distribution of wealth and resources are possible.

Four Fables: Chapter Outline

The first part of this book, "Dreamworlds of Development: Cold War Imaginaries in Franco's Spain", includes the chapters "Fables of Intervention" and "Fables of Outer Space", which examine the cultural logics surrounding the processes of capital circulation that began in 1950 with the US intervention in Spain and the subsequent integration of the country into the Western capitalist system. The second part, "Providential Capitalism", includes the chapters "Fables of Chance" and "Fables of Grace", and focuses on the processes of distribution of wealth and resources through the dynamics of gambling and charity in a country that lacked a welfare state. Chapter One examines literary and media accounts of unidentified airspace phenomena reportedly sighted after the Spanish–American Pact of Madrid in 1953. Through this geopolitical alliance, the Francoist government agreed to an ongoing US military presence in Spain (materialized by an integrated network of military bases, transit facilities and oil pipelines) in exchange for economic aid. Focusing on shifting imaginaries of aerospace technologies —

---

21 See Luisa Elena Delgado.

24 *Fables of Development*

and specifically on the varied connotations attributed to flying saucers— this chapter discusses this alliance and the political position of Franco's Spain in the Cold War global order. In this context, some figurations of alleged or fantasized sightings of flying objects in Spain included the consideration of outer space as a locus of colonization, as an extension of the Christian skies, or as a place for barely-disguised allegories for the government's dream of a Marshall Plan that would fall like "manna" from the sky. The interpretations of unidentified aerospace phenomena by renowned writers such as Camilo José Cela, Gabriel Celaya, Jacinto Benavente or Noel Clarasó were manifold. Unlike conventional military threats, these unidentified activities could not be acknowledged without calling national sovereignty itself into question. It must also be noted that some reported sightings included military aircraft carrying cutting-edge nuclear technology across the Spanish sovereign airspace, so they were on many occasions identified as such. However, unidentified flying objects were most commonly interpreted in Spain as providential signs that regulated the appearance of unknown agents, who, regardless of their origin, provided the terrestrial inhabitants with unexpected gifts or threats. That is why they are studied side-by-side and in connection with accounts of other miraculous and supernatural visions, which were very frequent in the period and equally inspired by the Catholic doctrine of grace. If anything, what makes Spanish narratives of UFO sightings different is their tendency to link the military and economic presence of the United States with the convenient discovery of uranium and petroleum deposits in national soil. Such (real or imagined) reserves were meant to revalorize the country after the failure of the autarchic regime. These "hidden treasures", which would turn Spain into a desirable ally, were the subject of news stories, comic books and cinematic productions, such as José Luis Sáenz de Heredia's film *Todo es posible en Granada* (1954 [Everything's Possible in Granada]) and Rafael Salvia's *¡Aquí hay petróleo!* (1955 [There's Oil Here!]).

Chapter Two explores space science fiction literature and comics as a locus of enunciation for the representation of otherness in Franco's Spain. In parallel with the constant reports of UFO activity, space technologies and alien worlds portrayed in novels, theatre and comics were popular fictional devices used to re-imagine social antagonisms as well as varied utopian longings. Spanish outer space imaginaries displaced the ideological coordinates of American science fiction that had proliferated during the height of the Cold War. In those narratives, aliens threatening to invade the Earth shared many traits with the communist infiltrators as popularized by the so-called "Red Scare propaganda". In this sense, Spanish outer space fictions displayed new interpretations of extraterrestrial life determined by

Introduction   25

the political position of Franco's Spain as the Fascist "Other" incorporated into the democratic capitalist bloc. This chapter examines utopian science fiction novels in which different political and social orders were imagined. On the one hand, the kiosk novels *La saga de los Aznar* (1953-1958 [The Aznar Saga]) by Pascual Enguídanos (George H. White) depicted the politics of outer space as a socialist utopia under the guise of Christian values. On the other, Falangist writer Tomás Salvador's novels *La Nave* (1959 [The Ship]) and *Marsuf, vagabundo del espacio* (1962 [Marsuf, the Space Wanderer]), developed political allegories of the post-war Spanish "national reconciliation" by depicting a fictional Spanish–American spacecraft in which a national community was built upon providential grounds. Other examples of utopian worlds, in which a fictional National-Catholic Spain played an increasingly prominent role in a new "interplanetary order", are examined in popular *Diego Valor* radio-theatre series and comics (1953-1958). "Fables of Outer Space" contends that some comic creators who suffered an "inner exile" within Spain used space science fiction to convey utopian visions of the future in which the characters of their works and the artists themselves — who can be considered "alien" citizens in Francoist Spain— were portrayed as extraterrestrial beings. In this sense, I examine how the aerospace technology images displayed in their comic books and strips unveiled the real poverty and scarcity in everyday life along with the collective desires for new industrially produced consumer goods. In a context in which all forms of media were controlled by the state, those visual imageries became a parody that revealed the real material conditions of existence behind the façade of the regime's desire for technological modernity. To conclude, the chapter proposes an analysis of Antonio Buero Vallejo's opera libretto *Mito* (1967 [Myth]). In this play, Buero's reinterpretation of the Don Quixote myth in a science fiction key engages the reader to imagine a democratic community to come. This community, in which extraterrestrial beings mimic human appearance, successfully infiltrates society to introduce democratic practices in an imagined dictatorial nation-state.

Chapter Three studies the social ontology of chance in Franco's Spain by examining cultural objects that revolve around the representation of national lotteries, raffles, radio contests and games of chance. In this context, those social and cultural institutions configured a society of potential consumers in which the socialization of gains was achieved through gambling. By opening a collective horizon of economic expectations, those games of equal chance found a willing audience in a population eager to experience material gains after a long period of material deprivation. In this way, hope in chance became a "secularized" faith that projected gamblers into future settings. I then move to explore this dimension of immanent transcendence in gambling through the examination of fictions in which the expectations of experiencing an out-of-the-ordinary turn of events in daily life allowed Spaniards to transcend the sense of static time under the Francoist regime. The circulation of capital and goods —or at least its growing representation in media— allowed Spanish citizens to recover a notion of contingency in which chance became a non-theological *primum movens* that could drive new social hopes. In contrast with the secular notions of randomness and chance, National-Catholic discourses about gambling reinforced the presence of divine providence as a force that intervened in state lotteries —whose main beneficiary was the state as the collector of revenues— and in charitable raffles sponsored by the Spanish Catholic Church and other organizations. The collective fantasies around equal chance gaming grew in parallel with the social inequalities promoted by the regime's economic policies, which rejected the public redistribution of wealth that was occurring in European welfare states. This confluence between the state policies and mass entertainment industries is examined in *Historias de la radio* (1955 [Radio Stories]), a film by José Luis Sáenz de Heredia. In this comedy, radio contests and raffles were portrayed in providential narratives where the absence of collective welfare state protection was fictionally replaced with the "invisible hand" of divine providence. The effects of gambling are also examined in films such as *Esa pareja feliz* (Bardem and Berlanga, 1951 [That Happy Couple]) and *Felices Pascuas* (Bardem, 1955 [Merry Christmas]), in Antonio Buero Vallejo's play *Hoy es fiesta* (1956 [Today's a Holiday]), and in Juan Goytisolo's novel *Fiestas* (1958). These cultural objects challenged the Francoist figure of the consumer-citizen, whose well-being was based on the access to consumer goods that games of chance made possible. In contrast with this model, these works considered distribution of wealth to be the main principle of the moral economy of communities organized around relations of social solidarity. Lotteries, raffles and contests were portrayed by these anti-Francoist creators as the opposite of what they were supposed to be; therefore, prizes were understood as punishments, and losses became moral rewards. By displacing both theological and market-based notions of chance, those fables portrayed imagined networks of solidarity among the most vulnerable and precarious members of their fictional gambling communities.

Chapter Four proposes a study of "providential capitalism" as a set of symbolic structures and practices taking place at the conjuncture of the economic liberalization process in Spain. Opus Dei ministers and economists drew on influential neoliberal theorists, such as Wilhelm Röpke, to promote what they called "Christian capitalism", a form of putative economic liberalism that eschewed public distribution of wealth and resources. This

Introduction   27

chapter analyses the intersection of theological and political economies at the time, focusing on charity as the guiding principle of the "economy of grace" that determined the public distribution of resources developed by the State and the Catholic Church. The first part of the chapter examines the role of the Catholic Church as an agent responsible for charitable policies in the films *Cerca de la ciudad* (Luis Lucia,1952 [Close to the City]), *Marcelino Pan y Vino* (Ladislao Vajda, 1954 [Marcelino Bread and Wine]) and *Sor Citroën* (Pedro Lazaga, 1967 [Sister Citroen]). In the context of the 1953 Concordat with the Vatican, these films reinforced the idea that assisted citizens were not considered as holders of social rights, but as subjects who may be "redeemed" in a National-Catholic community. As an example of the changes within the Catholic Church brought by the Second Vatican Council (1962–1965), I explore the new technocratic, market-driven and market-oriented imaginaries of charity in Pedro Lazaga's comedy *Sor Citroën* (1967). In the second part of this chapter, counter-hegemonic narratives of private charity are examined in Luis Buñuel's *Viridiana* (1961). In this film, the protagonist's display of pastoral power collides with the desires of capitalist modernization embodied in the character of her cousin, co-owner of the estate in which Viridiana establishes her own Christian utopia. In the next section, I study the relationship between consumer and entertainment industries, charitable practices, and mass media in Luis García Berlanga's film *Plácido* (1961). Finally, I analyse the relationship between voluntary beneficence and the rise of the technocratic state in Juan Marsé's *La oscura historia de la prima Montse* (1970 [The Dark Story of Cousin Montse]). Although the novel was published in 1970, it could be considered an early example of a "memory novel" that covers the period from 1960 to 1970. By portraying the profound transformations that took place within Spanish Catholicism following the *aggiornamiento* recommendations of the Second Vatican Council, Marsé's novel depicted the cultural logics of charity in Catalan lay apostolate organizations in connection with the economic and political instances in the 60s.

I.

Dreamworlds of Development: Cold War Imaginaries in Franco's Spain

1

Fables of Intervention

On January 2, 1951, the Falangist newspaper *Imperio* presented General Franco's traditional New Year's message to the Spanish people on its front page. Next to a speech in which the achievements of the regime in a year that the dictator described as the "más fecundo" [most fruitful] of his mandate were described, a news item appeared with a surprising headline: "Bombas atómicas a bordo de platillos volantes" [Atomic bombs aboard flying saucers] [FIG. 1]. In his speech, the general blamed the country's economic difficulties on the lack of assistance from a Marshall Plan that had been helping to strengthen the economy of other European countries thanks to the aid received in the form of an "arbitraria lluvia de dólares" [arbitrary rain of dollars] ("Mensaje" 1).[1] While highlighting the obstacles that economic isolation entailed, Francisco Franco expressed his confidence that the country's integration into the international political and military markets and spaces would be expanding. He had reason to hope, since in November 1950 the United Nations General Assembly had declared that the sanctions that had weighed on the Spanish government since 1946 had been lifted, without, in the words of the Caudillo, "ningún cambio sustancial de posiciones doctrinales se haya producido en nuestra Patria, que ha continuado sirviendo al imperativo de nuestra misión histórica en el mundo" [any substantial change in doctrinal positions having taken place in our Homeland, which has continued to serve the imperative of our historic mission in the world] ("Mensaje" 3).

On the front page of *Imperio*, this speech was accompanied by two other news items. A press release from New York reported that the recent sightings

---

1 The plan was named after General George C. Marshall, Secretary of State. The US government understood that the economic recovery of Europe through the creation of a massive economic aid programme would help ensure political stability capable of protecting US economic investments and, at the same time, make the recipient countries less susceptible to Soviet pressures. See Gindin and Panitch (89–101).

Fig. 1. *Imperio: Diario de Zamora de Falange Española de las J.O.N.S.*, January 2, 1951. (Biblioteca Virtual de Prensa Histórica. Creative Commons [CC] licence).

of flying saucers in different parts of the planet had a technological-military origin: "Son proyectiles controlados por radio. En otras palabras, aviones sin piloto que pueden llevar bombas atómicas a ultramar sin arriesgar una sola vida" [They are radio-controlled projectiles. In other words, pilotless

Fables of Intervention

planes that can carry atomic bombs overseas without risking a single life]
("Bombas" 1). Another accompanying story, entitled "Defensa civil yanqui"
[Yankee Civil Defence] summarized a proposal by the US Congress to design
a programme of defence preparations, including the construction of shelters
"hacer frente a los horrores de posibles ataques con bombas atómicas,
de gas o de otras clases" [to cope with the horrors of possible attacks by
atomic, gas or other types of bombs]. In the inner pages of the newspaper,
General Franco continued to express his concern about the possibility of an
imminent global war scenario, emphasizing the strategic advantages that
the "providential" geographical situation of Spain offered: "Sería nuestro
deseo que una renaciente voluntad de resistencia revalorase el sistema
defensivo que el Occidente pretende presentar; pero si esto no se alcanzase,
hemos de agradecer a la Providencia nos haya deparado esta privilegiada
situación geográfica en este espolón occidental de Europa" [It would be our
wish that a renascent will of resistance would revalue the defensive system
that the West intends to present; but if this is not achieved, we have to thank
Providence for having given us this privileged geographical situation in this
Western buttress of Europe] ("Mensaje" 3).

The juxtaposition of the three news items placed readers before a
new juncture in which the regime's press began to praise the economic,
technological and military superiority of the United States. This superiority
was linked to the potential development of nuclear weapons and the capacity
of this country to assemble the centres of the global capitalist system
within its area of influence. This news was reported in the Spanish media
in the context of diplomatic negotiations aimed at achieving alliances with
the US government. The alliances had begun to consolidate in January
1950, when Secretary of State Dean Acheson urged all member countries
of the United Nations to send ambassadors to Madrid, a decision that the
General Assembly ratified in November (Bowen 108–110). While Franco's
government declared that it was willing to help contain the spread of
communism in Asia by sending military units to Korea, the US Senate
authorized the Export-Import Bank to issue loans to Spain with an initial
credit of $62.5 million (Lieberman 39; Garcés 157).

In 1953, the Spanish Government strengthened its alliance with the USA
through the signature of the Pact of Madrid, and in 1955 both countries
reached another agreement in matters of atomic energy. In 1952 talks had
begun to authorize the construction of twelve military bases in Torrejón
de Ardoz (Madrid), El Copero (Sevilla), Morón de la Frontera (Sevilla),
Zaragoza, Reus, Los Llanos (Albacete), Los Palacios (Sevilla), Alcalá and
San Pablo (Sevilla), Rota, Matagorda and San Cristóbal (Cádiz) (Viñas, "Los
pactos" 228–229). Together with the installation of a radar network and

34   *Fables of Development*

the construction of an oil pipeline from Rota (Cádiz) to Zaragoza, these US infrastructures were planned "ante todo y sobre todo como almacenes de abastecimiento y circulación aérea de armamento nuclear" [first and foremost as supply depots and aerial transport of nuclear weaponry] (Vilarós 45). In the Pact of Madrid the building and use of four permanent military bases in Spanish ground was finally agreed upon: three of them would be air bases, the ones in Morón, Zaragoza and Torrejón de Ardoz, and the one in Rota would be a naval base. Although these military bases should be used by way of mutual agreement, the US government reserved the right to use the bases unilaterally "en caso de evidente agresión comunista" [in the event of overt communist aggression] threatening the security of the West (Carr, "La época" 222). According to historian Carlos Barciela, should an armed conflict between the two superpowers have broken out, Spain would have been most seriously affected (Barciela and Escudero 29). It was, therefore, an alliance that put the whole of the Spanish population at risk, exposing civilians to the possibility of a military attack and to the problems derived from the use of atomic weapons. A few years later, in 1966, a serious nuclear accident took place in Palomares (Almería), when a B-52 crashed with a KC-135 coming from the Air Base in Morón de la Frontera (Sevilla) and dropped 4 thermo-nuclear bombs. The same operation had been carried out 140,000 times over the Spanish population without a single accident.[2]

The concessions made by the Francoist dictatorship to its US allies in terms of sovereignty were extraordinarily broad, although the agreements were publicized at the time as a trial of resistance by the dictator, who had defended "palmo a palmo, pulgada a pulgada, la integridad y la independencia españolas ante el intervencionismo de los Estados Unidos" [inch by inch Spain's integrity and independence in the face of US interventionism] (Alfaya 142). The US financial help represented less than 1% of Gross Domestic Product (GDP) between 1953 and 1963, a loan which was used primarily to cover the expenses of the US military and strategic needs (Viñas, "Los pactos" 271). In the 1960s, Spain's geographical location also made it one of the first destinations for NASA control centres located outside the United States. Since the 1940s, the National Institute for Aerospace Technology (INTA) had established solid contacts with American scientists and, in March 1960, participated in the signing of the agreement for the construction of the first

---

2 On October 19, 2015, the Government of Spain and the United States signed a document on the disposal of nuclear waste in the geographic area surrounding the Spanish town of Palomares (Almería). According to the investigations produced that same year, the area presents increasing levels of americium, a by-product of the plutonium transported by the four nuclear bombs (Rejón). See Moreno Izquierdo.

NASA station in Spain, which was located in Maspalomas (Gran Canaria). In 1961 the first antenna for the Mariner IV launch programme to Mars was placed at the Robledo de Chavela Tracking Station (Madrid), a facility now known as the Madrid Deep Space Communication Complex (Moriente 121).

During 1953, the year of the signing of the Pact of Madrid, the Spanish press continued to link information on the economic and military achievements of the United States with information on sightings of unidentified aircraft. Thus, on the front page of the *Imperio* newspaper of January 9, 1955, news with titles such as "Más aviones yankis que nunca en Occidente" [More Yankee planes than ever in the West] or "La VI Flota yanki visita España" [The 6th Yankee Fleet visits Spain] shared space with information about the increasingly common sightings of aircraft in news such as: "Otros dos platillos volantes 'vistos' en Orense" [Two more flying saucers 'spotted' in Orense].[3] Along with this information, there were also hopeful news items describing discoveries of mineral resources throughout the national territory with headlines such as "Parece que darán buen resultado las explotaciones petrolíferas de Granada" [It seems that the oil exploitations in Granada will give good results] and "Un coto de uranio se explota en Sierra Morena desde hace año y medio" [A uranium reserve has been exploited in Sierra Morena for a year and a half]. Taking into account such a recurrent presence of news about unidentified flying saucers in the Spanish media, the Spanish government's attitude is really striking: not only did the government not censor this information but it promoted the representation of an extremely sophisticated military technology coming from outer space. After all, this representation challenged the sovereignty and autonomy of the Francoist state in an area such as that of national airspace, now intervened by strange spaceships. As Raymond Duvall and Alexander Wendt state, the presence of flying saucers globally challenged the notion of modern sovereignty, a notion that in the context of the Cold War was especially at stake in the dominance of airspace. In their opinion, it is the very idea of sovereignty that the unidentified flying objects called into question: "Like Achilles, the modern sovereign is a warrior whose function is to protect ... from threats to the norm. Unlike conventional threats, however, the UFO threatens humans' capacity to decide those threats, and so cannot be acknowledged without calling modern sovereignty itself into question" (628).

In the early 1950s, the threat of nuclear war had not shaken global confidence in the feasibility and desirability of large-scale technoscientific

---

3 The US VI Fleet became a constant presence in Spain from January 9, 1951, when thirty ships arrived simultaneously at the ports of Barcelona, Palma de Mallorca, Cartagena, Alicante, Málaga, Valencia and Tarragona.

projects, which included the peaceful use of atomic energy. Thus, the two major technoscientific projects of the second half of the twentieth century, the exploration of outer space and the use of nuclear energy, were inextricably intertwined, not only in sectors of institutionalized knowledge but also in popular culture (Geppert 338).The impending human expansion towards outer space, commonly discussed with such imperialistic terms as "exploration", "exploration", "conquest" or "colonization", as well as the new technological achievements became an integral part of the global belief in the powers of both scientific and technological progress, drivers for the economic development and growth of nations. Thus, the UFO myth fed on the Cold War tensions and the fear of a nuclear massive destruction; on occasion, it also toyed with the soteriological beliefs of alien intervention as a way of offering some remedial answer to these threats.[4] In these revived versions of the plurality-of-worlds debate, spacecraft crew members could operate as agents of redemption in the face of the threat of atomic peril, but they were also imagined as potential agents of conquest and annihilation for humans (Landes 391–396; Roush 15–38; Battaglia 1–33; Lepseter 46–79; Roth 38–93; Eghigian 621).

This chapter examines the debate on the origin of unidentified aircraft in Franco's Spain, a debate whose interpretations included the consideration of outer space as a place of colonization, as an extension of the Christian skies, as a sign of the plurality of inhabited worlds, or as a place to represent thinly disguised allegories about the dream of a Marshall Plan that would fall like "manna" from the sky. In parallel, flying objects were commonly interpreted in Spain as providential signs, which is why they will be examined in connection with other miraculous and supernatural visions inspired by the Catholic doctrine of grace. Thus, in the 1950s and 1960s, flying saucer sightings began to populate the pages of the national press along with news that highlighted the discoveries of mineral deposits such as oil and uranium, energy resources that, according to these reports, would make the country a potential key bastion in the Atlantic Axis, not only because of its geostrategic position, but also because of the value of its possible exports. After the agreements with the United States, these natural resources acquired a recurring significance in some fictions of popular culture, comics, cinema and literature, where the prodigious or magical appearance of hidden capitals translated into a recapitalization of the nation's own image vis-à-vis its economically and militarily superior allies. These cultural fables were organized around processes of "enchantment" that took place simultaneously both in the sky and in the subterranean

---

4 See Flaherty and Pasulka.

Fables of Intervention

spaces of the national territory. In this way, "enchantment", understood as a fantasy-constructing mechanism in modernity (Bennett 3–16), progressively shifted towards outer space, a new frontier for colonization that masked the costs of the technological and scientific processes of a terrestrial warlike escalation that was played out in the control of airspace (Tiryakian 89). As will be analysed in the last section of this chapter, the representation of both real and imaginary energy reserves aimed at revaluing Spain's image after the failure of the autarchic regime were a central theme in the press of the period, as well as in films such as *Todo es posible en Granada* (1954 [Everything's Possible in Granada]) by José Luis Sáenz de Heredia, and ¡Aquí hay petróleo! (1956 [There's Oil Here!]) by Rafael Salvia. The fantasy of a possible Spanish national "treasure" coveted by the Americans thus gave shape to a series of fictions on the economic and military intervention of the United States in which the sublimation of national capital acquired the very form of a hidden treasure.

The Debate in the Spanish Press: Writers and Intellectuals in the Face of Flying Saucers

During the 1950s and 1960s, aircraft sightings had a recurrent presence in the Spanish press, both in news reports that collected the testimonies of witnesses and in articles in which writers, intellectuals and experts offered explanations about the complexity of the phenomenon. The global dissemination of flying saucer sightings had begun in 1947 with the report by American civilian pilot Kenneth Arnold on the appearance of nine flying objects at Mount Rainier. In this context, news of the transatlantic phenomenon of sightings began to spread at about the same time as the emergence of the United States' containment strategy against the international expansion of communism (Gabilliet 6). From 1950 onwards, there was a proliferation of news in the Spanish press about the collective visions of unidentified aircraft, popularly known as *platillos volantes*, a literal translation of the English term "flying saucers" that Arnold had used in his description of the sighted objects.[5] The news in the official Francoist press presented the flying saucers as objects whose military origin could be perfectly "identified". According to these reports, they could be

---

5 In this chapter, the expression "flying saucer" is used as a term in fashion in Spain during the 1950s. Although the term O.V.N.I. —which stands for the English acronym UFO or Unidentified Flying Object— was coined in 1952 by Edward J. Ruppelt, director of Project Blue Book of the United States Air Force (USAF) for the study of ufological phenomena, the popular spreading of this denomination occurred later in Spain.

Fables of Development

"proyectiles de pequeño tamaño [small-sized projectiles] ("Los platillos" 4), "aparatos de fabricación norteamericana" [American-made devices] ("Ya no son" 2), "fragmentos de bombas –cohetes estalladas en la estratosfera por las fuerzas aéreas" [fragments of bombs – rockets exploded in the stratosphere by the air forces] ("Opinión" 2), and even "bombas atómicas a bordo de platillos volantes" [atomic bombs aboard flying saucers] ("Bombas" 1) crossing international airspace. According to these reports, the strange aircraft sighted carried cutting-edge nuclear and computer technology that corresponded to the weapons development of the US allies. Their presence made it possible to think of a globalized sky in which aircraft incursions were multiplying at the same time as fantasies about the capital flows of Marshall Plan aid, financial investment, and trade with the new hegemonic power were circulating among the countries linked to the Atlantic Axis. This was a scenario that Manuel Vázquez Montalbán summarized in his *Crónica Sentimental de España* as follows:

> Los extraños signos en el cielo, los extraños signos en el mar. De pronto, sobre las ciudades y los calveros, sobre los plantíos de repoblación forestal y sobre los pantanos, sobre las alzadas cabezas de España entera, aparecieron estelas de humo en los cielos en otro tiempo imperiales. Los cazas americanos dejaban extrañas líneas paralelas del humo más blanco de todos los humos. (112)

> [Strange signs in the sky, strange signs in the sea. Suddenly, over the cities and the glades, over the reforestation plantations and over the marshes, over the towering heads of all Spain, smoke trails appeared in the once imperial skies. American fighters left strange parallel lines of the whitest smoke.]

In the 1950s, the escalation of political tensions between the United States and the USSR began to be played out in the control of airspace and cosmic space. Both dimensions were included in what Carl Schmitt called the "pluralismo de grandes espacios" [pluralism of large spaces] (4) in 1962, the same year in which Minister Manuel Fraga appointed him honorary member of the Institute of Political Studies. For the German thinker, the new conflict between blocs did not take place on "campos de batalla abiertos" [open battlefields] but in "los espacios multidimensionales de la guerra fría" [the multidimensional spaces of the Cold War] (31). It was an expansion of the dominion of the so-called "politics of verticality" (Weizman), in which states gave a relevant role to the gaze from above as a criterion for observation and intervention on the population. The

Fables of Intervention

deployment of new control, security and surveillance devices took place in a global airspace which, in Schmitt's opinion, encompassed zones and regions of very different density and permeability: state territory, the area of influence of the Monroe Doctrine, NATO's sphere of defence and the UN's global space. These were spaces that formed "campos de fuerzas magnéticas de energía y de trabajo humanos" [fields of magnetic forces of energy and human labour], which articulated a new "nomos de la Tierra" [nomos of the Earth] ("El orden" 21) or new world order that was defined by three phenomena: anti-colonialism, the conquest of space and the "desarrollo industrial de las zonas subdesarrolladas por los desarrollados" [industrial development of the underdeveloped zones by the developed] (21). According to Schmitt, the control of one of these spaces had repercussions on that of the others, so that the "invasion" of outer space became one of the most important geopolitical objectives for the opposing powers: "Solamente quien domine la tierra dominará los nuevos espacios cósmicos, que se hacen accesibles al hombre gracias a los nuevos medios técnicos. Y al revés: cada paso que se dé en la toma del espacio cósmico significará un paso en la dominación de la tierra para el poder que lo efectúe" [Only he who dominates the Earth will dominate the new cosmic spaces, which are made accessible to man thanks to the new technical means. And vice versa: every step taken in the seizure of cosmic space will mean a step in the domination of the Earth for the power that takes it] (23).

Two years after the end of World War II, the Cold War had entered its second phase when the alliance between the United States and the Soviet Union broke down. When Harry S. Truman began his term as president, the relationship between the two world powers, now pillars of the UN, resulted in a total division of the world that was articulated around the friend-enemy political logic, and all that remained of the old project of a unified world in the face of fascism were the old progressive utopias and technicist fantasies. In this context, the Spanish press in exile also echoed the sightings of the mysterious airships flying in the sky, relating them to the advances and threats of the US military industry, in which the so-called "Marshallization" of science, as exiled journalists called it, would play a key role:

> Desde que la Unión Soviética declaró poseer el arma atómica, la inventiva yanqui no tiene fronteras. La bomba de hidrógeno, los platillos volantes, el gas destructor de los centros nerviosos, la bomba atómica de bolsillo y, según la revista *Ciencia para todos*, "armas ultra-secretas que permiten helar los mares e incendiar la atmósfera". ("La ciencia yanki" 95)

40 *Fables of Development*

[Since the Soviet Union declared that it possessed the atomic weapon, Yankee inventiveness has known no bounds. The hydrogen bomb, flying saucers, nerve centre destroying gas, the pocket atomic bomb and, according to the magazine *Ciencia para todos*, "top-secret weapons that can freeze the seas and set the atmosphere on fire".]

In the early 1950s, the first American aid to the Spanish population was donations of food such as powdered milk, cheese and butter distributed by the Catholic organization Caritas. Humanitarian aid that, as a consequence of institutional corruption that favoured the existence of the black market, was quickly purchased by middle-class families who bought the products from citizens in real need.[6] As stated in a joke published in the exile press in 1950, the economic loans granted to the government did not help to alleviate the pressing needs and hunger of the population, which received simultaneously to its daily poverty the visit of the "flying saucers" in the Spanish skies:

– En la tertulia de un café, pregunta uno:
– ¿Se han enterado ustedes de lo de los platillos volantes?
– Ya lo creo, responde uno, como que España ha pasado a ser la mayor potencia aérea del mundo.
– No exagere.
– Pero que no le quepa la menor duda. ¿Es que no tiene Franco 28 millones de platos en el aire? ("El humor" 96).

[– In a café conversation, one of them asks:
– Have you heard about the flying saucers?
– Sure I have, one replies; in fact, Spain has become the greatest air power in the world.
– Don't exaggerate.
– But don't you have any doubt. Doesn't Franco have 28 million saucers in the air?]

---

6 "Nos llegó una especie de grosera caricatura de Plan Marshall para pordioseros famélicos: leche en polvo, queso y mantequilla salada, regalo de Caritas norteamericana para los necesitados españoles (inmediatamente, en toda España surgió un pequeño mercado negro generalizado: las familias de clase media compraban por cuatro perras esos productos a sus pobres, cuyas necesidades primarias no tenían nada que ver con el concepto de ayuda de los yanquis" (Reyes). [We received a sort of crude caricature of the Marshall Plan for starving beggars: powdered milk, cheese and salted butter, a gift from the American Caritas for the needy Spaniards (immediately, a small generalized black market arose all over Spain: middle-class families bought these products for four bucks from their poor, whose primary needs had nothing to do with the Yankees' concept of aid).]

Fables of Intervention

While most of the Spanish population was trying to survive hunger and poverty, the mysterious airships expressed the daily desires related to the improvement of food and living conditions in the carnival imaginary recreated by the comics and the humour of the illustrated magazines. Thus, together with the possible military uses of aerospace technology, the so-called illustrated *Almanaques* [Almanacs] included in their forecasts and prophecies for the year 1951 a representation of flying saucers as a vehicle to express the most pressing collective concern at that time, namely, the desire for more abundant and nutritious food: "Cuando sepan en Marte que en la Tierra hay países que pasan hambre, mandarán platos volantes colmados de buenos alimentos" [When they know on Mars that there are countries on Earth that are starving, they will send flying saucers full of good food] (quoted in Guiral, "TBO" 103). These wishful illustrated "prophecies" continued in 1952, despite the fact that the regime had withdrawn the food rationing cards in order to reaffirm the supposed successes of its economic policy. In the words of one of these comic strips expressing wishes for better food: Es posible que aparezcan platillos volantes provistos de cuchillo y tenedor. Y algunos hasta con alguna chuleta y todo" [It is possible that flying saucers with knives and forks will appear. And some even with a chop and everything] (quoted in Guiral, "TBO" 105).

The dissemination of news following the first sightings of unidentified flying objects in 1947 had given rise to various interpretations around the world. In the first survey published on the phenomenon in the United States, the responses of the participants pointed to different hypotheses about the origin of the aircraft, among which their extraterrestrial nature was not contemplated: "On August 15, 1947 a Gallup poll revealed that 90 percent of Americans surveyed were aware of the flying-saucer sightings and that most believed that US or foreign secret weapons, hoaxes, and balloons were responsible" (Bartholomew y Howard 191). The extraterrestrial hypothesis and doubts about the responsibility of states in managing information about the phenomenon began to gain strength after the publication of essays such as *The Flying Saucers Are Real* (1950), by military aviator Donald Keyhoe, or *Behind the Flying Saucers* (1950), by journalist Frank Scully. The media around the world echoed these opinions, displacing the possible military origin of the aircraft from public debate. As Pierre Lagrange points out in his comparative study of the first flying saucers in the United States and the ghost-rockets sighted in Norway and Sweden in 1946, the social history of ufology must consider the frameworks of interpretation employed at the time by witnesses to sightings in different places (224–244). In this sense, in the Spain of the 1950s, the population's experience of civilian bombings during the Civil War was connected to the popular knowledge of

42 *Fables of Development*

military agreements with the United States, as well as to the proliferation of nuclear weapons, events which all determined the interpretation and public discussion of the nature of aerial objects.

In 1954, Alfredo Kindelán, general in charge of Franco's air force during the Spanish Civil War, summarized for the newspaper *ABC* the explanations that until then were contemplated: "Alucinación colectiva. Misterio. Confusión con globos, aerolitos y estrellas. Consecuencia de las explosiones atómicas. Ensayos de armas secretas y visitas de seres o de artificios extraterráqueos" [Collective hallucination. Mystery. Confusion with balloons, aerolites and stars. Consequence of atomic explosions. Tests of secret weapons and visits of extraterrestrial beings or artifacts] ("Platillos" 3). Kindelán even raised the possibility of "plantas superinteligentes" [super-intelligent plants] that could invade the planet, an argument reminiscent of the film *The Thing from Another World* (1951), released a few months earlier in Spain. The general finally opted for the hypothesis that they could be secret remote-controlled weapons.[7] Two years earlier, Kindelán had dealt with this issue in another article entitled "Las preocupaciones extranjeras y las nacionales" (Foreign and National Concerns), in which he placed the national controversy about the saucers in relation to other issues of "universal interest" such as "el rearme, la Unión Europea, el Pacto del Atlántico, la posible tercera guerra, la paz en Corea y los experimentos atómicos" [rearmament, the European Union, the Atlantic Pact, the possible third war, peace in Korea and atomic experiments] ("Las preocupaciones" 3).

The discussion on the origin of the airships sparked a debate in the Spanish press in which, along with the hypotheses of scientific and military experts, several writers expressed their opinions on the puzzling phenomenon. As early as 1950, Nobel Prize winner Jacinto Benavente summarized the possible alternatives that had been considered in his article "El asunto del día" [The issue of the day]. In this article, Benavente drew a comparison between the arrival of airships and the aid sent to Europe by the Marshall Plan, in which the saucers took on an "enchanted" dimension whereby they became donor agents descending from the sky to generously provide for humans:

> Respecto a los platillos volantes, tenemos de un lado a los razonables y de otro a los imaginativos. Entre los primeros, están en primer lugar, los incrédulos, los que no creerán en tales platillos mientras no los vean, los palpen, se den cuenta de su mecanismo y sobre todo de

7 The North American experimental aircraft Vought V-173 and XF5U, also known as "Flying Flapjack", have been traditionally pointed out as one of the possible objects seen collectively.

Fables of Intervention

su utilidad . . . Entre los razonables están también los que atribuyen la supuesta visión de los platillos a una psicosis de guerra, un caso de sugestión colectiva y epidémica, como lo fue el terror milenario en su tiempo y en los suyos la licantropía y los aquelarres . . . A las explicaciones, más razonables y científicas, que se trata de aerolitos por parte de la Naturaleza, que anda también un tanto desquiciada en estos tiempos, o por parte de los hombres, de nuevos artefactos de guerra en maniobras de ensayo. Pudiera objetarse que para ser aerolitos son demasiados y habría que suponer en el sistema planetario un sobrante de existencias de las que no saben cómo deshacerse, como es el caso de los Estados Unidos. Y tal vez los platillos volantes procedan del plan Marshall de algún planeta tan generoso y desprendido como los Estados Unidos. (5)

[Regarding flying saucers, we have on one side the reasonable and on the other the imaginative. Among the former, there are first of all the incredulous, those who will not believe in such saucers until they see them, feel them, realize their mechanism and above all their usefulness ... Among the reasonable are also those who attribute the alleged vision of the saucers to a war psychosis, a case of collective and epidemic suggestion, as was the millenarian terror in its time and lycanthropy and covens in their own time ... There are also more reasonable and scientific explanations, that it is a matter of aerolites on the part of Nature, which is also somewhat unhinged in these times, or on the part of men, of new war artifacts in rehearsal manoeuvres. It could be objected that for aerolites there are too many of them and it would be necessary to suppose that there is a surplus of stock in the planetary system which they do not know how to get rid of, as is the case of the United States. And perhaps the flying saucers come from the Marshall plan of some planet as generous and detached as the United States.]

The writer used in his text the same narrative motif that populated other fictions in the early 1950s, which showed the reception of gifts or goods that appeared as "manna" falling from the sky. In this sense, the representation of communities receiving a sudden abundance of goods from airspace was common to three European films: *Passport to Pimlico* (Cornelius, 1949), *Miracolo a Milano* (De Sica, 1951 [Miracle in Milan]), and *¡Bienvenido, Mr. Marshall!* (García Berlanga, 1953 [Welcome Mr Marshall!]). The common element in all of them was their ability to construct fables about the longed-for "miracles" in a Europe where hunger and rationing cards still survived. This was the case of the political fiction recreated in Luis García

44 *Fables of Development*

Berlanga's comedy, in which the residents of a small town celebrated the imminent arrival of the American delegates of the Marshall Plan with the aim of attracting the aid of the European Recovery Program. According to its authors, they decided to make a film "cuya intención encajaba de lleno en la postura política y diplomática española frente a la psicosis mundial de Reyes Magos creada por la mal aprovechada ayuda americana" [whose intention was fully in line with the Spanish political and diplomatic stance in the face of the worldwide psychosis of the Three Wise Men caused by the ill-used American aid] (Pérez Perucha 325). In the context of the incipient relations between the two countries, the film offered a reflection on the role of the Francoist state in the imaginary construction of a credit that was portrayed as the prize of a geopolitical "lottery" that would spill over the territory.

In the film, the Castilian village of Villar del Río becomes the simulacrum of an Andalucían village in order to please its visitors and ends up incurring an enormous debt with the expenses of this celebration (Woods 9–26, Marsh 97–121, Martín 73–80, Pavlović 169–174). In the denouement, not only do the townspeople fail to obtain the goods that the town authorities have forced them to request on the petition lists intended for the Americans, but they must also socialize the payment of the credits they have requested for the celebration, which in the narrator's words translate as "unas peticiones al revés" [some backwards petitions]. On the night before the arrival of the American visitors, a farmer who has told the authorities of his wish to receive a tractor, dreams that this gift is part of a shipment of goods transported by US Army planes. In his dream, those responsible for the delivery of these goods are three US military personnel dressed as the Three Wise Men, emblematic donor figures in Catholic tradition. This was a depiction that had been recurrently used in the 1950s to represent Americans as the donor agents in post-war Europe, an allegory in which President Eisenhower himself was described as one of "Rey Mago y el prestamista del mundo" [Magi and the lender to the world] ("La administración Eisenhower" 58). In the dream of *¡Bienvenido, Mr. Marshall!*, it is precisely three American "Wise Men" who parachute from their plane the goods requested as part of an economic plan from which Spain was finally excluded.

This cargo granted by a higher authority can be analysed from a symbolic logic that in the field of anthropology is called "cargo cults". "Cargo cults" were especially popular belief systems after World War II in Pacific communities that developed superstitious rituals in the hope of attracting goods supplied by more technologically advanced nations. In these rituals, celebrated in societies that had seen intervention by foreign powers, participants developed infrastructures designed to attract desired cargo. Anthropologists such as Marvin Harris or Lamont Lindstrom have pointed

Fables of Intervention

out how cargo cults would be nothing more than a way of capturing the link between the unequal distribution of wealth enjoyed by some nations that extract natural resources and human capital from others. It is also a means of articulating the right to demand the products of industrialized nations from communities that cannot afford them. From this logic of cargo cults, the neighbours' requests in *¡Bienvenido Mr. Marshall!* can be interpreted as donations expected from the United States, a country that the characters sensed would benefit in return for the European aid of the Marshall Plan. Historians and anthropologists have analysed the ufological phenomenon in the light of the millenarian and providentialist narratives of the cargo cults, establishing the points of convergence between beliefs in visitors from outer space and these rituals (Landes 391–420; Trompf 221–238; Grünschloß 423–424).

Following the logic present in the text "El asunto del día" [The Issue of the Day] by Jacinto Benavente, cited above, the extraterrestrials aboard the observed flying saucers would be creatures coming from a civilization technologically superior to our own and bringing with them a salvific "cargo". In some of these narratives, this "cargo" would consist of a kind of evolutionary wisdom that would help humans overcome the political hostility of the atomic age. This is precisely the same narrative logic through which the writer Noel Clarasó showed his fascination with the phenomenon of sightings in his 1950 article "Platillos volantes cruzan el sueño" [Flying Saucers Cross the Dream]. In this text, Clarasó claimed the possibility of generating a more hopeful look at the future of the planet; a look that was possible to vindicate by imagining the existence of other civilizations for which the idea of technological progress would not lead to destruction, but to the dream of other possible worlds:

> ¿No es una especie de juventud del alma esta aparición de los platillos que nos invitan a soñar en otros mundos, donde las velocidades supersónicas son el paso de tortuga, la palabra hablada y escrita se cita como símbolo de antiguas civilizaciones, y la energía atómica ya no se usa para fines destructivos? El hombre se está convirtiendo en un ser escéptico y ensoberbecido por exceso de confianza en su propia técnica. No está de más que otros seres raros le demuestren que es un niño recién salido del colegio. (7)

> [Is it not a kind of youth of the soul, this appearance of saucers inviting us to dream of other worlds, where supersonic speeds are the turtle's pace, the spoken and written word is cited as a symbol of ancient civilizations, and atomic energy is no longer used for

46   *Fables of Development*

destructive purposes? Man is becoming sceptical and conceited through overconfidence in his own technique. It is not superfluous for other rare beings to show him that he is a child just out of school.]

In contrast to the utopian projections of Noel Clarasó or Jacinto Benavente, the writer Camilo José Cela expressed his rejection of the imaginative excesses that the UFO phenomenon provoked in his article "Los platillos volantes o un mundo con astigmatismo" [Flying saucers or a world with astigmatism]:

Mientras tanto los platillos volantes siguen deambulando por los aires como fieles fantasmas escoceses, y lo malo empezará cuando uno de ellos con el rumbo perdido, se estrelle contra las gentes y contra las casas de una ciudad. Será algo así como si tomaran cuerpo las "moscas volantes" de los astigmáticos y, en vez de seguir volando, se le colasen por los ojos y por los oídos con ánimo de anidarle en el cerebro. Nadie se sienta seguro ante los discos voladores. Malo, si son de duro hierro. Pero peor, mucho peor, si son de la humosa carne del fantasma. Porque los sueños de la imaginación—nadie lo olvide—engendran monstruos. (4)

[Meanwhile, flying saucers continue to wander through the air like faithful Scottish ghosts, and the bad part will begin when one of them, with its course lost, crashes into the people and houses of a city. It will be something like if the "flying flies" of the astigmatics take shape and, instead of continuing to fly, slip through the eyes and ears with the intention of nesting in their brains. No one feels safe in front of flying discs. Bad, if they are made of hard iron. But worse, much worse, if they are of the smoky flesh of the phantom. Because the dreams of the imagination —no one should forget it— spawn monsters.]

It is highly significant that Cela, who had worked as a censor a few years earlier, used the sentence framing Goya's *Capricho 43* as a warning to sanction the freedom of the imagination. The Aragonese painter, who had given testimony in his painting of the collective sightings of hot air balloons in the eighteenth century, had also recreated in a utopian way in his *Proverbios* (1819) some technological devices thanks to which men were able to soar and fly. Goya's sentence served Cela to frighten the public with his interpretation of the visions, opening the way to the utopian potential of an aerospace imaginary that, as the painter recreated, also served to project the visions of an alternative social model. Two years later, Cela wondered about a possible encounter between aliens and humans, establishing a comparison with the conquest of America in 1492; a simile in which the vulnerability

Fables of Intervention

of the indigenous people in the face of the military and technological superiority of the conquerors was ignored:

> Con este raro cuento de los platillos volantes podemos calcular nuestro miedo, pero no debemos tampoco echar en saco roto el miedo que deben pasar los pobrecitos aviadores, o lo que sean, marcianos, venusianos, jupiterianos, saturnianos o de los mismísimos infiernos. Con el descubrimiento de América debió pasar algo por el estilo, y si los indígenas al ver desembarcar a los españoles, tenían sus reservas, los españoles al tropezarse con los primeros indios que asomaron sus plumas a la playa, tampoco debían tenerlas todas consigo. ("Tres hombrecillos" 7)

> [With this strange tale of the flying saucers we can figure out our fear, but neither should we ignore the fear that the poor little aviators, or whatever they are, Martians, Venusians, Jupiterians, Saturnians or from the very underworld, must have had to go through. With the discovery of America, something similar must have happened, and if the Indians had their reservations when they saw the Spaniards disembark, the Spaniards must have had their concerns, too, when they met the first Indians showing their feathers on the beach.]

The conquest of America was also used by the press in exile as an emblematic image to analyse the imperialist project of space conquest. Thus, in the "Poema terrestre dedicado a los habitantes de la luna" [Terrestrial poem dedicated to the inhabitants of the moon], published in the anarchist newspaper *Solidaridad Obrera: A.I.T. Órgano del movimiento libertario español en Francia* in 1959, an anonymous author launched a series of warnings to the Selenites, converted in his allegory into indigenous populations facing the process of dispossession resulting from colonial projects, including that of space colonization:

> Hoy la competencia está en llegar tal o cual bando el primero en vuestros dominios lunares, tan tranquilos, quedando el invasor dueño y señor de vuestros ensoñadores dominios para sembrar ellos la venenosa planta del egoísmo, trasplantar el deseo voraz de adquirir del vecino sus montañas de metales preciosos, oro a ser posible, a lanza y espada de ser necesario, como antaño en las Indias. Hoy de las Indias no se habla, pero indios, nuestros grandes ambiciosos parecen idearlos en la Luna, y por eso os alertamos. Tendréis que velar por vuestros valores y vuestras vidas, el bien más precioso. Pero, por desdicha vuestra, parece que cuando nuestros cohetes os alcancen habréis de cederlo

48 *Fables of Development*

todo si no disponéis de máquinas infernales y arrasadoras como así son las nuestras. (2)

[Today the competition is for this or that side to arrive first in your lunar domains, so calmly, leaving the invader lord and master of your dreamy domains to sow in them the poisonous plant of selfishness, to transplant the voracious desire to acquire from the neighbour his mountains of precious metals, gold if possible, with spear and sword if necessary, as in the Indies of yore. Today we do not speak of the Indies, but Indians, our great ambitions seem to devise them on the Moon, and that is why we are alerting you. You will have to watch over your values and your lives, the most precious asset. But, unfortunately for you, it seems that when our rockets reach you, you will have to give up everything unless you possess infernal and devastating machines such as ours.]

The representation of subaltern populations through an extraterrestrial imaginary thus expressed the concerns that ufological beliefs shared with other progressive traditions of a millenarian type and their yearnings for salvation and collective transformation (Wojcik 73–79). At the juncture of the Cold War and especially in the context of Franco's dictatorship, this simile took on new meanings as it was recreated by beings from an extraterrestrial world that could mark the beginning of a new era of peace and enlightenment.

Celestial Visions in Franco's Spain

The first sightings of flying saucers in Spain date back to 1947, when people from the towns of Bazalote (Albacete), Azpeitia (Guipúzcoa), and Montequinto (Sevilla) claimed to have witnessed different visions (Jiménez 25–33). The testimonies continued in the following years until reaching their zenith during the wave of strange celestial apparitions that took place between March and April 1950 (Geppert 2012, 340). The press collected numerous statements from witnesses, as is the case of Máximo Muñoz Hernáiz, a fourteen-year-old shepherd who in 1953 formulated his encounter with aliens in these terms: "Creí que era un 'globo grande' de esos que se tiran en la feria. Luego me di cuenta de que no: relucía mucho . . . Se abrió una puerta y empezaron a salir tietes . . . Muy pequeñetes. Eran amarillos y los ojos estrechos . . . (Vestían) igual que los músicos en la fiesta" [I thought it was a 'big balloon' of those that are thrown at the fair. Then I realized that it wasn't: it shone very brightly. A door opened and tiny little guys started to come out . . . Very tiny. They were yellow and their eyes were narrow. . . (They dressed) just like the musicians at the fiesta] (quoted in García Blanco

Fables of Intervention 49

40–42). The use of such a carnivalesque imaginary to describe contact with extraterrestrial beings was common throughout Europe, as evidenced by testimonies like those analysed by the psychoanalyst Carl Jung in his essay *Flying Saucers: A Modern Myth of Things Seen in the Skies* (1958), where they are related to narratives from popular folklore and mythology.

In the accounts of Spanish testimonies we find mythopoetic motifs such as the trope of the ghost ship or vessel. This was the case of the vision of Miguel Sevil, a resident of Lécera (Zaragoza) who in 1954 declared having seen "dos hombres muy rubios, que hablaban un lenguaje extraño" [two very blond men, who spoke a strange language] descending from "un barco luminoso, lleno de antenas y hélices" [a luminous ship, full of antennas and propellers] ("Un platillo con tripulantes" 36). The town of Lécera belonged to the region of Campo de Belchite, a locality —bombed in 1938 by the Condor Legion of the III Reich— where the anarchist collectives of Aragón constituted during the Civil War had been in charge of the construction of small airfields like the one that would have served as landing strip in this case. A week later, the *ABC* newspaper offered a scientific explanation that put the matter to rest: "Se trata de un globo de procedencia inglesa o francesa, de los que se utilizan para observaciones meteorológicas" [It is a balloon of English or French origin, one of those used for meteorological observations] ("Un platillo volante resulta ser un globo" 19).

Although the press made an effort to deny some of these testimonies, on some occasions the media gave publicity to informants who claimed to have had direct contact with beings or objects from other worlds. This imagination about the supposed encounters with extraterrestrials materialized in findings such as the one announced in 1955 by the newspaper *El Alcazar*: "Marte coloca en Madrid su primera piedra" [Mars places its first stone in Madrid] (1). The "proof" of alien existence, a stone with nine enigmatic inscriptions, became the foundational event of ufology in Spain. Fernando Sesma, a fan of the UFO phenomenon who had published a series of articles in the newspaper *Madrid* under the epigraph "Los Platillos Volantes vienen de Otro Mundo" [Flying Saucers Come from Another World], gave wide media and literary coverage to this event, which became the centre of the debate surrounding the creation of the Sociedad de Amigos del Espacio in 1954 (Bravo 12–15). It was a ufological association that had its regular gathering at the Café Lyon in Madrid, in the neuralgic centre of a dictatorship that explicitly restricted the right of assembly.[8]

---

8 In its basements, the Café Lyon had a German salon known as "La Ballena alegre", a place where the gatherings of the Falangist circles were held during the Second Republic.

50 *Fables of Development*

In May 1967, Sesma made public the revelation of a finding that would change the history of ufology in Spain in the following decades: letters in which extraterrestrials warned of their presence in Madrid since the previous year as well as of future landings. It was the beginning of the so-called "Ummo Case", a scam that fed the ufological fantasies about the presence of extraterrestrial beings in Spain. Ummo would be the name of an exoplanet from which a civilization would hypothetically come from, and which would have contacted humans through documents and letters sent to groups of people fond of ufology. In this case, the utopian imagination of the previous decades would have become a fraud that came to be used by sectarian groups in the late 80s (Bravo 161–183).

In parallel to the experiences of aircraft sightings and the rise of science fiction, ufology emerged in Spain as a space for debate around which study groups and associations such as the Society of Friends of Space Visitors or the Center for Interplanetary Studies were created (Cabria 143–163). These organizations formed a place for meeting and discussion in a public sphere where the right of assembly and association was severely regulated. According to Jodi Dean, ufology emerged as a venue for the management of alternative knowledge generated by civil society in reaction to the discourse of scientific, political and military authorities. Ufology had initially emerged in the United States as a space for the production of social practices and knowledge that challenged the official narratives built around the space programme; these were narratives in which the advances in the conquest of outer space were promoted as a sign of the superiority of American liberal democracy over its Soviet competitors. Ufologists' associations developed a populist agency that challenged the presumed authority of the Cold War containment culture while generating a series of scientific and political hypotheses about the origin of airships. In this way, discussion groups questioned the limits of the very notion of modern sovereignty:

> Ufology was doing something; it wasn't just spinning an outlandish conspiracy tale. At the very least, it was publicizing an outlandish conspiracy theory that used outer space and the possibility of extraterrestrial visitations to challenge military and scientific hegemony. Indeed, Tom Englehardt suggests that, precisely because it was "beyond the pale," flying saucer society was able to attack the government without being accused of communism. From the perspective of the dominant culture, ufology was silly. Nonetheless, precisely because it was outside the constraining equation of truth with security and identifiability, ufology was free to focus on the unknown, to indicate the limits of governmental authority and validate

Fables of Intervention

the experiences of witnesses without necessarily claiming that it could identify or establish the object of their experiences. (42)

The collective sightings of strange airships in the Spanish skies were not a phenomenon that had begun in the 1950s, since the country had a long tradition of visions in modernity. Throughout the eighteenth century, the interpretation that had been made of these phenomena as omens of events determined by the signs of a divine order gave way to new scientific hypotheses. Thus, in 1729, the religious polygrapher Benito Jerónimo Feijoo dedicated the conclusion of his speech "Duendes y espíritus familiares" [Goblins and familiar spirits] to dismantle one of the "cuentos de viejas" [old wives' tales] that had circulated years before about the appearance of three "aerial postillions" over the sky of Galicia:

> Los años pasados corrió por Galicia, que cerca del Cabo de Finis Terrae se vio venir volando de la parte del Norte una nube, de la cual salieron tres hombres cerca de una Venta, y después de desayunarse en ella, volvieron a meterse en la nube, y continuaron el vuelo hacia la parte Meridional. Por ser esto en aquel tiempo en que las Potencias coligadas contra nosotros solicitaban entrar en su alianza a Portugal, se discurría que aquellos tres eran Postillones aéreos de alguna Potencia del Norte, que llevaban cartas a aquel Reino. (100)

> [Last years a rumour ran through Galicia, that near the Cape of Finis Terrae a cloud was seen coming flying from the Northern part, from which three men came out near an inn, and after having breakfast in it, they went back into the cloud, and continued the flight towards the Southern part. Since this was at the time when the Powers in league with us were requesting Portugal to enter into their alliance, it was thought that those three were air postilions of some Northern Power, who were carrying letters to that Kingdom.]

In the popular imagination, the vision of these phenomena was linked to mysterious technologies that expressed fear of an external invasion, as was the case when Feijoo wrote his essay in the context of the Anglo-Spanish War (1727–1729). Visions of strange aerial apparatuses also occurred continuously in Europe and the United States throughout the nineteenth century, coinciding with political crises that anticipated future military conflicts. Thus, the wave of sightings that took place in the United States between November 1896 and May 1897 (Clark 122) was interpreted from Spain through a discourse that considered the phenomenon as an invention of the sensationalist press to mobilize public opinion: "Por

52 *Fables of Development*

esta vez tócale el turno al interesante problema de la navegación aérea, resuelto victoriosamente por cierto misterioso personaje que, como *Robur el Conquistador*, de la novela de Julio Verne, paséase a bordo de su aerostato a través de todo el territorio norteamericano" [This time it is the turn of the interesting problem of aerial navigation, victoriously solved by a certain mysterious character that, like Robur the Conqueror, from Jules Verne's novel, flies his aerostat across the entire North American territory] ("La navegación" 2). Following this tradition of unidentified flying objects, in 1909 Ramiro de Maeztu narrated for the readers of *La correspondencia* the sightings of "ghost-balloons" that had flown over the British sky and that had also been sighted in the north of Spain, in the city of Vitoria. Later, during the 1930s, the stories about the visions of mysterious airships focused on stories about "ghost planes", which came to be related to the uprising against the monarchy led by Ramón Franco, brother of the future dictator, on the military airfield of Cuatro Vientos.[9]

During the Civil War, and coinciding with the beginning of the offensive of the Republican troops in the Battle of the Ebro, the military of Franco's side also witnessed a sighting in the so-called "Pinar de los muertos" [Pine forest of the dead] near Guadalajara, a vision that was interpreted as an 'invento aeronáutico alemán o de los "rojos"' [a German aeronautical invention or an invention of the Commies] (Ballester 30). In a parallel way, in the providential story that General Franco elaborated about the Civil War, understood as a Crusade, the success of the military victories was also associated with another type of visions, such as those of the divine apparitions that helped the fascist army in emblematic dates:

> Es en nuestra misma Cruzada la sucesión de hechos portentosos, que coinciden en su gran mayoría con las fiestas más señaladas de nuestra Iglesia, una nueva muestra de aquella protección. El paso del Estrecho tiene lugar el día de la Virgen de África, bajo la vista del Santuario de Ceuta. La batalla de Brunete tiene su crisis victoriosa en el mismo día

---

9 "La gente, en su fantasía, relaciona la fuga del comandante Franco con la aparición del avión misterioso que solía volar de noche sobre Pontevedra. De este avión fantasma dimos cuenta a los lectores de POLÍTICA. Ahora hay quien dice que el avión y la avioneta que voló sobre Madrid esta madrugada, son el mismo aparato y que en él se ha marchado el comandante Franco al extranjero. Naturalmente, sólo a título de fantasía acogemos el rumor." [People, in their fantasy, relate the escape of Commander Franco with the appearance of the mysterious plane that used to fly at night over Pontevedra ... Now there are those who say that the plane and the light aircraft that flew over Madrid early this morning are the same apparatus and that Commander Franco has gone abroad in it] ("El avión misterioso" 5).

Fables of Intervention

de nuestro santo patrón, Santiago de los Caballeros. La ofensiva de nuestro enemigo sobre Cáceres se detiene ante los muros del santo monasterio de Guadalupe, que cobijan a la Virgen, Señora de nuestros descubrimientos. ("Palabras del Caudillo" 242)

[It is in our same Crusade where the succession of portentous events —which coincide in their great majority with the most important feasts of our Church— is a new sign of that protection. The crossing of the Strait of Gibraltar takes place on the day of the Virgin of Africa, under the sight of the Sanctuary of Ceuta. The battle of Brunete has its victorious crisis on the same day of our patron saint, Santiago de los Caballeros. The offensive of our enemy on Cáceres stops before the walls of the holy monastery of Guadalupe, which shelter the Virgin, Lady of our discoveries.]

In Europe, and in Spain in particular, sightings of unidentified aircraft were also associated with collective visions of a religious nature. This relationship of the UFO phenomenon with the sacred dimension was one of the axes of the analysis that Carl G. Jung developed in *Flying Saucers: A Modern Myth of Things Seen in the Sky* (1959). Jung understood the mass sightings as a modern myth that captured the anxieties of a collective unconscious that constructed around the strange apparitions a vernacular religious response to the fears of the nuclear age. In his view, extraterrestrials would operate in certain ufological narratives as "technological angels" ("Collected" 322) who intervened to save humanity from its path to atomic destruction. Jung thus connected the flying saucer sightings with a historical tradition in which collective visions of supernatural phenomena were related, as in the case of Franco's discourse on the Civil War, to the unfolding of war events. The psychoanalyst listed, among others, the experience of "the crusaders in the siege of Jerusalem, that of the fighters of Mons in the First World War, that of the believing people of Fatima, [and] that of the border troops in the interior of Switzerland during the Second World War" ("Flying Saucers" 20).

In this sense, Terenci Moix (1942–2003) recalled in the first volume of his memoirs, *El peso de la paja. El cine de los sábados* (1990) the fictions that accompanied him in his childhood. The Catalan writer explains how in his imagination the narratives about the visions of prodigious phenomena such as Marian apparitions were confused with the "Martian" visions that populated the fictions and the press of the time:

Aquella semana se me antojaba ver *La señora de Fátima*. Reconozco que mi elección era insólita . . . Una vez más, la explicación proviene de

54   *Fables of Development*

la ignorancia. Las películas de milagros y apariciones encendían mi imaginación porque las asociaba con las historias de marcianos. Una señora que les caía del cielo a tres niños palurdos no era cosa que ocurriese todos los días, por lo menos en mi calle. Tendría algo que ver con los platillos volantes. (182)

[That week I was in the mood to watch *The Lady of Fatima*. I admit that my choice was unusual ... Once again, the explanation comes from ignorance. Movies of miracles and apparitions fired my imagination because I associated them with stories of Martians. A lady falling out of the sky to three uncouth kids was not an everyday occurrence, at least not on my street. It would have something to do with flying saucers.]

During the 1950s, the visions of airships in the Spanish skies coincided with the spread of miraculous apparitions in the country. These religious visions were promoted by the media and denounced by director Luis García Berlanga in his film *Los jueves, milagro* (1957). As historian William A. Christian Jr points out, descriptions of supposed Marian apparitions in Europe had been circulating in Spanish religious magazines since the end of World War II (259). Thus, the magazine *Iris de Paz* published in 1948 the testimony of the Dutch visionary Ida Peerdeman about her contact with the Virgin Mary, who revealed herself to her as "Lady of All Nations", and expressed in prophetic language her concern about the terrors of the new atomic age: "The explosion of atom bombs on Hiroshima and Nagasaki, the V-2 rockets of Peenemunde, the possibility of germ warfare, signaled a new era in the technology of destruction in which all were vulnerable, and in which death would come from the sky" (Christian 259). As Daniel Wojcik examines, during the twentieth century the apocalyptic warnings issued by the Virgin Mary operated similarly to the "avertive beliefs" associated with flying saucers, so that in both belief systems their adherents believe that "if people change their behavior as prescribed by otherworldly beings —put an end to violence, save the environment, become spiritually attuned, or work for the transformation of planetary consciousness— the world may be saved" (72). This relationship between aerospace technology and the transcendent dimension was also explored by Carl G. Jung, who argued that the possibility of space travel made "the unpopular idea of a metaphysical intervention much more acceptable" ("Flying Saucers" 22–23).

Spain was one of the countries where this confluence between the beginning of the Marian apparitions in Southern Europe and the first testimonies about the wave of transatlantic sightings since the end of the 1940s took place: "The months of June and July 1947, when the European

Fables of Intervention

wave of visions began, were also the beginning of the great American saucer scare" (Christian 258). We can find an example of this coincidence at the time in the reports of unidentified flying objects with the tradition of Marian apparitions in the Falangist newspaper *Imperio*, specifically in two news items that appeared together on the same page in its April 6, 1950 edition: "Un platillo volante sobre nuestra provincia" [A flying saucer over our province] and "Visita de la Virgen de Fátima y Santas Misiones" [Visit of the Virgin of Fatima and Holy Missions]. The celebration of the Holy Missions of Fatima in Spain emerged as a practice connected to the emergence of a new pastoral order at the beginning of the Cold War. It was the proposal of a parish priest from Berlin that a statue of Our Lady of Fatima would travel through the episcopal cities of Europe to the Russian border to convey the Marian message about the need for the Soviet Union to convert to Catholicism. According to Christian, these "missions" also coincided with a series of miraculous visions and apparitions throughout Spain. In his analysis of the cases documented in the first half of the 1950s, he views these experiences as "conversion dramas" that expressed in public the transformation of religious and political identities in a context marked by cruel repression (254–255).

The news item next to these "Santas Misiones" [Holy Missions], headlined "Un platillo volante sobre nuestra provincia" [A flying saucer over our province], described the sighting of a strange circular apparatus travelling in the direction of Portugal by some children and several peasants. In this case, any connection with a religious phenomenon like the one that gave rise to the visions of Fátima was discarded in the news and the possible veracity of the event would rest on the supposed ignorance of the witnesses with respect to these phenomena: "La noticia es digna de todo crédito por tratarse de personas ajenas a toda sugestión periodística, pues como hemos podido comprobar estas sencillas gentes ignoraban la existencia de cuantas informaciones de la Prensa acerca de los platillos volantes" [The news is worthy of all credit as it is about people alien to any journalistic suggestion; we have been able to verify that these simple people ignored the existence of all the information of the press about the flying saucers] (3). Whether or not they were aware of the published news, the truth is that —as one of the chronicles published in April 1950 in the same newspaper stated— the sightings were part of the daily conversations of the Spaniards, so it was not necessary to have access to the press to be informed of their existence: "the favourite topic at gatherings these days has revolved around the impressive details provided by our correspondent about the alleged beings fallen to Earth from other worlds" [el tema preferido en las tertulias de estos días ha girado en torno a los impresionantes pormenores suministrados por nuestro corresponsal acerca de los presuntos seres caídos a la Tierra desde otros mundos] ("La crónica-reportaje" 4).

At the beginning of the 1960s, the relationship between technology and Catholic religiosity continued in a context in which the existence of inhabited worlds was even contemplated as a possibility not discarded by Pope Pius XII at the VII Congress of Astronautics in 1956 (Cortes-Cavanillas 45). The *Revista de Enseñanza Media*, issued by the Dirección General de Enseñanza Media, published in 1962 a booklet entitled "Astronáutica y Espíritu" [Astronautics and Spirit], which was to serve as a complement in the education of high school students in Spain. The essay, written by the engineer Vicente Roglá, proposed "la adquisición universal católica de la espiritualidad y la moral a través del imperativo de la colonización espacial" [the universal Catholic acquisition of spirituality and morality through the imperative of space colonization] (Moriente 127). Following the vision that accompanied the developmentalist project, Roglá proposed a pragmatic techno-Christian rationale in which the development of aerospace science and technology would culminate in the welfare of the population and the end of class struggle (22-23).

Fig. 2. "Cae un platillo volante en Madrid." *Imperio: Diario de Zamora de Falange Española de las J.O.N.S.*, December 30, 1954, p. 3. (Biblioteca Virtual de Prensa Histórica. Creative Commons [CC] licence).

Fig. 3. Student Pepe Sales at La Salle Bonanova (a school in Barcelona), 1962. Courtesy of Martí Sales and LaBreu Edicions.

58   *Fables of Development*

This combination of aerospace imaginary and Catholicism also found expression in the popular culture of the period. The Christmas period was especially propitious for this type of amalgam of ufology, the sacred and a carnival-like visual repertoire. Thus, a flying saucer "landed" in the centre of Madrid to the astonishment of passers-by as part of a publicity prank held on Fool's Day (December 28) 1954 ("Cae un platillo" 3) [FIG. 2]. Another peculiar image that can help us understand the circulation of techno-Catholic imaginaries in the context of the incipient developmentalism can be found in a series of Christmas postcards made at La Salle Bonanova in Barcelona, dated 1962 [FIG. 3]. These are images in which the children photographed hold in their hands an object that represents an aerial artifact, a hybrid between a spaceship and an interplanetary missile that houses the figure of Baby Jesus. In this sense, it is worth remembering how in some areas of Spain the Baby Jesus is the equivalent of the Three Wise Men or Santa Claus as the bearer of gifts and toys for children during the Christmas period. The donor character of this figure was combined in the image with the representation of an aerospace technology that, as in the case of the previously analysed cargo cults, could guarantee peace, but also lead to the destruction of the inhabitants of the earth.

The relationship between aerospace technology, spirituality and art was also explored by sculptor Jorge Oteiza and filmmaker José Val del Omar. Both devoted part of their work to a spiritual interpretation of the figure of Soviet astronaut Yuri Gagarin, the first human to make a space flight in 1961. Oteiza established connections between Yuri Gagarin's ascent and the baroque pictorial vision of El Greco, represented in the figure of the Count of Orgaz. According to Oteiza, Gagarin's purely physical flight was an artistic equivalent to the suspension of gravity in El Greco's characters. In his vision, the weightlessness achieved by the astronaut was connected to a mystical state of liberation beyond everyday time and space that the sculptor sought to achieve through aesthetics. For his part, the filmmaker Val del Omar had seen in the transmission capabilities of the first artificial telecommunications satellite Telstar (launched into orbit in 1963) a prophetic guide, and he also found in the figure of Gagarin a source of inspiration. Thus, in the handbill of his short film *Fuego en Castilla*, awarded at the Cannes Film Festival in 1961, the filmmaker reflected on the recent space flights from the mystical tradition that guided his project of "expanded cinema": "¿A dónde se orienta la bóveda de luz sideral? La Tierra... ¿en qué cielo se apoya? He aquí el camino del firmamento ardiente de la Mística. ¡Viva Yuri Gagarin y viva Alan Shepard, que acortan las etapas de nuestra pasión!" [To where does the sidereal vault of light orient itself? The Earth...on which sky does it rest? Here lies the path of the fiery firmament of Mysticism. Long live Yuri

Gabriel Celaya's poetry book *Entreacto* (1957) also expressed this crossroads between the Catholic ideological matrix and the techno-scientific one through poetic discourse. His poem "Cuestión de nombres" [A question of names] posed how this double ideological matrix would finally be overcome in the secularizing process that displaced the old transcendent imaginaries. The poem distinguishes between things that are "noticed", such as flying saucers, and those phenomena that "can no longer be seen", such as "an angel named Gabriel":

Un piano líquido, una mujer transparente;
eso, puede verse.
Un golpe de luz ausente, un platillo volante;
eso, todos lo advierten.
Pero un ángel que se llame Gabriel y tenga dos alas,
eso, ya no puede verse.
Y si alguien lo ve, lo llama "Spitfire", "Mig" o "Douglas".
Porque no puede creerse. (64–65)

[A liquid piano, a transparent woman;
that, you can see.
An absent stroke of light, a flying saucer;
that, everyone notices.
But an angel whose name is Gabriel and has two wings,
that can no longer be seen.
And if someone sees it, he calls it "Spitfire", "Mig" or "Douglas".
Because it cannot be believed.]

In this sense it is significant that Gabriel is the name of the messenger bearer of news such as the annunciation to the Virgin Mary or the revelation of the Koran to Muhammad, but also the name of one of the archangels, chiefs of the heavenly militia. As Giorgio Agamben's research has shown, in the medieval tradition the angels played a bureaucratic and military role as collaborating agents in the divine government of the world (*opus gubernationis*) (149). Celaya describes in his poem the displacement of this Catholic imaginary coming from the feudal tradition in the face of the deployment of the new technological devices of the Cold War. Angels, mediating agents intervening in the governance of the world, can no longer "be seen" in the skies of the late 1950s. Instead, the celestial visions in which the inhabitants of the city of God were once believed to be glimpsed will be interpreted on the basis of categories from war technology using the designations "Spitfire" and

"Douglas", the names of British and American fighter aircraft, and "Mig", a Soviet fighter plane. It is these new secular forms that allow the enunciation of celestial apparitions because the fact of a divine messenger can no longer be "believed" in the horizon of both the author's historical expectations and those of his community of contemporaries.

Six years after the signing of the Pact of Madrid, General Franco addressed a speech to President Eisenhower during his visit to Madrid on December 21, 1959. The regime had inherited from Catholic political theology a providentialist narrative that dated back to the mid-nineteenth century, a time when the Church had developed a vision that attributed to each nation a mission in the project of divine providence —a narrative that confronted both the principle of liberal-constitutional nationality and socialist internationalism (Botti 197). The Caudillo elaborated on that occasion a messianic narrative in which he praised the role of the United States as an ally of Spain, a nation "chosen" as the spiritual reserve of the West. In his allusion to his transatlantic allies, Franco turned the Americans into "angels", messengers announcing a new time of peace and prosperity whose mediating function between God and the capitalist world-economy was narrated as a theodicy in the key of prodigy:

> Es la primera vez en la Historia que el Presidente de los Estados Unidos viene a España y la Providencia ha querido que ello ocurra en un momento en que nuestras relaciones alcanzan un punto de madurez y de comprensión y en el instante en que nuestros dos países están alineados en el mismo frente de defensa de la paz y de la libertad . . . Vuestro viaje se acaba, señor Presidente, bajo un signo cercano y alegre de paz, bajo el signo, tierno y poderoso al mismo tiempo, de la Natividad de Cristo, cuyos Ángeles prometieron hace veinte siglos Paz en la tierra a los hombres de buena voluntad. Vos sois uno de ellos y estoy seguro de que este augurio feliz ha de premiar vuestro esfuerzo, y os ha de dar una larga y fecunda vida. (*Discursos* 701)

> [It is the first time in History that the President of the United States comes to Spain, and Providence has willed that this should happen at a time when our relations are reaching a point of maturity and understanding and at the moment when our two countries are aligned on the same front in defence of peace and freedom ... Your journey ends, Mr. President, under a close and joyful sign of peace, under the sign, tender and powerful at the same time, of the Nativity of Christ, whose Angels promised twenty centuries ago Peace on earth to men of good will. You are one of them and I am sure that this happy omen will reward your efforts and give you a long and fruitful life.]

Since the beginning of the 1950s, flying saucers had made their appearance in the Spanish skies, in comic books, in popular novels, in cinemas and in radio voices. The writer Gloria Fuertes drew on this display of aerospace imagination in everyday life in a poem titled "Credo", included in her own poetic history, *Historia de Gloria*. In the poem, Fuertes associated the appearance of the saucers with the aluminium foil (also known in Spain as "papel de plata") that covered chocolate bars: "Creo en los platillos volantes/ Creo en las platillas que envuelven el chocolate" [I believe in flying saucers/I believe in the silver enveloping chocolate] (84). In her childhood, the writer would have had the opportunity to know the origin of these connections between the extraterrestrial imagination and chocolate, at a time when flying saucers, which did not yet have that name, were already imagined through the collections of trading cards that were given away with the cocoa bars; for example, the prints of the collection *Los secretos del Planeta Marte* [The Secrets of Planet Mars], published in the 1930s by the chocolate factory of the Colonial Company of Africa. At the beginning of the 1950s, the increasing diffusion of industrially processed foods, such as condensed milk, cocoa powder and chocolate bars, made it possible to support the insufficient diet of Spanish children with a supplement of calories around which circulated new collections of trading cards with a renewed aerospace imaginary. These fantasies, produced in times of scarcity, not only invented windows that opened onto an outer space through which devastation or the conquest of new territories could penetrate, but also created the capacity to dream of other possible worlds.

Signs in the Sky and Underground Treasures

With the arrival of the technocrats to the government in 1957, General Franco began to consider the potential that the development of nuclear and space technology could have for the modernization and international recognition of the country. In this sense, the speech he gave on October 9, 1957 at the inauguration of the Escombreras Thermal Power Plant in Cartagena (Murcia) —still impressed by the USSR's launch of Sputnik I five days earlier— was particularly significant. The dictator deviated from the speech he had prepared to express his admiration for the technical advances that had made possible the Soviet achievement, the result of the "political unity", the "principle of authority", the "efficiency" and the "discipline" of the "new Russia" (quoted in Franco Fernández 80–81). The Stabilization Plan of 1959 and the First Development Plan of 1963 gave a new perspective on the energy needs of an accelerating economy in which the expansion of nuclear energy and aerospace technology was promoted. At the beginning of the 1960s, the governments of Spain and the United States signed an agreement to establish NASA satellite ground stations in Gran Canaria and Robledo de Chavela (Madrid) and, in 1964, the Spanish government approved the construction of the only non-experimental plutonium reactor at the Vandellós 1 Nuclear Power Plant (Tarragona). Vandellós 1 was conceived as a dual civilian and military use plant and became the third plant located in Spain, after Zorita (Guadalajara), and Santa María de Garoña (Burgos), both with American enriched uranium technology.[10]

As diplomatic negotiations with the United States took place, news of flying saucer sightings began to fill the newspapers along with information highlighting the discoveries of supposed mineral deposits that would make Spain a key bastion in the new geopolitical scenario, not only because of its strategic position but also because of its natural resources. After the Pact of Madrid, the narratives about the providential and unexpected appearance of these hidden "treasures", present both in fiction and in the daily life of Spaniards, contributed to recapitalizing the image of the nation in front of its allies. The fantasy of a possible national treasure that was coveted by the Americans was recreated in a series of fictions in which the sublimation of capital in the very form of the "hidden treasure" transferred to the imaginary plane the measure of the value of potential capitals that had not yet been put into circulation in the form of merchandise or money. In this sense, on the part of the regime, but also on that of the left-wing press in exile, a type of fantasy was constructed around the existence on Spanish soil of numerous underground mineral treasures, capable of supplying the country's needs in the context of the Cold War. The idea of a sudden appearance of mineral resources thanks to which the endemic problems of the national economy would be solved had already been present in moments of crisis during the Second Republic. Thus, for example, Dionisio Pérez published in 1934 the report "El milagro del oro que podría salvar a España" [The miracle of gold that could save Spain] in the newspaper *ABC*, where he speculated on this possibility: "He aquí la leyenda dorada de la asombrosa abundancia y riqueza de España que resurge ante nosotros, precisamente cuando el presupuesto en déficit de nuestro Estado y la cifra de casi un millón de obreros en paro forzoso piden a la Providencia que restablezca el equilibro económico de la

10 The threat of the irruption into everyday life of objects of unknown origin and intentions had been the protagonist of works of fiction such as Pedro Salinas's dystopian novel *La bomba increíble* (1950) —written during his exile in the United States— since the early 1950s. In the novel, the protagonist couple defies the instructions of a "Government of the Technical Scientific State" that decides to establish a political order in which citizens can be sacrificed in the name of a new cult of technology.

Fables of Intervention

nación" [Here is the golden legend of the amazing abundance and wealth of Spain that resurfaces before us, precisely when the deficit budget of our State and the figure of almost a million workers in forced unemployment ask Providence to reestablish the economic balance of the nation] (178). Immediately after the end of the Civil War, Franco resumed this type of narrative based on a kind of "cornucopianism" which, according to his estimates, would make it possible to maintain Spain's energy autarchy. This type of discourse was taking place in a post-war period in which energy independence had become a priority objective for a regime that was constantly announcing solutions that would providentially save the precarious national autarchic economy. In addition to press accounts that identified the aerospace technology of the first sightings with devices of North American origin, other cultural fables of the period were organized around other processes of "enchantment" occurring simultaneously both in outer space and in national subterranean spaces. In this way, alongside the experiences of sightings, the fictions of the period would be populated by citizens who threw themselves into the "fever" of mineral and energy discoveries in the form of uranium or oil deposits.

In 1953, the same year of the signing of the Pact of Madrid, the US Geological Survey sent a team of geophysicists to locate uranium in Spain and, the following year, the Compañía Ibérica de Petróleos, a company dedicated to hydrocarbon research, was created (Camprubí 191). Since Spain was not an oil producer and depended on other countries, the use of uranium was encouraged as a national energy whose access was restricted to the state. In 1948, the Junta de Investigaciones Atómicas [Atomic Research Board] was created, an organization dedicated to the study and exploitation of uranium deposits and the development of techniques related to the physics of uranium, which was replaced in 1951 by the Junta de Energía Nuclear [Nuclear Energy Board] (Presas 198–199). This Board was one of the three foundations, together with the Consejo Superior de Investigaciones Científicas [Spanish Scientific Research] and the Instituto Nacional de Técnicas Aeronáuticas [National Institute of Aeronautics], on which the Spanish science and technology system was built after the war. Thus, the discovery of considerable, although magnified, uranium metal reserves, which placed the country in fifth place in the world ranking, was used as a decoy by the regime's authorities to gain international collaboration.[11]

11 Spain participated from the start as an associate or full member in the main international agencies and forums: "it joined the IAEA of the UN; the European Nuclear Energy Agency (ENEA); the European Society for Chemical Treatment of Irradiated Fuels (Eurochemic), under the ENEA; the European Atomic Forum

64 *Fables of Development*

In December 1951, the United States generated electricity from nuclear energy for the first time, and in December 1953 President Eisenhower gave the famous speech "Atoms for Peace", in which he defended the civilian uses of this energy at the United Nations General Assembly. At that time, only four nations —the United States, the United Kingdom, Canada and the Soviet Union— possessed the atomic secret and many of the developing countries were beginning to struggle to find a solution to the dilemma posed by the atom: being at the same time the greatest danger known to mankind and having the potential to become, as Winston Churchill stated, the "perennial source of world prosperity" (quoted in De la Torre and Rubio-Varas 17). Like other countries, the Spanish nuclear programme aspired to combine the civil and military dimensions, that is to say, the production of electrical energy with access to atomic weapons. In July 1955, Lewis L. Strauss, director of the Atomic Energy Commission, and the Spanish ambassador in Washington, José María de Areilza, signed in the US capital the bilateral collaboration agreement on "civilian uses of atomic energy", which in turn conditioned Spanish civil nuclear development as dependent on the US, both in terms of equipment and the supply of enriched uranium as fuel for research reactors or electricity production.[12] The agreement included the supply of an experimental reactor, which came into operation in 1958, and the transfer, on lease, of enriched uranium, as well as the transfer of American nuclear technology to Spain and the arrival of scientific and educational material. The United States was thus carrying out a strategy that it later replicated in many other countries: in order to curb national nuclear energy programmes it sold, at very cheap prices, nuclear reactors manufactured in the United States that worked with enriched uranium, which led to dependence on US material. Thus, what began as a project to achieve Spain's energy independence based on nuclear energy ended up falling into the orbit of dependence on US production.[13]

After the signing of the Pact of Madrid, Spain's dependence on its partners in energy policy conditioned the intervention of American companies in the investigation of natural resources in the peninsula and, in the following three years, "the number of American prospectors in Spain doubled, helping it to find two rich pitchblende veins" (Adamson, Camprubí and Turchetti 29). The sudden discovery of uranium is the basis of the plot of *Todo es posible*

(Foratom), established in 1960 by the six member countries of the EEC; and the European Centre for Nuclear Research (ECNR)" (De la Torre and Rubio-Varas 392).

12 In 1963, the director of the JEN, José María Otero Navascués, commissioned the so-called "Islero Project", a study on the country's possibilities of building an atomic bomb without alerting the international community.

13 See Romero de Pablos and Sánchez-Ron, and Presas.

en Granada (1954), a movie directed by a filmmaker who was sympathetic to the regime, José Luis Sáenz de Heredia, who adapted one of the original stories from Washington Irving's *Tales of the Alhambra* (1832) to construct a plot that revolved around the discovery of uranium in some land near Granada. The film tells the story of the expropriation negotiation process that the American technicians of a company called "Pan-American Mining Company" carry out with the owner of the land after the agreements to extract uranium with the United States. The information about the Pact of Madrid appears from the beginning of the film through the exhibition of images from newspapers, newsreels and photographs that recreate the dissemination of the news. From there, two story lines are followed. On one side, the negotiation of the Americans to change the mind of the owner of the land, who refuses to put it up for sale arguing that he has a parchment from his ancestors that attests to the presence of a hidden treasure belonging to King Boabdil. On the other side, the love story that, little by little, develops between the landowner and Miss Folson, a worker of the company in charge of negotiating the expropriation. The denouement of the film recreates the discovery of the real treasure hidden in those lands: Boabdil's jewels. Within the framework of representation of the stereotypes about the folklore and history of Andalucía that are recreated throughout the film, the treasure symbolizes the presence of the cultural legacy of a country that yields to the desires of the American giant without losing an iota of an identity based on the exoticization of the country that foreign travellers and authors like Irving had recreated since the nineteenth century. Following this discovery fever, the finding of a supposed oil field in a Castilian town by an American prospecting company was the main theme of Rafael Salvia's film *¡Aquí hay petróleo!* (1955). When the local people decide to begin the search for oil by their own means, they find a hidden chest containing a message warning of the real treasure in the subsoil, which is none other than a subterranean water spring, a fundamental asset for the development of the Spanish countryside and for the development of the government's hydro-electric project. This was a clear regenerationist message that underlined the idea that, despite external aid, progress could only be achieved through the efforts of Spaniards and the exploitation of the country's natural resources.[14]

14 Another example of these fantasies can also be found in the novel *Las ratas* (1962) by Miguel Delibes, which is set during the mid-50s. In its plot, the protagonist spills a barrel of petrol that belongs to the mayor of the village, which leads the neighbours to believe that they are living above a "mar de petroleo" [sea of oil] (123). When they find out that there is no oilfield there, the mayor transforms his speech into an appraisal of the virtues of the agrarian sector, a pillar of the economy of the first Francoist period: "Campesinos: habéis sido objeto de una broma cruel. No hay

Fig. 4. Josep Renau. *España y la paz*, September 28, 1954. (Biblioteca Virtual de Prensa Histórica. Creative Commons [CC] licence).

Fables of Intervention

In June 1953, the US Air Force commissioned the construction of the country's first intercontinental jet bomber, the B-52, which was capable of dropping hydrogen bombs on Soviet targets. In this sense, Spaniards were not aware of the direct consequences of the government policies on airspace management that the regime had agreed in 1953 until the nuclear accident that took place in Palomares in 1966: an accident in which four hydrogen bombs with a destructive power equivalent to about 75 times that of Hiroshima fell on Andalucían territory. Although the population was never informed of the seriousness of the accident, the press in exile had been alerting Spanish readers of the consequences of the military agreements with the United States since the beginning of the decade. In 1954, the magazine *España y la Paz*, published in Mexico City, called for "Action by all Spaniards in defence of peace, life and the independence of Spain" using an illustration by the communist artist and cartoonist Josep Renau [FIG. 4]. Under the title "Haremos de España un porta-aviones insumergible (de la prensa americana)" [We will make of Spain an unsinkable aircraft carrier (of the American press)], the illustration represents Spain as a small town floating suspended between a sky furrowed by jet planes and a sea in which a boat turned into a kind of mother ship floats, imprisoning the territory with its claws. This recreation of a Spanish village was very similar to that of the coastal town where the characters lived in *Calabuch*, a film by Luis García Berlanga released in 1956. In this pacifist utopia, Berlanga turned the fishing village of Peñíscola (Castellón) into an imaginary territory that served as an allegory of the communities that had to be preserved from the destruction and terror of what Roland Barthes called at that time "atomic death" ("Eiffel" 29). The film's protagonist, an American scientist who flees his country to avoid participating in the manufacture of more atomic bombs, spends his days helping the town's neighbours and uses his knowledge to manufacture fireworks hidden in this small place in Spain. Despite his attempts to go unnoticed, the American intelligence services find the researcher and take him back to his country.

In 1952, the connection between the saucer sightings and a possible extraterrestrial intervention concerning the mineral and energy resources of

petróleo aquí. Pero no os desaniméis por ello. Tenéis el petróleo en los cascos de vuestras huebras y en las rejas de vuestros arados. Seguir trabajando y con vuestro esfuerzo aumentaréis vuestro nivel de vida y cooperaréis a la grandeza de España. ¡Arriba el campo!" [Peasants, you have been the target of a cruel joke. There is no oil here. But don't be disheartened by this. You have the oil in the casks of your plowed land and in the meshes of your plowshares. Keep up the work, and, with your efforts, our living standard will grow, and you will cooperate with the greatness of Spain. Long live the countryside!] (125).

Fig. 5. *El Caso*, 1952. Courtesy of Grupo Editorial 33 and Princeton University Library.

Fables of Intervention

the country occupied a central place in the reports of the weekly newspaper *El Caso*, one of the most widely read in Spain [FIG. 5].[15] In this newspaper, stories about the possible existence of visitors from outer space were included among its regular reports on crimes, miraculous apparitions, and also among the news about alleged discoveries of gold mines and oil wells in Spanish territory. In one of its reports, an alien mission from the planet Gemide, whose purpose was to invade the planet for extractive purposes, was narrated in great detail: "Desvelado el misterio de la presencia de los gemiditas en la Tierra. Necesitan nuestros minerales" [The mystery of the presence of the Gemidites on Earth is unveiled. They need our ores] (quoted in Rada 99).

This feature invited readers to anticipate the consequences of an alien invasion aimed at extracting mineral wealth and other resources on Planet Earth. The invasion recreated by *El Caso* activated the imagination about military and economic intervention in Spanish territory, and the possibility of inhabitants being exposed to attacks and the theft of its natural resources. This analogy was especially significant in the context of Spain's alliance with the United States. As happened in this report, some stories about the presence of possible extraterrestrial visitors were narrated in terms that could well be extrapolated to the American actions in Spanish territory, imagined as an intervened territory. Thus, in the article "Algunas opiniones de calidad sobre lo que puede haber de realidad y de fantasía en torno a los famosos discos volantes" [Some quality opinions on what may be fact and fantasy surrounding the famous flying discs], published on March 31, 1950 in the newspaper *ABC de Sevilla*, this hypothesis about a future

15 *El Caso* was a pioneer in the narration of the black chronicle in the Spanish post-war period. Published between 1952 and 1997, the conditions imposed by censorship to control the news meant it could only include in its pages one crime each week. The role of the "event" was fundamental to understanding a type of mass culture tolerated by the Franco regime. These were stories whose variations in the plebeian public sphere would construct a complementary story to that of the regime's press in a popular key, sometimes alternative and even defiant. The "fait-divers", for Barthes, would preserve the notion of ambiguity in the construction of any system of cultural signification, which would allow its circulation under the control of censorship:

But in the fait-divers, the dialectic of meaning and signification has a historical function much clearer than in literature, because the fait-divers is a mass art: its role is probably to preserve at the very heart of contemporary society an ambiguity of the rational and the irrational, of the intelligible and the unfathomable; and this ambiguity is historically necessary insofar as man still must have signs (which reassure him) , but also insofar as these signs must be of uncertain content (which releases him from responsibility). ("Critical Essays" 194)

colonization of the planet was launched. In its description of the situation of the earthlings, it warned that, at the present time, the planet would be facing "el preludio de una ofensiva interplanetaria en la que la Tierra, algo atrasada ciertamente en materia de estrategia sideral, no pasaría de ser territorio propicio para la ocupación, base de ulteriores operaciones militares astronómicas" [the prelude to an interplanetary offensive in which the Earth, certainly somewhat behind in terms of sidereal strategy, would not be more than a favourable territory for occupation, a base for further astronomical military operations] (Menéndez Chacón 9).

These news items, generally published as notes in the local press, were parodied in opinion columns, in which the daily vision of airships was recreated as a palpable sign of Spanish integration into the geopolitical "normality" of the international community: "En multitud de naciones, de un mes a esta parte, se disfrutan visiones parecidas. Es raro el día en que los periódicos no anuncian el paso de estos artefactos sobre el cielo de diferentes países. Es más, un pueblo en donde sus vecinos no han visto un "platillo volante", es poco menos que un pueblo atrasado" [In many nations, from one month to the present, similar visions are enjoyed. It is a rare day when the newspapers do not announce the presence of these artifacts over the skies of different countries. Moreover, a town where its neighbours have not seen a 'flying saucer' is little less than a backward town] ("La moda" 1). At the same time as alien invasion narratives were spreading, Spain's rapprochement to the Atlantic Axis accelerated the construction of a series of fantasies about the nation based on the economic development and future investments of its new allies. As has been examined in these pages, the imaginaries about aerospace technology opened a profound social debate about the possibilities of the role of intervention in Spanish territory by other terrestrial or extraterrestrial communities. Questions about the limits of national sovereignty, the threats of a possible external attack, the extractivism of resources or new security and surveillance technologies were intertwined with fantasies about a utopian hope for the existence of new forms of life in space in the time of dictatorship

2

Fables of Outer Space

One of the main characters in Carlos Saura's film *La Caza* (1966 [The Hunt]) is a science fiction literature fan; during the rabbit hunt that gives the film its title, he takes advantage of his time off to read a science fiction novel titled *El quinto planeta* [The Fifth Planet]. The reading of this novel takes place in a country house which, years before, became a battlefield where the protagonists met one another when fighting on the Falangist side during the Spanish Civil War. In the middle of the hunt, Luis, as the character is called, speculates about a future time in which the extermination of the human species as a consequence of an invasion of rabbits as the dominant species will give rise to a new civilization in which social classes will disappear: "Llegará un día en que los conejos se coman al género humano. Nos invadirán y formarán una nueva civilización. Como son más pequeños que nosotros, habrá lugar para todos, la lucha de clases desaparecerá y no habrá más envidia. Y así se arreglará el mundo" [There will come a time when rabbits will eat the human race. They will invade us and make a new civilization. As they are smaller than us, there will be enough room for all of them, class struggle will disappear and there will be no more envy anymore. And so the world will be set right]. At several moments of this political fantasy, Luis quotes passages from St John's *Apocalypse* as if they were part of *El quinto planeta*. The interchangeability between both texts might initially seem just a simple iconoclastic gesture on the part of Saura; however, the superposition of both discourses is given new meaning in the light of the recurrent presence of providential narratives in Spanish science fiction during the 1950s and 1960s.

By 1966, science fiction had become one of the genres that could best map the imaginary coordinates of the Cold War as a global conflict which projected its cultural and technological battles into outer space. As a result of the economic-military alliance with the USA, Spain had come to occupy a key geographic position in the escalation of the space and weapon race, which began to be regulated in the Outer Space Treaty signed by the USA, the United

72   *Fables of Development*

Kingdom and the USSR on January 27th, 1967. Before the signing of the treaty, both the USA and the USSR had begun to feel the threat that both countries would begin to design satellites with which to launch its own bombs (Grego 8–11), a shared fear that led to trials with the creation of anti-satellite weapons (ASAT). Given Spain's particular situation in this scenario, the representation of otherness and alien life in space science fiction produced under Franco's regime was inevitably conditioned by the country's situation as a fascist dictatorship that embodied an "otherness" within the bloc of liberal democracies, and who also opposed a communist "Other", imagining those on the far side of the Iron Curtain to be threatening. Considering the particularity of the Spanish case, this chapter analyses the providential narratives that shaped the production of science fiction under Francoism as an expression of the overlapping of the cultural logics of global capitalism during the Cold War on the ideological matrices historically given in Spain during the 1950s and 1960s. The representation of both the otherness and difference of outer space was expressed in the Spanish collective imaginary through this ideological superposition while encouraging different political positions in the reading public. In this sense, this chapter will pay special attention to the authors' political stance when analysing the development of imaginaries of the economic and social development from the science fiction perspective.

The genre faced the challenge of imagining new social formations that projected the idea of progress in a future time. Spanish military leaders who fought against the totalitarianism of extraterrestrial civilizations, visionaries who maintained the utopian hope in the creation of an egalitarian social order in other inhabited worlds, or citizens who believed it was possible to reach a higher level of progress through contact with beings from other planets, were some of the characters who starred in science fiction stories during this period. At the beginning of the 1950s, the genre began to be very popular in Spain thanks to its diffusion in the cinema, the radio theatre, and the so-called "kiosk" literature or "novelas de a duro" (the Spanish version of the "American dime novel") as well as in comics or "tebeos". In 1953, three collections of novels dedicated to the contributed to consolidating the diffusion of the space opera subgenre: "Futuro", published by Ediciones Futuro, "Espacio", published by Ediciones Toray, and "Luchadores del Espacio", published by Editorial Valenciana (Canalda and Uribe-Echeberría 19). The first two were mainly made up of translations of stories such as those in the US magazine *Weird Tales* (1923–1954) (Santoro 319). For its part, Editorial Valenciana housed the work of Spanish authors who published their novels under an Anglophone pseudonym. This was the case of Pascual Enguídanos (George H. White), author of the popular

Fables of Outer Space

series of novels *La Saga de los Aznar* (The Aznar Saga) (1953–1958), and other writers such as José Luis Benet (Joe Bennett), José Caballer (Larry Winters), Ramón Brotóns (Walter Carrigan), Miguel Nieto (Mike Grandson) or Fernando Ferraz (Professor Hasley) (Canalda and Uribe-Echeberría 23). In this sense it is worth remembering how some creators of the collection "Luchadores del Espacio", like writer and cartoonist Alfonso Arizmendi, were Republican artists who had suffered reprisal by Francoism and were given the opportunity to publish their work under a new identity.

The possibility of imagining fictional worlds in outer space allowed these authors to go back to the utopian genre and use it as a variety of science fiction with which to propose alternative social and economic imaginaries to the existing order. Within a political regime that had a stern control over everything that could be made visible in the public sphere, speculations on the realization of alternative social and political projects to the dictatorship found a means of representation in the characteristic forms of science fiction; these are what Fredric Jameson calls "strategies of indirection" ("Archaeologies" 87), which allow readers to acquire the experience of approaching their own reality through a distanced approach. In this sense, it should be remembered that the science fiction utopian narratives in this period were part of the literary and audiovisual productions of the anti-Franco creators as well as of the work of authors ideologically close to the regime, as is the case of Falangist writer Tomás Salvador, author of the novel *La Nave* (1959) or of General Enrique Jarnés, scriptwriter of both the comics and radio programme based on the popular series *Diego Valor* (1953–1958), namesake of the space hero.

The success of the genre in Spain was greatly conditioned by the diffusion of American cinema and literature. Although there was no national film production dedicated to science fiction, from the beginning of the 1950s viewers could see emblematic films such as *The Thing from Another World* (1951), released in 1952 with the title *El enigma de otro mundo*, or *Earth vs. the Flying Saucers* (1956), found on billboards under the title of *Platillos voladores*. In these films, the threat of intelligent beings invading the planet and imposing their totalitarian programmes or infiltrating society and turning humans into emotionless automatons came from outer space.[1] The traumatic core of

---

1 Susan Sontag describes the depiction of the alien's depersonalization in 1950s science fiction cinema in her essay "The Imagination of Disaster":

For science fiction films may also be described as a popular mythology for the contemporary negative imagination about the impersonal. The other-world creatures which seek to take "us" over, are an "it," not a "they." The planetary invaders are usually zombie-like. Their movements are either cool,

74 *Fables of Development*

antagonism inherent in any social formation was expressed in the United States at the beginning of the Cold War in narratives such as these, which harboured the fears of a nation "beset by fears of infiltration both from without and from within" (Hendershot 1). These were fictions produced under the propagandistic effects of a Red Scare in which the characteristics that served to imagine aliens as depersonalized beings, capable of mentally controlling others, coincided with the construction of stereotypes about the infiltrated communist "Other".[2] The narrative category of the "Other", whose metaphor in science fiction was the alien motif, thus operated as a representation of the imaginary enemy but also as an emblem of radical otherness.[3]

In Franco's Spain, numerous cultural producers were great fans of science fiction literature and in some cases, such as Antonio Buero Vallejo, they even had a wide knowledge of the activities of ufological associations (Jiménez 201). In the work of these authors, representation of otherness and difference was embodied in the alien, which became an emblematic figure of the period as it allowed these writers to express the collective wishes and anxieties of Cold War control societies as well as of the surveillance society of the Francoist dictatorship. Fredric Jameson, in his analysis of science fiction history in the Anglo-American sphere, explained the transformation of the alien motif in this period; it is his view that during the 1950s the alien embodied "an isolated monster, a kind of aberration" ("Archaeologies" 323), whereas in the next decade its representation included the attempt to depict

> mechanical, or lumbering, blobby. . . If they are human in form dressed in space suits, etc.-then they obey the most rigid military discipline, and display no personal characteristics whatsoever. And it is this regime of emotion-lessness, of impersonality, of regimentation, which they will impose on the earth if they are successful . . . The attitude of the science fiction films toward depersonalization is mixed. On the one hand, they deplore it as the ultimate horror. On the other hand, certain characteristics of the dehumanized invaders, modulated and disguised -such as the ascendancy of reason over feelings, the idealization of teamwork and the consensus creating activities of science, a marked degree of moral simplification-are precisely traits of the savior-scientists. (221–223)

2 On the interpretation of the alien as the Cold War Other in the realm of popular culture, see studies by Lucanio (1987), Hendershot (2002), Seed (2011) and Rose (2013).

3 As Tom Engelhardt recalls, "In a 1950s civics textbook of mine, I can remember a Martian landing on Main Street, USA, to be instructed in the glories of our political system. You know, our tripartite government, checks and balances, miraculous set of rights, and vibrant democracy. There was, Americans then thought, much to be proud of, and so for that generation of children, many Martians were instructed in the American way of life" (3).

"entire alien cultures or societies, to imagine what a whole alternative form of collective life might be like" (323). At the end of the 1950s, Roland Barthes also referred to this same transformation in "Martians", one of the sections of *Mythologies* (1957); according to the French semiologist, the flying saucer had come from being considered a "Soviet-propelled saucer" to a "Martian engine" ("Eiffel" 27). In a context where Western mythology conferred on the communist world "the very otherness of a planet", the USSR had become "an intermediary world between Earth and Mars" (27). The fantasies of an airspace invasion gave way to what Barthes called "the myth of the Identical" (28), according to which the Earthly society was projected in outer space. In this way, aliens stopped being a threat to Planet Earth and became a "Super-Nature from the sky", a "third Onlooker" whose function was to witness the confrontation between the Western and the Eastern blocs:

> Only, in this process, the marvelous has changed meaning; we have shifted from the myth of combat to the myth of judgment. Mars, as it happens, until further notice, is impartial: Mars lands to judge Earth, but before condemning, Mars wants to observe, to understand. The great USSR/USA standoff is henceforth perceived as a guilty state, since the danger is out of proportion to any justification; whence the mythic recourse to a celestial surveillance, powerful enough to intimidate both sides. (27)

In the final part of his essay, Barthes points out the limitations of imagination on outer space when it comes to representing earthly identity and difference regarding alien life. In his opinion, the heterogeneity embodied by earthly existence usually becomes simplified as it is transformed into a mere reflection of the dominant ideology: "Every myth inevitably tends to a narrow anthropomorphism and, what is worse, to what might be called a class anthropomorphism. Mars is not only Earth, it is a petit bourgeois Earth, it is the little district of mentality cultivated (or expressed) by the popular illustrated press" (29). In this way, the extraterrestrial "Other" could be represented either as a discovery of radical difference or as a projection of the hegemonic ideology of the historical period. This was therefore an ambivalent interpretation which reproduced the same dialectics which had enunciated the representation of the exotic "Other" in the colonial rationale which had permeated the foundational narratives of the science fiction genre in the mid-nineteenth century.[4]

4 On the relationship between the colonial project and the emergence of science fiction literature, see Rieder (2012), Milner (2012), Hopkinson (2010), Roberts (2016), Bould (2012) and Miéville (2009).

76   *Fables of Development*

Following up on George Lukács's *The Historical Novel* (1936), Jameson analysed the emergence of science fiction in the middle of the nineteenth century, once the historical genre was beginning to show its inability to record in a critical way the links with the past of the different nation-states. In the face of the decadence of the historical novel, science fiction became the ideal means to revitalize progress narratives as it was able to portray "some nascent sense of the future" in the space "on which a sense of the past had once been inscribed" ("Archaeologies", 286). In the second half of the twentieth century, outer space had become the new frontier towards which the imperialist impulse was shifting. Representations of the new conquests were also imbued with the exotism that had accompanied previous colonizing projects: "the exotism of outer space not only has psychological and economic functions (for example, generating important objects of consumption in a consumer society) but also may have similar political functions of legitimating enormous expenditures for space exploration, colonization, and military defense" (Tiryakian 89).

In their essays on science fiction in Spain, Pablo Santoro Domingo and Benjamin Fraser have emphasized the social dimension of the genre, as it centres on the description of contemporary problems rather than on scientific or technical issues. Such emphasis brings the genre close to the costumbrism already present in the work of pioneers such as Nilo Maria Fabra, whose short story "En el planeta Marte" [On planet Mars] (1895) is analysed by Fraser in connection with Benito Jerónimo Feijóo's "Si hay otros mundos" (1745 [If There Are Other Worlds]) (3). As will be pointed out later in this chapter, a great deal of the science fiction produced under the Francoist regime was heir to this tradition of a social and costumbrist nature, which was especially clear in both comics and comic scripts. Space science fiction puts forward a political imagination about the present through the reinvention of social phenomena which in real life take place over extended periods of time. In its capacity to transform the present "into the determinate past of something yet to come" (Jameson, "Archaeologies" 288), science fiction turns out to be a useful tool for the representation of a complete social ontology. Critic Darko Suvin characterized the genre on the basis of the principle of "cognitive estrangement" (61), a notion that took up the proposals of Russian Formalism as well as Bertolt Brecht's *Verfremdungseffekt* (effect of alienation or distancing). Through the use of this "estrangement", speculative imagination allows for a transformation of the readers' experience of historical temporality. This is a hypothesis that Suvin summarized with these terms: "The aliens —utopians, monsters, or simply differing strangers— are a mirror to man just as the differing country is a mirror for his world. But the mirror is not only a reflecting

Fables of Outer Space 77

one, it is also a transforming one, virgin womb and alchemical dynamo: the mirror is a crucible" (5). This reflection is consistent with the sociologist Jesús Ibáñez's analysis of the use of differential temporalities, which allow the genre to formalize new historical narratives: "Los mundos posibles que explora son los que están contenidos –como pasados abolidos o futuros abortados– en el presente del mundo real. No trata del futuro: trata del presente, contemplado desde una perspectiva u-tópica y/o u-crónica" [The possible worlds it explores are those that are contained —as abolished pasts or aborted futures— in the present of the real world. It doesn't deal with the future: it deals with the present, viewed from a u-topical and/or u-chronic perspective] (261).

During the dictatorship, fantasies about the future went together with a utopian memory about the recent past. Anti-Franco creators tried to avoid censorship when inventing societies which were confronting dictatorial models, whereas the cultural battle between the Falangist creators and those closer to National-Catholicism also took place regarding their ideas about the past. In this sense, it should be remembered that the Francoist state had outlined a model of national reconstruction based on an ideal of a future that referred to a mythical past: it encouraged the use of a melancholic rhetoric that identified the greatness of the country with a past whose foundational landmarks were the construction of the authoritarian nation-state by the Catholic Kings, and the imperialistic expansion of the Counter-Reformation.[5] Thus, the linear time of progress was replaced by a rhetoric in which past and present merged into an anti-evolutionary utopia. According to David K. Herzberger, for the Francoist ideology "time (history) is perceived not as a progression or as a becoming, but rather as a static entity anchored in all that is permanent and eternal" (33).

This nostalgic rationale is helpful to understand how fictions about the future were linked to the historical periods which science fiction creators identified with a loss object. Thus, those who were defeated in the Civil War projected their ideals in the return of the political utopias of the Second Republic. Novelists, cartoonists and comic scriptwriters who were living an inner exile remained faithful to a repertoire of narratives and aesthetic forms coming from Republican popular culture. This was the case of novelist George H. White (Pascual Enguídanos), author of the galactic epic story *La saga de los Aznar* (1953–1958), of playwright Antonio Buero Vallejo, author of the opera libretto *Mito* (1967 [Myth]), and of many comic creators. Among Francoist authors, the links with the past depended on their ideological adhesion to one of the two political projects confronting each other in their struggle for

5 See Herzberger (1995), Labanyi (1989) and Medina (2001).

hegemony: the fascism of the Falange and National-Catholicism of *Acción Española* and its epigones, the Opus Dei technocrats. The following sections are devoted to the analysis of the differences between the ideas of the past held by Falangist writer Tomás Salvador, author of the novel *La Nave* (1959), and a representative of National-Catholicism, General Enrique Jarnés, scriptwriter of the series *Diego Valor* (1953–1958). These differences will be crucial in order to understand the cultural and institutional battle held by both political factions.

Military Utopias in Outer Space: Diego Valor and La saga de los Aznar (1953–1958)

Fig. 6. *Diego Valor. Almanaque 2055*, Ediciones Cid, 1955. Courtesy of Universidad Internacional de Andalucía and Princeton University Library.

In 1953, the year when Franco's government signed both the Concordat with the Vatican and the Pact of Madrid with the USA, the Spanish audience was able to get acquainted with the first instalments of two space operas: the children's radio series *Diego Valor*, and the epic novels *La saga de los Aznar*. Their corresponding protagonists, Mayor Diego Valor and Lieutenant Miguel Angel Aznar, were military leaders in an interplanetary system as convulse as the earthly order at the beginning of the Cold War. Despite these similarities, the political imaginations that informed both series were complete opposites. The scriptwriter of *Diego Valor* was Enrique Jarnés Bergua, a general who combined his work as chief of the Army General Staff Publishing Service with a prolific literary activity [FIG. 6]. On the other hand, George H. White was the pseudonym that Valencian writer Pascual Enguínados had chosen to publish a series of novels focused on recreating a socialist utopia and which managed

Fables of Outer Space 79

to bypass censorship. The author himself admitted some years later that "La idea de la Saga era el desarrollo de un mundo socialista que la censura, o no se dieron cuenta, o no les pareció tan mal" [the idea of the Saga was the development of a socialist world which censorship didn't catch on to, or didn't disagree with that much] (quoted in Mars 122).

Diego Valor became a very popular media phenomenon addressed to a child audience in the 1950s. Comics, toys, stickers and costumes of the space hero were used as accessories to the daily broadcast of a programme that had incorporated the latest publicity techniques.[6] The phenomenon had begun in 1953, when the advertising agency Cid, linked with radio station Cadena Ser, bought the rights for a Radio Luxembourg serial; a programme based on the comics *Dan Dare* and *Pilot of the Future*, published in the British magazine *Eagle*. *Diego Valor* was so successful in Spain that it lasted 4 seasons, from 1953 to 1958, with a total of 1200 episodes of 15 minutes each. The content was also adapted for the stage (three plays were premiered between 1956 and 1959) and for TV (20 episodes were released between 1958 and 1959), as well as being published as a comic —168 instalments came out between 1954 and 1957, scripted by Jarnés himself and illustrated by Adolfo Álvarez-Buylla and Braulio "Bayo" Rodríguez. *Diego Valor* was set in the 50s of the twenty-first century, and it told the adventures of a group of military personnel whose operations centre was at the Interplanetary Astroport placed in Alcalá de Henares (Madrid). From here, mayor Diego Valor, together with his comrades, scientist Beatriz Fontana, lieutenant Hank Hogan and French lieutenant Pierre Lafitte, fought against the evil inhabitants of the planet Venus, the wiganes, led by Gran Mekong.[7]

6 Andrew Milner explains how the commercial phenomenon related to the series spread to several European countries:

Colonel Daniel McGregor Dare was the star of the British weekly comic, of the hardback Eagle Annual, of *Disco Volante* (*Flying Saucer*) and *Il Giorno dei Ragazzi* (*Children's Day*) in Italy, of the Adelaide Advertiser's Australian Eagle, and the inspiration, too, for a welter of metal and plastic toys, from ray guns to walkie-talkies. My older cousin, Colin, even listened to Dare's adventures on the 'wireless', as radio was known in those days, where Noel Johnson played the title role and Francis De Wolfe the Mekon, broadcast by Radio Luxembourg from 1951 until 1956. In Australia they were broadcast by Radio 4AK, in Spain, with Spanish actors, by Cadena SER. (4)

7 In *Dan Dare, Pilot of the Future*, the protagonist's companions are American Captain Hank Hogan and French Major Pierre Lafayette, who reminded British readers of the volunteer squadrons of the Eagle Squadrons and the Forces Aériennes Françaises in 1940.

80 *Fables of Development*

The Spanish series coincided with the namesake British collection in that in both a Venusian tyrant was designated as enemy, named Mekon in the British comics and Gran Mekong or Mhee Kohng in the Spanish ones. He was a character that reminded readers of other villains such as Fu Manchu or Ming the Merciless, whose characterization embodied the Western xenophobic and racist attitudes of the so-called "Yellow Peril" discourse prior to World War II. The most recent fears towards both Maoist China and the development of the war in Korea converged in Diego Valor's portrayal of the enemy, who was described as a tyrant who "durante toda su vida política se dedicó, apoyado en una dictadura absoluta y cruel, a la ilusión de su vida: conquistar el Universo y hacer esclavos suyos a todos los seres" [had devoted all his political life, supported by an absolute and cruel dictatorship, to his lifetime dream: the conquest of the Universe and the enslavement of every human being] (Álvarez-Buylla and Jarnés 31). Like in the British series, the defence of alien populations by the military personnel was carried out in the name of the intervention principle known as the Truman Doctrine which the USA advocated to intervene in those countries likely to come under the influence of the communist bloc.[8] In the fulfilment of these space missions, the most striking similarity between *Diego Valor* and *Dan Dare* is the role played by their leading female characters: Professor Jocelyn Peabody, who in the British comic is the brains behind the operations, has been replaced by Beatriz Fontana, a Spanish female scientist. Bearing in mind the position of subordination of women in the public sphere during the dictatorship, the presence of this character may be explained in terms of her service and dedication to the mission, understood as military values.

In *Diego Valor*, the content of the British comics was adapted to the Spanish audience for the National-Catholic ideology. The main difference between the Spanish series and the British one lies in the role played by Catholicism as the main social cohesive factor within the galactic community. Thus, readers were able to find in *Almanaque 2055* (1954) a section titled "Notas de sociedad en Venus" [Venus Social Events], which featured the news inspired by the usual contents in the Spanish press of the time [FIG. 7]. The first note in this gossip column contained information about a Catholic christening in the community of the alien allied inhabitants: "En el templo de Turkéal,

---

8 The principle had been formulated in 1947 by the President of the United States in these terms: "I believe it must be the policy of the United States to support free peoples who are resisting attempted subjugation by armed minorities or by outside pressures". In the British series *Dan Dare*, the character who played the "Prime Minister of Earth" also justified the protection of threatened extraterrestrial populations under this framework of intervention: "We are morally committed to help the Therons and Atlantines and to try and foil the Treens" (Chapman 69).

Fig. 7. *Diego Valor. Almanaque 2055*, Ediciones Cid, 1955. Courtesy of Universidad Internacional de Andalucía and Princeton University Library.

completamente reconstruido después de terminada la guerra artil-wigán, se ha celebrado con gran pompa el bautizo del primer hijo del general Targas, presidente del Gobierno de Mekongta y de la encantadora Lúa" [The temple of Turkéal, completely rebuilt after the war artil-wigan came to an end, has witnessed the pompous celebration of the christening of General Targas, president of the Mekongta Government, and his charming wife Lua's first son] (Álvarez-Buylla and Jarnés 18). The reflection of everyday religious practices in this society of the future can be analysed using Roland Barthes' ideas on the way in which other planets were represented as "a petit bourgeois Earth" ("Eiffel" 29). Accordingly, Venus became a world that had "the same nations, the same wars, the same scientists, and the same inhabitants as ourselves ... the same religions as well, especially our own" (28).

The year before the publication of this *Almanaque*, the Francoist government had signed a Concordat with the Vatican which turned Spain into a guarantor of the Christian pastoral. In a geopolitical scenario where the containment of communism determined the strategies of the capitalist bloc, the Spanish regime could present itself as a pioneer state in the defence of "Western civilization". In *Almanaque 2055*, the social events note

82 *Fables of Development*

which referred to a christening in 2055 came with another piece of news informing of the incorporation of Coronel Sondar "como embajador del Gobierno General de las Naciones Terrestre" [as ambassador to the General Government of the Earthly Nations] (Álvarez-Buylla and Jarnés 18). It was a diplomatic appointment which coincided with the impending official entry of Spain in the United Nations, which took place in December 1955. The same body which in 1946 had stated that general Franco was guilty of conspiring to trigger off World War II were now ratifying a decision which had begun to be forged in 1950. In this sense, the simultaneous support given to the Francoist government by both the United States and the Vatican in 1953 was crucial in driving this UN decision, which resulted in the international recognition of the dictatorship.

In this context, *Diego Valor* conferred new meaning to the role played by the Spanish army, now portrayed as a hegemonic presence inside the allies bloc fighting against totalitarian expansion —a bloc united by political interests where Catholicism became the religion practised by both earthlings and the allied extraterrestrial populations. The comic was thus reclaiming the old ideal of the Christian European community which had been suggested by ideologues such as Rafael Calvo Serer and Florentino Pérez Embid. The desire to regenerate Europe on the basis of Catholicism —an idea already expressed in France by Charles Maurras, the ideologue of Action Française, and in Spain by Ramiro de Maeztu, founder of Acción Española— became a recurrent motif in this period. According to Calvo Serer, in a world whose future seemed to offer only two paths, both of them rejectable from a Christian perspective —"la sovietización o la americanización" [Sovietization or Americanization] (Calvo Serer, "España" 29)— the Spanish people had the chance "pasar de nuevo a ser actor principal en la historia de Occidente" [to become once again a main actor in the history of the Western world] (Calvo Serer, "España" 170). In these circumstances, Catholics were called to drive a new era in which the "Europa racionalista y marxista" [the rationalist and Marxist Europe] (Calvo Serer, "Una nueva generación" 337) could be replaced by a new Christianity where Spain would hold "un papel rector en el mundo del espíritu" [a guiding role in the spiritual world].[9]

---

9 Catholicism as an element of cohesion among European states was also the idea behind the "Latin Empire" project proposed at that time by Alexandre Kojève, philosopher and future advisor to the European Common Market. In the memorandum "L'Empire Latin: Esquisse d'une Doctrine de la Politique Française" (1945), Kojève had advised French President Charles de Gaulle to encourage the creation of a transnational political unity between France, Spain, Portugal and Italy. Such a union would not only help preserve geopolitical balance in the face of an Orthodox Soviet empire and a Protestant Anglo-Saxon one, but also counter

Fables of Outer Space

In this context, the *Diego Valor* series contributed to the dissemination of military propaganda aimed at children; a propaganda that promoted adherence to the values of National-Catholicism taking into account the new project of capitalist modernization, whose objective was the incorporation of the country into the economic and military spaces of the Washington–Rome Axis. In this sense, the theme song with which the tune of the radio programme began became an example of the new nationalizing pedagogy promoted by the serial:

> ¡Adelante soldados de la tierra!/ ¡Volad hacia el espacio misterioso!/ No temáis los azares de la guerra./ Mostrad en otros mundos vuestro ardor,/ que os guía, valiente y victorioso,/ el gran Diego Valor./ ¡Diego Valor!/ ¡El piloto del espacio!/ ¡El guerrero sin temor!/ ¡Diego Valor!/ ¡De los cielos caballero,/ de malvados el terror!/ Marte y Venus conocen nuestra gloria,/ que vibra en el vacío sin fronteras./ Viviréis en el libro de la historia,/ escritos vuestros nombres con fulgor. (Álvarez-Buylla and Jarnés 19)

> [Forward soldiers of the Earth!/ Fly towards mysterious space!/ Don't fear the mishaps of war! / In other worlds show your courage / because the one who guides you, valiant and courageous, / is the great Diego Valor / Diego Valor / the pilot of space / the fearless warrior! / Diego Valor! / A heavenly knight, terror of villains! / Mars and Venus know our glory / which trembles in the frontierless void. / You will live in the history books / your names written down with brightness.]

Imitating the Falangist songs and military anthems which children learnt at school, the theme song took on a warlike sense that had been diluted as the post-war period progressed. The world of Diego Valor became a military utopia in which the new space "knights" fought together with European fellows and alien populations in a war for the control of political order in space. Children were the target audience for this promotion of military values —hierarchy, discipline, cohesion, sacrifice— in the defence of security, progress and interplanetary confessional unity. In this way, the representation of these space missions reinforced the permanence of a combative style that fitted in with the regime's plans for its insertion

---

the influence of potential German economic power. Just as, for Spanish reactionary nationalism, Catholic unity was the defining essence of the national community, for Kojève Latin unity was in a sense already accomplished or updated in and through the unity of the Catholic Church.

84   *Fables of Development*

in institutions such as the European Economic Community and NATO.[10] Between 1953 and 1958, when *Diego Valor* was broadcast, writer George H. White (Pascual Enguídanos) published the thirty-three novels that make up the first cycle of *La Saga de los Aznar* [The Aznar Saga].[11] The first instalment of the series introduced Miguel Angel Aznar, Spanish lieutenant of the US air force, as the pilot in charge of investigating the appearance of some strange flying saucers over the Himalayas. In the next novels, Lieutenant Aznar accomplishes several missions on board a spaceship whose speed is capable of modifying the time experience of the protagonists. In *La horda amarilla* (1954 [The Yellow Horde]) he returns to Earth and discovers that six centuries have passed, and that the planet has been divided into four super-powers: North-America, the Iberian Federation, the Asian Empire and the African Union. Despite the threats, the inhabitants of the Western world live in idyllic subterranean cities, susceptible to being used as atomic refuges. A social model has been set up where both money and private property have been abolished, which constitutes to a communist utopia defined by the author as "Christian" in order to avoid censorship:

> Gracias al maquinismo de esta era super-civilizada podríamos vivir cada cual en nuestro país sin necesitar del vecino. Ya no quedan pretextos comerciales para emprender una guerra. . . Cada hombre y mujer de los Estados Unidos trabaja un año y vive el resto de sus días sin trabajar. El Estado, que es el único dueño de las fábricas, de las máquinas, de los edificios, centros de distracción y demás, atiende al sustento de sus súbditos. Les proporciona habitación, comida, ropas, muebles, distracciones y centros de cultura. Hace tiempo que desapareció el dinero. Cada cual va a los almacenes y toma más de lo que necesita . . .
> – ¿Comunismo?
> – Cristianismo -dijo la coronela sonriendo. (26–27)

> [Thanks to the mechanization of this super-civilized era, we are all able to live in our own country without the need of a neighbour. There are no trade excuses to start a new war...Each man and woman living in the United States works for a year and lives the remaining days of their life without working. The State, who is the only owner of the

10 In February 1962, Spain submitted its first application for membership in the European Economic Community, a request that was denied because the organization demanded that its members must be democratic states.

11 On the work of George H. White (Pascual Enguídanos) see García Bilbao and Sáiz Cidoncha (2002; 2004).

Fables of Outer Space   85

factories, of the machines, of the buildings, of the leisure centres, and so forth, cares for the sustenance of its subjects. It provides them with a room, food, clothes, furniture, distractions and cultural centres. Money disappeared a long time ago. Every person goes to the storehouses and takes more than is needed...
– Communism?
– Christianism, answered the Colonel (Ina Peattie) with a smile]

During their cosmic tour, this socio-economic model will be defended by the Aznar family in their fight against the threat of an extraterrestrial dictatorship. By the same token, White uses recurrently religious discourses to confer a providential vision on the mission of humans in the interplanetary conflicts. The fifty-six novels that make up *La Saga de los Aznar* recreate more than a million years of future history where readers could find references that connected with the history of Spain. The novels may be said to become a kind of "National Episodes" —emulating the genre created by Benito Pérez Galdós— that took place in outer space. These episodes included happenings that could be linked with political events in recent history, such as the proclamation of the First and Second Republic of Valera, name of the planet where the protagonists live.[12] In the sixth instalment of the series, *La abominable Bestia Gris* (1954 [The Abominable Gray Beast]), White tells about the first war between humans and aliens after the last of the earthly world wars. The enemy coming from Mars, known as "The Gray Beast", invades the Iberian Peninsula and ends up occupying Asturias, thus getting rid of the main earthly civil insurgency hotbed. The last resistance site is the city of Madrid, which is being besieged with nuclear missiles from the Guadarrama Mountains. The similarities between the events narrated about the defence of Madrid and the fight against fascism in the period ranging from the Asturian miners' strike of 1934 and the 1939 Republican defeat would be familiar to readers. Emulating the fall of Madrid at the hands of the Francoist troops, the survivors taking refuge in the spaceship "Lighting" must leave into exile while observing the defeat of their compatriots:

Un millón de valientes madrileños y aguerridos soldados se aprestaron a la defensa, contestando al asalto thorbod con el tronar ensordecedor de sus ametralladoras atómicas . . . Cada edificio, cada planta, cada

12 The First Spanish Republic was the political regime in force from February 11, 1873 to December 29, 1874. The Second Republic was proclaimed on April 14, 1931 and concluded at the end of the Civil War, on April 1, 1939, with the victory of the military rebels.

86 *Fables of Development*

hogar era un baluarte. Junto a las puertas de sus casas, mujeres vestidas de hierro aguardaban con un fusil entre las manos la llegada del invasor. . . . Madrid sería la piedra negra en la brillante campaña militar de la abominable bestia gris . . . El Rayo daba comienzo a su aventura. En su sala de control, una muchacha llamada Lola Contreras se arrojaba sollozando entre los brazos de Miguel Ángel Aznar . . . sus pupilas brillantes de lágrimas se clavaban en la pantalla de televisión, donde la Tierra se empequeñecía por momentos.
– ¡Adiós, Tierra amada! -murmuró-. ¡Jamás te volveré a ver...! (98)

[A million courageous Madrileños and brave soldiers got ready for the defence, answering the Thorbod assault with the deafening thunder of their atomic machine-guns...Each building, each floor, each home was a bastion. By the doors to their home, women dressed in iron awaited the arrival of the invader holding a rifle in their hands... Madrid would be the black stone in the outstanding military campaign of the abominable gray beast..."Lighting" was the beginning of their adventure. In the control room, a girl called Lola Contreras threw herself in the arms of Miguel Ángel Aznar...her pupils shining with tears fixed on the tv screen, where Earth became smaller rapidly.
– Goodbye, dear Earth! she murmured. I will never see you again...!]

Vladimir Lenin had suggested, in an interview carried out by writer H. G. Wells in 1920, that the discovery of other inhabited worlds would allow nations to revise the social models in a scenario where revolutionary violence would no longer be necessary: "If we succeed in making contact with the other planets, all our philosophical, social, and moral ideas will have to be revised, and in this event these potentialities will become limitless" (quoted in Buck Morss 44). In the work of George H. White, the war between planets recreated the continuity of a violence which was still necessary for the expansion of the socialist model in the galaxy. Writing in this way about the memories of the violence of the Civil War was also a manner of challenging the Francoist censorship, and such memories could not be portrayed differently from the defeated side. As philosopher Ernst Bloch explained in *The Spirit of Utopia* (1918), the remains of past utopias survive in the form of a "utopian surplus" (196) which surfaces in social and cultural practices, activating new potentialities for emancipation. In this sense, the science fiction written by Pascual Enguídanos, one of those defeated in the war, allowed it to reassume the political function of a genre which managed to preserve and bring up to date the utopian thrust of the Second Republic's political ideals.

Tomás Salvador's Science Fiction Work: A Vindication of the Falangist Utopia in the Face of the Triumph of Technocracy

In March 1959, Ediciones Destino published *La Nave*, a novel considered by its author, Tomás Salvador, the first science fiction work written in Spain after the Civil War.[13] In the prologue the author carried out a defence against the reviews that stated that science fiction was a minor genre which had become fashionable thanks to the success of both "literatura de kiosco" [kiosk literature] and "historietas infantiles" [children's comics] (13). Tomás Salvador was a Falange Española militant who had fought in 1941 in the campaign against the USSR carried out by the División Azul (Blue Division), a unit of volunteers from Francoist Spain within the German Army; this military experience was the basis for his novel *Division 250* (1954). In the prologue of *La Nave*, Salvador explains that his aim was to recreate "un proceso de experiencia humana" [a process of human experience] (11) through the representations of a community that would have been travelling in space for more than seven hundred years. The novel became a pioneering work in the use of the "generational spaceship" motif, which Robert A. Heinlein y Clifford D. Simak had developed in their short stories at the beginning of the 1950s.[14] The motif of the lost ship in space allowed for a preservation of verisimilitude in the sense that covering vast stellar distances requires a great amount of time, and that the only way of doing this is by populating huge ships with generations of families that live and die there. At the height of the space race, Salvador thus explained his aim of reproducing in a ship a whole social ontology, a complete world:

> Mi "Nave" es una Nave espacial: americanos y rusos están sembrando el espacio de satélites y exploradores. ¿Cuánto tiempo tardarán las aeronaves, con tripulación humana, en viajar por lo menos dentro de nuestro sistema solar? Muy poco: una o dos generaciones . . . "La

13 Salvador describes pre-war Spanish science fiction production in these terms: "Antes de 1936 teníamos al Coronel Ignotus; después algunas cosas sueltas de Cargel Blaston, Eduardo Texeira, sendas novelas de Carlos Rojas y Antonio Ribera . . . Al enfrentarme, pues, con una carencia de obras nacionales, me enfrento con una carencia de clima" [Before 1936 we had Colonel Ignotus; then some loose things by Cargel Blaston, Eduardo Texeira, a novel each by Carlos Rojas and Antonio Ribera ... So, faced with a lack of national works, I am faced with a lack of climate] (16).

14 One of the most famous novels of the genre, *Non-Stop* (1958) by Brian Aldiss, has similarities with Salvador's novel, which was written during the same year. It was published in Spanish in 1961.

88   *Fables of Development*

Nave" lleva setecientos años perdida en la inmensidad. Los hombres que la crearon, lanzaron y gobernaron primeramente han muerto. Han muerto también sus sucesores hasta la veintitrés generación. ¿Qué les queda, entonces, a los habitantes de "La Nave" cuando tomo la narración? Nada. Es decir, una remota raíz humana ... Dejemos que la "Nave" sea una nación, un planeta, un cosmos, con derecho a buscar su propio renacimiento. (16–20)

[My "Ship" is a space Ship: both Americans and Russians are sowing space with satellites and explorers. How long will it take for airships, with a human crew, to travel inside our solar system? Very little: one or two generations ... "the Ship" has been lost for seven hundred years in the immensity. The men who created, launched and governed it at the beginning have died. Their successors up to the 23rd generation have also died. What, then, are the inhabitants of "the Ship" left with when I take over the narrative? Nothing. That is, a very remote human root... Let's let "the Ship" be a nation, a planet, a cosmos, with the right to look for its own renaissance.]

Salvador's novel takes the main plot as well as some narrative motifs from Clifford D. Simak's short story "Spacebred Generations" (1953), translated into Spanish in 1955. As happens with *La Nave*, in Simak's short story the main character discovers the origin and subsequent decline of a society that travels adrift by reading a book with the history of the ship which he only can access. The use of hydroponic gardens as a means of obtaining food, the use of birth control or the fact that the inhabitants of the Ship have forgotten their earthly origin are some of the themes which Salvador borrows from Simak's fiction. *La Nave* also made use of other literary motifs from H. G. Wells' *The Time Machine*, a classic of the genre. Foremost among these is the decay of a community, represented by the Eloi, that has culturally regressed despite technological progress, as well as the existence of another human species, the Morlock, described as a race which lives in a subterranean world.

In the spaceship imagined by Salvador, there are two communities living apart and in conflict: the Kros and the Wit. The former are the species who have mastery over technology and control over the Wit, whereas the latter live in the bottom part of the ship and are the workforce maintaining the supply of food. The members of the Wit community are banned inhabitants who, in the original crew, were "specialized workers but not wise, settlers or technicians" (146). The image of this subterranean community refers to the experience of the primitive Christians who took refuge in the catacombs,

Fables of Outer Space

but also to a narrative motif which can be found in Fritz Lang's *Metropolis* (1927), one of the first science fiction films, and based on a novel of the same title which had great success in Spain.[15] This motif, present also in traditions such as Germanic folklore, is none other than the presentation of the productive process as an action that takes place underground, away from the public gaze.

The protagonist of *La Nave* is Shim, a Kros who is the chronicler or "Hombre de Letras" [Man of Letters] (142). Together with Mei-Lum-Faro, master of the Ship, Shim has exclusive access to the book where the history of this community is recorded. After reading the testimonies of his predecessors, Shim gathers knowledge of a history unknown to the rest of the inhabitants of the ship. According to the chronicles, the vehicle was launched to space in 2317, carrying a crew of three thousand people chosen among the population of the so-called "Federación Euro-americana" [Euro-American Federation] (157). In this original population, the Hispanic presence was really important, considering that the language spoken by the settlers of the ship was the "Anglo-Hispanic" language (98). The crew failed in its colonizing mission because they never managed to find the "campo magnético" [magnetic field] or "pasillo" [passage] (1959, 75) that was needed to continue their journey. 15 years after launching the ship, when the inhabitants discovered that they were travelling in space without the possibility of returning to Earth, the "Primera Revolución" [First Revolution] (75) broke out. A second revolution took place in 2390, when most of the objects coming from Earth were destroyed and most of the crew had unsuccessfully attempted immolation.

At the very moment when Shim begins to learn in the Book about the origin of the division between the Kros and the Wit, the confrontation between both species gets worse. The Wit threaten the Kros with declaring a hunger strike if their demands —having some living space in the top part of the ship and improving their working conditions— are not met. After the Wit representatives are given a death sentence by the Ship Council, Shim decides to intercede on their behalf by addressing leader Mei-Lum-Faro with the following plea: "Perdónalos, Señor, porque los Wits son igual a nosotros y los necesitaremos" [Forgive them, Lord, because the Wits are equal to us and shall be needed] (105). As a consequence of this request, the chronicler is tortured and banned to the subterranean space. His arrival in the cellars of the ship is interpreted by the seven

15 Domingo Santos recalls how in the 1940s the novels of Thea von Harbou, including *Metropolis*, were published in Spain, a publishing phenomenon described by this author as a fashion "attributable to our Germanophilia of the time" (8).

90 *Fables of Development*

family clans of Wit in terms of the apparition of the promised messenger by the "Señor de los Símbolos" [Lord of the symbols]; it is one the Earthly mythical representations kept by the Wits in the manner of prophecies which announce the arrival of a Messiah who will die to save them.[16] Shim, who had discovered the meaning of the concept "God" in his readings of the history of the Ship, is unanimously elected as their leader by the Wit clans (239).

During this period, the chronicler explains to the different chiefs of the Wit clans the knowledge he has acquired about the origin and history of their species, at the same time as he reflects on his own mission: "No podré cambiar el destino de la Nave, pero sí enseñar a mis hermanos el camino de la regeneración" [I won't be able to change the fate of the Ship but I will be able to show my brothers the way of regeneration] (71). Shim rejects the revolutionary violence proposed by the Wit clan of the warriors as a solution to conflicts with the Kros and suggests that they should recover the unity with the inhabitants of the ship, which has been lost. That's why he proposes to get rid of the notion of antagonism which is well rooted in both communities; he tries to convince them both of the idea that "Lo enemigo puede ser amigo" [the enemy can be a friend] (51). After the Lord of the Ship's death, Shim brings forward a project of reconciliation between Kros and Wit, which is worded as a pact of oblivion of the past. It is a pact which, in the chronicler's words, will allow them to begin a new era of peace where "sólo el Amor puede vencer a la Ley" [only Love can defeat the Law] (154). When he is on the point of being made leader of the Ship, Shim is murdered at the hands of the warriors of the Wit clan, who reject the pact of reconciliation between both communities.

The killing of the main character, which had been announced in the Wit's prophecies, offers a clear parallelism with Christ's death, understood as a sacrifice for the redemption of the community. Salvador explains in the prologue that Shim's death becomes "el obligado tributo de sangre que los idealistas o soñadores de la utopía han pagado siempre al lento progresar de los mediocres" [the mandatory blood tribute that idealists or dreamers of utopia have always paid for the slow progress of the mediocre] (18).

---

16 "Os dejaré algunos de mis símbolos y al cabo de mucho tiempo, os enviaré otro mensajero. Será un hombre diferente a vosotros, un hombre que os dará lástima, os amará, pero al que terminaréis matando. No importa. Será necesario que muera por salvaros. Se anunciará con la gran luz y la luz se lo llevará" [I will leave you some of my symbols and after a long time, I will send you another messenger. He will be a man different from you, a man you will pity, he will love you, but whom you will end up killing. It does not matter. It will be necessary for him to die to save you. He will be announced with the great light and the light will take him away] (165).

Fables of Outer Space 91

According to the author, the seven clans of the Wit community are the custodians of the knowledge upon which this community's regeneration should be founded: "El pueblo Wit, el más primitivo de los dos que pueblan 'la Nave', condenado a vivir en cámaras tenebrosas, descubre la luz, la danza, el culto a los muertos, el curanderismo y el simbolismo" [The Wit people, the most primitive of the two that inhabit the ship, sentenced to live in gloomy chambers, discover light, dance, cult of the dead, folk medicine and symbolism] (19). The narrative motif put forward by H. G. Wells in *The Time Machine* regarding entropy and the decadence of a society once it has reached the highest point of technological development is used by Salvador in his representation of the Kros people. This community is described as "una raza degenerada en un mundo automático" [a degenerated race in an automatic world] (19) which has forgotten its origins, regressing to "casi la Edad de Piedra, o mejor un feudalismo sin raíces" [almost a Stone Age or rootless feudalism] (19). Salvador himself points out that the persistence of earthly vestiges among the people is an opportunity for the regeneration of the ship.

The narrative revolves around the central axis of Falange's fascist ideology: the myth of the renaissance or regeneration of a nation after a period of decay or misery. In this sense, the Wit represent the organic community claimed by the Falangist project: an "eternal" people in which the intra-historical essences survive, the basis of all regeneration. Shim's death thus turns him into the first martyr of a new era. The parallelism between the life of a political leader and the figure of Christ had also been conveyed through the exaltation of the founder of the Falange, José Antonio Primo de Rivera, executed in 1936. Primo de Rivera was presented in the post-war Spanish press as "El Jesús de España" [the Jesus of Spain] (quoted in Botti 48–49), a Messiah who had shed his blood for the redemption of the country. According to writer Dionisio Ridruejo, the leader of the Falange fulfilled his mission to inspire unity, order and willpower in a Spain torn by social and partisan splits —a sacrifice that, in his opinion, embodies a similarity with Christ's life: "José Antonio vino a España con un destino trágico, para morir crucificado" [José Antonio came to Spain with a tragic fate, to die crucified] (37). Still in 1964, Tomás Salvador raised the figure of José Antonio to the category of myth on the occasion of the inauguration/ unveiling of a monument in Barcelona: "José Antonio tiene una memoria segura. Murió joven y limpio y eso vale para la eternidad" [José Antonio's memory will surely last. He died young and clean/pure, and that is worthy for eternity] (quoted in Morán 371).

In his novel, Salvador reenacts the consolidation of an organic community as well as the connection of this process with a charismatic

92 *Fables of Development*

leader, called on to fulfil an epic and supernatural mission. Comparing the nation with a ship, Primo de Rivera described such a mission as follows: "El jefe es el que tiene encomendada la tarea más alta, es él el que más sirve. Coordinador de los múltiples destinos particulares, rector del rumbo de la gran nave de la patria" [The chief is the one who is entrusted with the highest task, he is the one who serves the most. Coordinator of the multiple particular destinies, rector of the course of the great ship of the homeland] (156). In the novel, the ship is defined by the different characters as a "cuerpo autárquico" [autarchic body] (27), a "nación" [nation] (20) and a "Patria" [Homeland] (149) which must restore its lost unity along its "eterno viaje" [eternal voyage] (21) across time and space. The Falange Española took the idea of Spain as a nation from José Ortega y Gasset, who had formulated the concepts of both historical project and "comunidad de destino" [community of destiny] and turned them into the foundational items of the movement.[17] The writer Dionisio Ridruejo, Tomás Salvador's comrade in the Blue Division, also followed this conceptual framework to explore the idea of the nation as a community bearing eternal values and a historical mission, a community which moves in time and space:

> Una Patria "no es un agregado de tierras", es un haz de gentes que caminan juntas. Caminamos. El espacio hace aquí el papel de tiempo. Somos "unos" porque lo somos hacia el porvenir, en el destino más que en la procedencia. Y porque lo somos de cara a "otros", junto a ellos o frente a ellos; en lo universal. He aquí esta unidad de destino en lo universal atravesando la Tierra hacia el combate, tal y como España – lo soñamos—va a atravesar el tiempo. Cierto: la División es una España andante, nuestra España. (Quoted in Saz 364)

> [A Homeland "is not an addition of lands", it is a bundle of people who walk together. We walk together. Space plays here the role of time. We are "some" because we are towards the future, in destiny rather than in origin. And because we are with regards to "others", together with them or in front of them; in what is universal. Here lies this unity of destiny in what is universal while crossing the Earth towards combat,

---

17 "España no es un territorio. . . es, ante todo, una unidad de destino . . . Una entidad, verdadera en sí misma, que supo cumplir –y aún tendrá que cumplir– misiones universales" [Spain is not a territory ...it is, above all, a unity of destiny .... An entity, true in itself, which knew how to fulfil —and will still have to fulfil— universal missions] (Primo de Rivera 31).

Fables of Outer Space   93

just like Spain —we dream— is going to cross time. True: the Division
is a walking Spain, our Spain.]

The idea of a "walking Spain", similar to the term "España Peregrina"
[Pilgrim Spain] used by those in exile, will also be used by Salvador in
his allegory of the nation that crosses time and space. In his novel, Shim's
proposal of reconciliation between races necessarily implies overcoming
differences through mutual acknowledgement as human beings, and religion
is proposed as the main cohesion element between both communities. Shim
plans this community's redemption through confessional unity, an aim
which had also been present in the imperial Spanish project and which
reemerges in the space journey of these descendants of the "discoverers".
Just as the chroniclers state in the book of the Ship, "Calmo Berlhengui,
cronista de la quinta generación, dice que el hombre se dividía en cuatro
etapas: descubridores, aventureros, colonizadores y habitantes...Para volver
a empezar otra vez, un poco más lejos. Y decía Calmo: Nosotros somos
descubridores" [Calmo Berlhengui, chronicler of the fifth generation, says
that man was divided in four stages: discoverers, adventurers, settlers and
inhabitants ... To start again, a little further away. And Calmo said: We are
discoverers] (83).

In May 1958, a month before Tomás Salvador started writing *La Nave*,
the recent Law of Fundamental Principles of the National Movement
proclaimed in its first article that Spain had a "unidad de destino en lo
universal" [unity of destiny in the universal]. The document had been
initially requested from José Luis Arrese, Secretary of the Movement.[18]
The proposal freed both the Movement and its National Council from
its dependence on the future Head of State. With this law, the Falangist
sector intended to play a hegemonic role in the government again, thus
becoming the sovereign body of control of the public authorities. The
monarchic sectors, as well as senior members of the armed forces and
the ecclesiastic hierarchy denounced the law as a totalitarian threat, as a
result of which the text was rejected. Falange proved once more incapable
of articulating a project for the future and did little more than repeat
the same political formula without possibility of renewal. Its autarchic
proposal also clashed with the Spanish economic needs and with the
strategies designed by the international organizations of which Spain
had become a member. The writing of a new document was entrusted to

---

18 On the debates surrounding the creation of the Law of Fundamental Principles
of the National Movement (1958) see Tatjana Gajić's *Paradoxes of stasis: literature,
politics, and thought in Francoist Spain*.

94 *Fables of Development*

both Laureano López Rodó, an Opus Dei jurist, and Gonzalo Fernández de la Mora, an ideologist close to the technocrats.[19] Following the failure of the members of Falange, in February 1957, Franco faced a government crisis and carried out the most important ministerial reshuffle: Arrese was relegated to the Housing Ministry, and José Antonio Girón de Velasco, Secretary of Labour, was dismissed after 16 years in office; two Opus Dei members were appointed Secretaries of Treasury and of Commerce, and Lopez Rodó became responsible for the Office for Economic Coordination and Planning. The Falangist sector began to lose political and cultural power, and the Opus Dei men were the ones finally chosen to lead a Catholic neoliberal project in Spain.

This institutional marginalization was counteracted by the Falangists with populist proposals which expressed the clash with their rivals. At the time when Tomás Salvador was writing *La Nave*, Falange practised an internal opposition inspired by the labour organizations and that connected with the social doctrine of the Church. Since the late 1950s, claims of social justice were the backbone of the consensus policies carried out by Falange from the Labour Ministry and the Housing Ministry, as well as from their own organizations (Molinero 93–110). Faced with this new situation, Tomás Salvador claimed in his novel the importance of the utopian Falangist impulse, still active when the technological utopia of the ship fails. The main character believes that it is possible to establish a peaceful coexistence based on a spiritual unity capable of guaranteeing harmony between the two opposing races. In this sense, Shim uses the discourse of social justice to claim before the Kros an improvement in the living conditions of the Wit: "El pueblo wit está escarnecido y humillado, condenado a vivir en las cuevas inmundas aplastadas por suelos de metal, sin aire casi para respirar, sin derechos humanos" [The Wit people are ridiculed and humiliated, condemned to live in filthy caves crushed by metal floors, with almost no air to breathe, without human rights] (148-149).

The protagonist included in his claim the legal terminology used in the 1948 United Nations Declaration of Human Rights. As a matter of fact, an excerpt of this Declaration had been disseminated during the student protests of April 1, 1956, in the context of the imminent meeting in

---

19 From 1938 onwards, the Falange Española had been subsumed in a political-social structure called Movimiento Nacional, whose most relevant aspect was its direct subordination to the Caudillo. The new 1956 document described the National Movement not as an intermediate phase in the conquest of the totalitarian state but as a "comunión de los españoles en los ideales que dieron vida a la Cruzada" [communion of Spaniards in the ideals that gave life to the Crusade] (quoted in Ross 92).

Fables of Outer Space

Madrid of the Executive Committee of UNESCO. On the back of the leaflet distributed to the students was included, together with the Declaration, a manifesto written by the Communist Party of Spain which expressed the idea of national reconciliation after the Civil War.[20] Two months later, the Communist Party of Spain (PCE in Spanish) published a document titled "Por la reconciliación nacional, por una solución democrática y pacífica del problema español" [For national reconciliation, for a democratic and peaceful solution to the Spanish problem]. The text, which appealed to decisions that the international community had adopted in order to promote peaceful coexistence in the Cold War, proposed a union among the forces opposing the dictatorship. Among these forces was included the sector of "falangistas disidentes" [dissident Falangists] (Oliver, Pagès, Pagès 1978, 284), a category under which Falangists such as Tomás Salvador could be classified. In this way, the PCE revealed itself at this juncture as an organization that could compete with the working-class sectors of Falange in its objective of integrating the proletarian masses into a national project.

In the project of reconciliation between the communities of *La Nave*, Salvador proposes the resolution of an antagonism that is never expressed as a conflict between social classes. The conflict ultimately confronts the owners of the means of production and military technology and the workers, who have developed an organization based on social corporatism. The Wit are grouped into "families" and "guilds", institutions that coincided with the Falange's corporate structures, based on the feudal mode of production. This would be the social model that Salvador would recreate in depth in

---

20 It reads as follows:

En este día, aniversario de una victoria militar que sin embargo no ha resuelto ninguno de los grandes problemas que obstaculizaban el desarrollo material y cultural de nuestra patria, los universitarios madrileños nos dirigimos nuevamente a nuestros compañeros de toda España y a la opinión pública. Y lo hacemos precisamente en esta fecha –nosotros, hijos de los vencedores y los vencidos– porque es el día fundacional de un régimen que no ha sido capaz de integrarnos en una tradición auténtica, de proyectarnos a un porvenir común, de reconciliarnos con España y con nosotros mismos. (Quoted in Mesa 346)

[On this day, anniversary of a military victory that nevertheless has not solved any of the major problems that hindered the material and cultural development of our homeland, we, the university students of Madrid, once again address our colleagues throughout Spain and public opinion. And we do so precisely on this date —we, children of the victors and the vanquished— because it is the founding day of a regime that has not been able to integrate us into an authentic tradition, to project us into a common future, to reconcile us with Spain and with ourselves.]

96   *Fables of Development*

his later science fiction work, *Marsuf, el vagabundo del espacio* (1962 [Marsuf, the Space Wanderer]), an anthology of stories for children.[21] In the story "Polizón a bordo" [Stowaway Onboard] Salvador describes a future time in which an imaginary Geneva Convention declares outer space free, in such a way that "ninguna potencia pudiera tener bases militares, derechos territoriales o colonias al viejo estilo" [no power would have military bases, territorial rights or old-style colonies] (30). After a period of war in which the terrestrial nation-states had financed colonial expeditions into space in defiance of the mandates of the new law, the clans of the so-called "merchants" decide to reach an agreement regarding the laws of the Merchants Guild. In this alliance, the old women of each ship organize the families in a manner similar to the Wit clans of *La Nave*. In keeping with his Falangist ideal, Salvador reinforces in his science fiction for children the institutions of the family and the guild as means of overcoming social and political antagonism. After the failure of the proposals by the Falange Española in 1957, Salvador used the space science fiction genre to update the fascist and Catholic ideology of the movement in a futuristic scenario.

Space Science Fiction in Comics: Technological Modernization and Development in a Humorous Tone

In 1957, an "Interplanetary man" wanders the streets of Madrid handing out advertising leaflets in a scene from the film *El tigre de Chamberí* [The Tiger from Chamberí], directed by Pedro Luis Ramírez. He is a boy disguised in a metallic "space" suit and works as an advertising man. On September 25 of that same year, Francisco Franco gave one of his speeches at the Empresa Nacional Siderúrgica de Avilés [Avilés National Steel Company], one of the possible places where the steel of this costume could have been manufactured. His words announced to the workers the end of the autarchic project and the definitive entry of the country into the circuits of international capitalism:

> España se está transformando. No podemos por ello temer al futuro: el futuro está en nuestra unidad, en nuestra disciplina, en nuestra fe, en creer y ser optimistas . . . Que digan los pesimistas que nuestra obra es una locura, que nos llamen, como a éste (señalando al Sr. Suanzes),

21 "La ballena alegre" was the name of the Editorial Doncel collection in which this anthology was published. It was also the name of the basement located in the Café Lyon in Madrid, a meeting place for Falangists during the Second Republic. This locale would also be the place where the Sociedad de Amigos de los Visitantes del Espacio, founded in 1955, held its crowded gatherings.

Fables of Outer Space

Julio Verne. ¡Qué importa, si España se transforma! ¡Bendita la locura que crea riquezas y las reparte, que crea ideales, levanta factorías como la que contempláis y echa los cimientos de nuestra futura exportación! (Franco, "Discursos" 359)

[Spain is undergoing a transformation. We cannot therefore fear the future: the future lies in our unity, in our discipline, in our faith, in believing and being optimistic . . . Let the pessimists say that our work is madness, let them call us, like this one (pointing at Mr Suanzes), Jules Verne. What does it matter, if Spain is changing! Blessed is the madness that creates wealth and distributes it, that creates ideals, that builds factories like the one you are contemplating and lays the foundations of our future export!]

In this speech, the Caudillo referred to the writer Jules Verne, the nickname by which the Secretary of Industry, Juan Antonio Suanzes, was known at the time. The figure of the French writer, whose science fiction novels had become an emblem of liberal utopianism, was used by the dictator to describe the new economic liberalization plans. In the context of the industrial boom of the late nineteenth century, Jules Verne's novels had been characterized by sublimating the values of productivity and technological progress without taking into consideration the relations of production. His fetishization of technological advances was expressed through an ideological displacement similar to that employed by General Franco in his description of capitalism as a "madness that creates wealth and distributes it". A metaphor in which the processes of capital distribution were represented on the basis of a providential logic that reinforced the supposed "impersonality" of capitalism, it concealed the exploitation of the labour force and the social costs.

The narrative that the regime was constructing about its own modernization process was promoted in the press and NO-DO, the cinema newsreels. In the news that appeared in these media, the rhetorical excess with which the activities of the national industry were described tried to hide the shortcomings of an obsolete technological park. In contrast to these official representations, the images of technological development that circulated in comics and humorous cartoons during the 1950s and 1960s parodically expressed the lack of material resources and the precariousness of industrialization. From a series of popular publications aimed at all types of audiences, parody and humour became powerful mechanisms to codify or distort a reality that thus made visible its material conditions. This transition to modernization in this period of Francoism can be analysed in the light of philosopher Gilles

98   *Fables of Development*

Deleuze's analysis of the transformation of political regimes in relation to the mutation of technology in different cycles of capitalism:

> Types of machines are easily matched with each type of society—not that machines are determining, but because they express those social forms capable of generating them and using them. The old societies of sovereignty made use of simple machines—levers, pulleys, clocks; but the recent disciplinary societies equipped themselves with machines involving energy, with the passive danger of entropy and the active danger of sabotage; the societies of control operate with machines of a third type, computers, whose passive danger is jamming and whose active one is piracy and the introduction of viruses. This technological evolution must be, even more profoundly, a mutation of capitalism, an already well-known or familiar mutation. (6)

Following the sequence proposed by Deleuze, the representation of aerospace technology in Spanish comics can be studied by examining the country's transformation from a capitalism of production to a capitalism of sales or markets. In the mid-1950s, some of the images of aerospace technology recreated devices that combined the use of what Deleuze called "simple machines" with "energetic machines". An illustrative example of this joint use of both types of machines can be found in the representation of the space suit included in the *DDT Almanaque para 1956*, a design that cartoonist Francisco Ibáñez reinterpreted in 1961.[22] [FIG. 8]. Both "suits" needed the body of the users and their labour power in order to function, thus showing the conditions of precariousness that underlay the representations of the "technological sublime" that the regime promoted. In the late 1950s, the economic activity of the Spaniards underwent a radical transformation thanks to the boom of the tourist industry, and both tourism and mass culture began to rely on some technology managed by the Ministry of Information and Tourism —a management that was possible thanks to the economic and technological aid resulting from the establishment of US military bases, built precisely to house nuclear technology. At a similar time, the "computer machines" mentioned by Deleuze began to be incorporated into the visual representations of technology in Spanish comics. This was the case of the illustration of a "Martian machine" that, according to its creators, would serve to improve their working conditions as cartoonists and scriptwriters "en Marte desde el año 2782" [on Mars since the year 2782]. In

---

22 The publication *DDT contra las penas* made its appearance in 1951. It ended up being called simply *DDT* (Lara 2002, 44–74).

Fables of Outer Space

Fig. 8. Francisco Ibáñez. "Traje especial para leer este número", Número especial de *DDT, ¡Brrrr! ¡Qué frio!!* (1961). Courtesy of Francisco Ibáñez and Penguin Random House Grupo Editorial.

100   Fables of Development

Fig. 9. Cifré (Guillermo Cifré Figuerola). *DDT contra las penas. Almanaque para 1956*, 6. Courtesy of Artists Right Society and Princeton University Library.

the cartoon, the comic creators work comfortably inventing jokes that they communicate to the machine. In real life, these cartoonists had to work intensively for a publishing house to which they were obliged to hand over all their copyrights and intellectual property rights over their characters. Given these abusive working conditions, the comic book machine expressed the cartoonists' emancipatory desire to free themselves from exploitation in their working conditions [FIG. 9].

A few months after the publication of this cartoon, the cartoonists Escobar, Cifré, Peñarroya, Conti and Giner founded the first cooperative of cartoonists —D.E.R. (Dibujantes Españoles Reunidos)— and left Editorial Bruguera to create their own magazine, *Tío Vivo*.[23] The experience materialized a possibility of collaborative work that had been anticipated in their cartoons

---

23 Paco Roca dedicated his graphic novel *El invierno del dibujante* (2010) to this process of emancipation of Bruguera's cartoonists. The essay *Historia social del cómic* (2007) by Terenci Moix and the works of Antoni Guiral (2005; 2011) are also essential to understand the field of cultural production in which the project of the Catalan publishing house was inserted.

about the future life in space [FIG. 10]. However, their career as freelancers was brief and they had to return to their old publishing house: "Aquella aventura fue un anticipo de las reclamaciones sobre los derechos de autor. Por primera vez en España y en Europa los dibujantes gestionaban su propia revista, pero Bruguera hizo todo lo posible para que *Tío Vivo* no funcionara y a finales de 1958 regresaron" [That adventure was a foretaste of the copyright claims. For the first time in Spain and in Europe, cartoonists managed their own magazine, but Bruguera did everything possible to stop *Tío Vivo* from working and at the end of 1958 they returned] (Barrios 2010).

In their cartoon, these creators represented themselves as "Martians" who dreamed of gaining control of the means of production, in a future time when technology would be put at the service of the production of popular culture. The cartoonists imagined their own magazine as a publication for a community of readers to come. As Manuel Vázquez Montalbán recalls, many creators who had suffered political reprisals were working for Editorial Bruguera, thus contributing during the dictatorship to the continuity of the popular culture produced during the Second Republic: "Fue una sorpresa enterarnos, años después, que gracias a ella habían sobrevivido intelectuales rojos, dibujantes y escritores que por las historietas y la subliteratura de Bruguera consiguieron pagar el alquiler, el *seiscientos,* una edición marxista literal del universo confiado en su condición de vencidos" (It was a surprise to learn, years later, that thanks to this publishing house, red intellectuals, cartoonists and writers had survived; and that through Bruguera's comics and sub literature they managed to pay the rent, buy a SEAT 600, a literal Marxist edition of the universe, confident in their condition as defeated) (1982). Hunger, exploitation, repression and the hollow aspirations of a middle class complicit with the values of the regime or the criticism of National-Catholic education, were part of the stories that these cartoonists and scriptwriters bequeathed to several generations of readers.

The space airships, as well as the planets and satellites imagined in these comics, became habitable worlds for those creators who, from an imagined outer space, survived in a kind of "inner exile" within Spain.[24] In a country where an aerospace industry could not be developed, the characters of the comics built their own ships to go to meet other beings beyond the terrestrial borders. The comics produced by these anti-Franco artists recreated countless saucers, spaceships, planets and satellites where all sorts of misfits, outcasts, rebels and dreamers could live differently. This is the case of the cover of

---

24 In his study of literature of Francoist Spain, Paul Ilie observes that inner exile may define itself "by the isolation endured by distinct groups vis-a-vis each other with respect to an entire culture" (47).

Fig. 10. Peñarroya (José Peñarroya Peñarroya). *DDT contra las penas. Almanaque para 1956*, 5. Courtesy of Mercè and Carmen Peñarroya and Princeton University Library.

DDT Almanaque para 1956, created by cartoonist José Peñarroya [FIG. 10]. The image depicts a cast of the magazine's characters soaring through the skies aboard an artificial satellite while waving to a passing child manning a rocket, symbol of the new year that is beginning. The precarious construction of the asteroid, made of sheet metal, is reminiscent of the shantytowns that grew up on the outskirts of Spanish cities in the 1950s and 1960s, as a consequence of the lack of housing faced by the thousands of workers who emigrated from the countryside in the so-called "rural exodus". Technology, a fictional device that makes possible the "estrangement" of readers and viewers of science fiction, was recreated in this image from the material conditions of a country in which imagination had to be fruitful when it came to solving the lack of material resources in everyday life. These visual imaginaries about aerospace technology could be read later in a costumbrist key, forgetting that their aesthetics corresponds to the material reality of a period marked by misery and poverty for a large social majority.[25]

At the end of the 1950s, the motif of the alien visiting Planet Earth appeared in cartoons such as those in the section of the magazine *Tío Vivo* named "Cartas a Marte" (1957) or the series "Doña Tomasa, con fruición, va y alquila su mansión" (1959 [Doña Tomasa, with relish, goes and rents out her mansion]), created by Josep Escobar. In them, the figure of the alien was used in a similar way to the figure of the foreigner in the costumbrist literature of the eighteenth and nineteenth centuries, as an effective poetic mechanism to defamiliarize national customs and habits. Like the images of the "Martians" that had populated the illustrated pages of the satirical press during the first third of the twentieth century, the figure of the "good alien" became a key character for understanding an ethics of experience with the unknown Other in a popular key. Thus, in one of the first Spanish comics that recreated the new phenomenon of the flying saucers in 1950, Don Berrinche, the irate and violent character created by Peñarroya, appeared as an emblem of the post-war fascists who did not cease in their efforts to exterminate the peaceful aliens. On the other hand, the motif of the alien as the colonized Other in an outer space conquered by earthlings would also be included in the images of comic books during the 1960s. In this way, the representation of violence through the aerospace imaginary made it possible to provide readers, many of them children and adolescents, with

---

25 The persistence of this precarious technological imaginary would be prolonged over time, as in the film *El astronauta* (Aguirre, 1970), in which the residents of a village in La Mancha put into orbit a domestic rocket manufactured by themselves from the SANA (Sociedad Anónima de Naves Aeroespaciales).

104 *Fables of Development*

aesthetic and political tools capable of counteracting the rhetoric of violence inoculated by Franco's nationalizing pedagogy.

In the 1960s, aerospace technology also served to recreate the economic transformations related to the consumer industries and mass tourism. Following the tradition of a carnivalesque imaginary —according to which the desired goods descend to earth literally, as if falling from the sky— the consumer goods longed for by Spaniards were represented in the "Pronósticos para el año 1960" [Forecasts for the year 1960] of the *DDT Almanaque* as objects coming from outer space: "En lugar de platillos volantes, durante 1960 cruzarán los espacios máquinas de coser, neveras, radios, etc. Objetos mucho más prácticos" [Instead of flying saucers, sewing machines, refrigerators, radios, etc. will cross space during 1960. Much more practical objects]. With respect to other countries, these goods arrived late to a population that would have been aware of them through their experience as spectators of images from cinema and advertising rather than through their actual presence in the market. Faced with the lack of definition of the origin that the aircrafts could have, the cartoonists imagined an invasion of those consumer objects in which technological advances would undoubtedly be much more useful and necessary for the population. The transformation of the country's infrastructures to handle mass tourism —a phenomenon that gave rise to what Sasha Pack called the "peaceful invasion"— was also linked in the popular imagination to the phenomenon of flying saucer sightings. Thus, in the pages of the Falangist newspaper *Imperio*, journalist Sergio Collado humorously wondered about the tourist potential of extraterrestrial visitors who might have arrived on Earth after a wave of sightings in the region:

> Nos place esa preferencia de los marcianos, pues aunque su turismo no deja, por el momento, divisas, hay que tener en cuenta que estos primeros viajes son de prueba y que no estará lejos el día en que aterricen bonitamente en el Campo de Coreses y nos hagan frecuentes visitas. Yo creo que los hoteles zamoranos ya se hallan preparados para recibir a tan extraños visitants. (1)

> [We are pleased with the preference of the Martians, because although their tourism does not leave, for the moment, foreign currency, we must bear in mind that these first trips are a test, and that the day will not be far off when they land nicely in the Campo de Coreses and pay us frequent visits. I believe that the hotels in Zamora are already prepared to receive such strange visitors.]

From 1962 onwards, the tourism industry began to dominate Spanish economic policies. From that year on, Manuel Fraga turned the tourism sector into what Justin Crumbaugh called, following Michel Foucault's terminology, an "art of governance" (13) that allowed the Francoist regime to consolidate its developmentalist project. Thus, by attracting foreign currency from foreign investors and visitors, the government was able to continue imposing its ultraconservative political agenda while at the same time boosting the legitimacy of its exercise through media promotion of its economic achievements and its own technocratic management. It is at this new juncture that cartoonist José Peñarroya recreated the technocratic policies in the adventures of one of his characters, the child prodigy Pitagorín. In one of his cartoons, Pitagorín travels to the Moon to convert the Selenites into collaborators whom he tries to convince of the advantages of his entrepreneurial tourism project:

> En la Tierra todos hablan de la Luna. Eso quiere decir que cualquier día comenzarán a llegar turistas y tenéis que prepararles alojamientos. Esto es un hotel para turistas. Estos hoteles tienen que llenarse por dentro de estos aparatos llamados muebles, cortinas, alfombras, teléfonos. ¡Manos a la obra y a trabajar! Espero que ahora estos pobretones de lunáticos que vivían metidos en esos agujeros tan feos, podrán disfrutar de muchas comodidades. (6)

> [Everyone on Earth is talking about the Moon. That means that any day now tourists will start arriving and you have to prepare accommodations for them. This is a hotel for tourists. These hotels have to be filled inside with these things called furniture, curtains, carpets, telephones. All hands on deck and let's get to work! I hope that now these poor little lunatics who were living in those ugly holes will be able to enjoy many comforts.]

Pythagorin's indoctrination of the Selenites coincided with the so-called "pedagogy of leisure" ("Horizonte" 318) postulated by Secretary Fraga in his projection of tourism as a collective mission, as a "national enterprise" ("Horizonte" 56) in which Spaniards should collaborate. Among his objectives for the expansion of the new industry, Fraga prioritized the formation of a consensus among Spaniards on the legitimacy of this project and on the need to participate as involved agents. Pitagorín's discourse thus became a parody of the pedagogical training of Spaniards in the new values of the leisure industry and technocracy by the state —a parody that transferred the colonization of the subjectivity of the Spaniards by the leisure and

106   *Fables of Development*

consumption industries and linked it to the developmentalist policies of the Franco regime to the imaginaries of outer space.

Science Fiction, Ufology and Democratic Utopia in *Mito* (1967) by Antonio Buero Vallejo

In January 1967 the composer Cristóbal Halffter proposed to the playwright Antonio Bueno Vallejo the joint creation of an opera based on a theme that should deal with "los más universales temas españoles: Celestina, Don Quijote, Don Juan" (the most universal Spanish themes: Celestina, Don Quixote, Don Juan) (1968, 73). The libretto, entitled *Mito*, was published the following year in the magazine *Primer Acto* together with the essay "Del Quijotismo al 'mito' de los platillos volantes" [From Quixotism to the 'myth' of flying saucers] (1968, 73). In this text, Buero explained why he had decided to make an interpretation of Don Quixote in a ufological key, comparing the Cervantes myth with the phenomenon of flying saucers. Buero considered this phenomenon as a "Mito de nuestro tiempo" [myth of our time] (1968, 73), an expression with which Carl Jung had formulated his hypothesis about collective sightings in *Flying Saucers: A Modern Myth of Things Seen in the Sky* (1958). The playwright from Madrid explained the meaning of his opera in these terms:

> Bajo la presión –o el vacío– de una sociedad grotesca y decadente, Don Quijote creó su fe en la Caballería. Bajo la insanía del mundo actual, ciertos seres de ánimo quijotesco crean su fe en los "platillos volantes" y en los Caballeros de Marte, de Venus o de algún lejano planeta perteneciente a otra estrella: divinos Caballeros que nos instan, desde arriba o confundidos entre nosotros, a deificarnos con ellos. Pues bien: los "platillos volantes" son un formidable mito de nuestra época y mi título también lo alude, al tiempo y no menos que al de Don Quijote. Y si la palabra va en singular es porque estos mitos pueden conjugarse y se conjugan de hecho; porque pueden formar y forman realmente, en ocasiones, uno solo. ("Del Quijotismo" 73)

> [Under the pressure —or the emptiness— of a grotesque and decadent society, Don Quixote created his faith in Chivalry. Under the insanity of today's world, certain beings of quixotic spirit create their faith in the "flying saucers" and in the Knights of Mars, of Venus or of some distant planet belonging to another star: divine Knights who urge us, from above or confused among us, to deify ourselves with them. Well then: the "flying saucers" are a formidable myth of our time and my

Fables of Outer Space 107

title also alludes to it, at the same time and no less than to that of Don Quixote. And if the word is in the singular it is because these myths can and do blend; because they can and do form, at times, a single one.]

As a writer interested in the phenomenon of unidentified flying objects, Buero was familiar with the debates that took place in the ufological organizations that had proliferated in Spain since the late 1950s. One of these, the Sociedad de Amigos de los Visitantes del Espacio, organized public gatherings at the Café Lyon in Madrid that Buero had occasionally attended (Jiménez 201). The presence of the "flying saucers" was as indecipherable in that context as was their ability to effectively challenge the notion of sovereignty while being relegated as an object of study by the scientific and political community. Buero's opera made sense of questions about the limits of governance through the eyes of its protagonist, an opera singer who believes in extraterrestrial existence just as Don Quixote believed in the reality of chivalric fables. *Mito* connects both characters by recreating the motif of the theatre within the theatre. Eloy, the protagonist, is a tenor who is part of an opera company that performs a musical adaptation of Cervantes' novel. After one of their performances, the company must remain locked in the theatre overnight, as the government has decided to conduct one of its "ensayos de defensa atómica contra un fingido ataque nuclear" [atomic defence rehearsals against a feigned nuclear attack] (150). These lock-ins become a source of suspicion for Eloy, who thinks that the government is covering up other kinds of events. In his opinion, some of the reasons the government would have for conducting the drills would include exposure to a real nuclear attack, the celebration of a clandestine strike or else the visit of extraterrestrial beings that the state is hiding from the citizens. The protagonist expresses his belief in the existence of a Martian community that would have long since invaded Planet Earth, anonymously infiltrating themselves among human beings:

Nos han mandado a quienes nos vigilan
y viven confundidos con nosotros.
Ignoráis que nos hablan cada día
bajo las más humildes apariencias.
La portera, el obrero, la maestra
de vuestros hijos, pueden ser marcianos.
¡Y en el mismo teatro puede haberlos! (118)

[We have been sent those who watch over us
and live in mingled confusion with us.
You ignore that they speak to us every day

108   *Fables of Development*

under the humblest appearances.
The concierge, the worker, the teacher
of your children, may be Martians.
And in the same theatre there may be some!]

In this way, Buero Vallejo reverses the Cold War imagery in which the figure of the alien embodied the figure of the imagined enemy to turn the extraterrestrials into members of a democratic community to come. A community that would have already materialized in the present, living day by day among the spectators. By incorporating the aliens into the human community, *Mito* proposes to the spectators the possibility of a new horizon of emancipatory universalism. In this sense, Eloy's character uses the aliens as a political fiction to imagine a new social organization in the same way as Don Quixote had interpreted the social order established by mercantilism on the basis of the feudal imaginary of the books of chivalry. In *Mito*, Buero disputes the meaning that the ideologues of the Francoist regime gave to Cervantes' novel. The appropriation of the quixotic myth for the project of reconstruction of the New Fascist State had begun in 1939, when the academics of several institutions had to take the oath of office before the Gospels and before a copy of Don Quixote bound with the Falangist symbol of the yoke and arrows (Lago 55). This was a consequence of the readings of the novel by Ramiro Ledesma and Ramiro de Maeztu in the 1920s, rescued by the ideologues of the pro-Franco regime in their attempt to resurrect some of the most elemental impulses of the work. In a Nietzschean key, Ledesma and Maeztu asked themselves: what would happen if Don Quixote's madness were not the symptom of the inadequacy of feudal production relations to a modern world, but the voluntarist exercise of its glorification, of the celebration of its anachronistic nature? This will of anachronism expressed during the first Francoism the need of the regime to put into practice a political model based on the feudal experience of modernity, formulated in the full and satisfied conscience of living a divergent temporality.

Buero Vallejo, on the contrary, established a parallelism between the beliefs of ufologists in contemporary times and the beliefs in the chivalrous world that Don Quixote recovered in his metamorphosis from poor gentleman to free knight. Through the parodic inversion of the literature of chivalry, Cervantes' novel closed a historical sequence —that of medieval feudalism— inasmuch as it succeeded in inaugurating another stage that remained irremediably open: that which is usually identified, broadly speaking, with the term "modernity." At a historical juncture in which the new mercantilist mode of production necessitated the freedom of individuals to sell their

Fables of Outer Space 109

labour power in the marketplace, the character of Don Quixote encountered freedom and assumed it completely, making the decision to choose his own life. In this sense, Buero's opera actualized the possibility of thinking of Cervantes' novel as an unfinished and ever-living event, as a long-lasting sequence that impatiently awaits the consummation of its premises.

The action of *Mito* takes place in an imagined contemporary nation-state that represses political dissidents like Ismael, a friend of Eloy's who has participated in one of the clandestine strikes during the nuclear attack drill. Before being captured by the security forces, Ismael escapes and hides in the theatre, where Eloy helps him to take refuge. His life is in danger from the moment the government accuses the strikers of having burned the "Old Palace" during the night, a situation that Buero builds following the events that led to the Reichstag fire in 1933, attributed by the Nazis to the communists. The government's actions recreated in *Mito* can be analysed in the light of the ideological figures that according to Roland Vegso legitimized the logic of exception in the name of national security during the Cold War period. Ideological figures such as the enemy (the unidentifiable figure threatening democracy), secrecy (the unrepresentable guarantee of national security) and catastrophe served to justify anti-democratic measures used to guarantee an order based on exceptionality:

> The "enemy" justified the expansion of a politics that increasingly relied on nondemocratic measures in the name of democracy. The "secret" allowed the withdrawal of executive power from the sphere of public deliberation. And the "catastrophe" institutionalized the rhetoric of "permanent crisis" that legitimated the militarization of civilian life. As the exception became the norm, war was turned into the standard mode of politics; secrecy became the standard terrain of sovereign power; and crisis became the standard of civilian life. (81)

In this sense, ufology questioned from civil society the secrecy and lack of transparency of both governments and the armed forces when it came to providing information, not only about the UFO phenomenon, but also about the control of the population in general. With respect to the management of the catastrophe, ufologists also wondered about the possibility that unidentified aircraft represented a threat to national security that the civilian population was unaware of. In the Spanish case, it is essential to remember how, the year before *Mito* was written, a nuclear accident took place in Palomares (Almería) in which, due to a collision between two United States Air Force aircraft, four thermonuclear bombs that failed to explode fell on this Andalucían village (Vilarós 45).

110   *Fables of Development*

In *Mito*, Eloy asks these same questions that ufologists asked about control and surveillance societies and constructs a vision in which aliens would not visit our planet as invaders, but as agents involved in the defence of earthly peace. In his view, aliens would be protective agents who transmit a "significado positivo de alarmas y advertencias" [positive meaning of alarms and warnings] (74) to those who are able to understand their message. In Buero's opera the scenography functions as a screen which projects images of disaster scenarios in recent history in which such warnings went unheeded. The appearance of the saucers is a reminder of how threats to the safety of the population come not from outer space, but from humans' own use of technology as a weapon of mass destruction: "Rápidas imágenes de platillos entran, enormes, en el campo visual . . . Sobre la negrura del fondo estallan ahora las imágenes de hongos atómicos, a las que sustituyen poco a poco numerosas visiones de exterminio: montones de cadáveres en campos de concentración..." [Rapid images of saucers enter, huge, into the visual field . . . Over the blackness of the background now burst images of atomic mushrooms, which are gradually replaced by numerous visions of extermination: piles of corpses in concentration camps...] (99). In the libretto, the protagonist appears as a reflection of Don Quixote, a figure that the tenor incarnated on stage some time ago. Just as the nobleman from La Mancha "reads" the world from the chivalrous imaginary, Eloy contemplates the reality that surrounds him in a ufological key. An example of this behaviour is his interpretation of "Yelmo de Mambrino" [Mambrino's helmet]—a piece of props from the opera about Don Quixote that they are performing— as "un objeto detector" [a detector object] (82) of extraterrestrial origin. For Eloy, the barber's basin that Don Quixote mistakes for a helmet would be shaped like a flying saucer and would be part of the array of devices used by space visitors to interact with earthlings. Eloy's character emulates Don Quixote until the end of the play and dies in the denouement. Like the protagonist of Cervantes' novel, Eloy chooses a radical ethical option and is shot dead by the police after impersonating his friend Ismael. When he dies, he confesses that his actions, like Don Quixote's wanderings in freedom, have not been in vain, since "los actos son semillas que germinan" [acts are seeds that germinate] (238).

At the juncture of late Francoism, Buero equated the capacity of Quixotism and ufology when it came to dissenting from official discourses and formulating fundamental ontological questions about the codes that regulated political and economic models in the nuclear era. In the words of the playwright: "El quijotismo no es siempre estéril o confuso –no en balde es 'andante'-, y la creencia en los 'platillos' es, a menudo, compatible con sanas y dinámicas conductas sociales" [Quixotism is not always sterile or confused —not for nothing is it 'andante'— and the belief in the 'saucers' is often compatible with healthy and dynamic social behaviours] (74). Along with the denunciation of the consequences of technological progress, Buero vindicates in his opera the value of myths as fantasies capable of activating a political imagination that projects itself into the future. In his essay on the value of mytho-poetic thought that accompanies the libretto, the writer claimed the creation of new myths from the "rubble" of existing ones: "Desmitificar es saludable y necesario, pero no es, creo, la fórmula definitiva de un arte finalmente desenajenado. Desmitificar es relativamente fácil; la dificultad – y el hallazgo– del arte consiste en volver a mitificar, de modo más real, con los escombros de las desmitificaciones" [Demythologizing is healthy and necessary, but it is not, I believe, the ultimate formula for a finally disengaged art. To demythologize is relatively easy; the difficulty — and the discovery— of art consists in re-mythologizing, in a more real way, with the debris of demythologizations] (73–74).

In *Mito*, Buero takes up the proposal formulated by Claude Lévi-Strauss on the capacity of mythical thought "to build its ideological palaces with the rubble of an ancient social discourse" (42). In this sense, the "debris" of the autonomous thought of the characters in Cervantes' novel and the "debris" of the discourses of science fiction and ufology, which already enjoyed an extensive trajectory in Franco's Spain by 1967, were used by Buero Vallejo to create new relationships with the imagination about outer space. The playwright vindicates science fiction and ufology as "myths" of his time, capable of activating a new historical consciousness. A consciousness in which, as reflected in this opera, the future would already be contained in a present time in which an extraterrestrial community was already present among the inhabitants of a democratic community to come. As I have examined in this chapter, Spanish science fiction of the 1950s and 1960s deployed collective desires and concerns about progress and development, including alternatives to dictatorship. In this way, the genre became an exceptional cultural artifact for mapping aesthetic and political imaginaries in which the global advance of the Cold War was intertwined with the social transformations during Franco's dictatorship.

II.

Providential Capitalism

3

Fables of Chance

In a text titled "Religion, the Lottery and the Opium of Poverty", the philosopher Antonio Gramsci pointed out an antecedent for the expression "opium of the people" (57), the metaphor on religion that Karl Marx had included in *A Contribution to the Critique of Hegel's Philosophy of Right* (1843). It was a description that Honoré de Balzac had used in the novel *Un ménage de garçon* (1842), in which he defined the lottery as an "opium of poverty" (67). In this novel, the French writer offered interesting reflections on the illusory promises of future that this game offered, fascinated by the enchanting power that chance exercised among the most underprivileged classes:

> No one has understood this opium of poverty. The lottery, all-powerful fairy of the poor, bestowed the gift of magic hopes. The turn of the wheel which opens to the gambler a vista of gold and happiness, lasts no longer than a flash of lightning, but the lottery gave five days' existence to that magnificent flash. (67)

In his analysis, Gramsci also examined the relationship between the lottery and the Catholic doctrine of grace present in Catholic countries and opposed it to the different conception of chance in communities with a Protestant tradition:

> There is moreover a close connection between the lottery and religion, wins showing who is among the "elect" or recipients of a particular grace of a Saint or the Madonna. One could make a comparison between the Protestants' activist conception of grace that provided the spirit of capitalist enterprise with its moral form and the passive and "good-for-nothing" (*lazzaronesca*) conception of grace typical of the Catholic common people. (58)

The social hopes that gambling encouraged were also a matter of reflection for many creators during the Franco regime. At the beginning of the

116 *Fables of Development*

1950s, many Spaniards were "waiting for the future", an expression used by Carmen Martín Gaite to title one of the books that best portrays that period: *Esperando el porvenir*. The writer was referring with this phrase to a tune hummed by her circle of friends, the group of young writers who collaborated in *Revista Española*. This was a publication in which authors such as Ignacio and Josefina Aldecoa, Rafael Sánchez Ferlosio, Alfonso Sastre and Martín Gaite herself defended the tendencies of existentialism and neorealism as a way of politically and aesthetically dissenting from the culture of the regime. The popular poem in question said: "Sentaíto en la escalera/esperando el porvenir/y el porvenir que no llega" ["Sitting on the stairs/waiting for the future/and the future that does not come"] (36). This *seguidilla* spoke of a recurring theme in the conversations of the time: anxiety about the future. According to the writer, the notion of the future expressed both the uncertain destiny of life trajectories marked by the harshness of the post-war period and the longed-for appearance of sudden financial opportunities: "Se hablaba mucho del porvenir, tal vez para conjurar las sombras del pasado, una palabra que hipotecaba el gozo del presente y que se oía a troche y moche... 'Un muchacho de porvenir'. 'El wolfram, eso sí que tiene porvenir'. Labrarse un porvenir" [There was much talk of the future, perhaps to ward off the shadows of the past, a word that mortgaged the joy of the present and that was heard at every turn... 'A boy of the future'. 'The wolfram, that really has a future'. To build a future for oneself] (35). The precarious situation of a social majority affected by poverty and repression, by the absence of a welfare state and by the harshness of the rural exodus, fuelled the illusion of finding providential solutions that could alleviate personal and collective poverty. Hopes for a more fortunate future were expressed in desires that ranged from the longed-for aid of the Marshall Plan credits to the eagerness to win some of the prizes offered In the numerous lotteries, contests, raffles and draws that proliferated during the 50s and 60s. It was a situation in which, as the writer Manuel Vázquez Montalbán pointed out, "pese a la sobrecarga de lo fatal, pese a las tumbas, los sabios y los dioses, todo el mundo esperaba el Gordo de Navidad" [despite the overload of the fatal, despite the tombs, the wise men, and the gods, everyone was waiting for the Christmas lottery jackpot] (38).

The progressive circulation of capital and credit —and the representation of its growing circulation in the press and in the fictions of the period— allowed the recovery of hopes in an idea of contingency based on chance. The increase in fiduciary circulation, which rose from 30 billion pesetas in 1950 to 65 billion pesetas in 1957 due to inflation (Ros 44), certainly contributed to this representation of the growing circulation of capital. Simultaneously, the proliferation of images of merchandise was promoted by the ubiquitous

Fables of Chance

presence of advertising, which sponsored contests and raffles that proposed to lift the contestants out of their poverty or to increase their expectations of access to consumption. It was a form of propaganda that contributed to forge an image of prosperity in which, contradicting the reality of scarcity in the supply of goods and purchasing possibilities, advertising acted "como si España fuese efectivamente una verdadera sociedad de consumo" [as if Spain were indeed a true consumer society] (Alonso and Conde 168) —so much so that by the end of the 1960s, the cost of advertising was already equivalent to 1.3% of national income (Martín Serrano 22–23).

As will be studied in this chapter, the representations of the circulation and distribution of capital through games of chance are very significant when analysing the transition from autarchy to the liberalization of the economy. Faced with an idea of the future that had been captured in theological terms by National-Catholic ideology, the contingency of ludic chance reopened, through capitalism, a new horizon of expectations. These expectations were perceived as potentially emancipating for a national subject who could express himself again as an autonomous individual in the sphere of gambling and consumption.[1] In this way, games made it possible to preconfigure a society of consumers who wished to obtain the prizes offered by the main managers of chance, such as the state, the Church, and the entertainment and mass consumption industries. In numerous cultural productions, chance was presented as a wealth-distributing device that made it possible to recreate the existence of communities whose cohesion resided in the fact of sharing participation in the games, and in the distribution of prizes or losses. In this sense, the collective practice of gambling became a central element for the representation of communities that materialized from what Antonio Gómez López-Quiñones has called a "social ontology of chance" (120). It is precisely the concrete way in which cultural logics were recreated around this circulation of capital that will allow us to elaborate diverse interpretations of chance in political terms. The following pages examine some productions by creators linked to the regime, such as the director José Luis Sáenz de Heredia, as well as the works of anti-Franco artists such as the filmmakers Luis García Berlanga and Juan Antonio Bardem, and the writers Antonio Buero Vallejo and Juan Goytisolo. In their works, these authors reflected on the emancipatory potential of gambling, betting and luck in different communities. These cultural artifacts proposed an aesthetic and political imagination about life

---

1 On the social practice of gambling and the Spanish bourgeoisie in the nineteenth century see Leigh Mercer's "The Games Men Play: The Stock Market and the Casino" in *Urbanism and Urbanity: The Spanish Bourgeois Novel and Contemporary Customs (1845–1925)*.

under dictatorship based on the recreation of the effects of gambling and the interdependent relationships generated by chance. In this way, they were able to challenge the narratives presented by the regime's media, which promoted a representation of the citizen-gambler who managed to get rich while justifying the distribution of benefits as an expression of the designs of divine providence.

Chance and Games in Franco's Spain

In the Spain of the 1950s and 1960s, a very specific type of contingency appeared in collective games, in which the logic of chance appeared as "a non-theological *primum movens*" (Gómez López-Quiñones 121). Chance can be understood in this context as a device capable of opening up the possibility of changes in the daily life of Spaniards under a dictatorship whose end was not in sight. Fortune appeared as a redeeming impulse that acted against all logical predictions, in such a way that the possibility of being one of those chosen by luck contained a quasi-miraculous and unprecedented dimension of time. This dimension was examined by Walter Benjamin, for whom chance would harbour the capacity to alter and disrupt the everyday experience and expectations of the players; it is his contention that "the wager is a means of conferring shock value on events [*Ereignissen*], of loosening them from the contexts of experience [*Erfahrungszusammenhängen*]" (513). The social hope in gambling that Vázquez Montalbán spoke of can be understood as a type of secularized faith —a faith that projected its effects in a dimension of immanent transcendence in which a stroke of luck would make it possible to overcome the everyday logic of capitalism. As the sociologist Roger Caillois argued in the 1950s, the chance present in games managed to "abolish natural or acquired individual differences" in order to put everyone "on an absolutely equal footing to await the blind verdict of chance" (18). In a context such as the Spanish one, in which post-war circumstances had made hope in luck a collective yearning, the institutionalization of randomness through gambling guaranteed a supposed equanimity when it came to distributing wealth. Collective participation in gambling thus made it possible to unify citizens around the epiphany of being able to perceive themselves as a community whose integration resided in the fact of sharing the randomness of bets, and in their involvement in the practice of gambling.

Social fantasies based on access to material reward grew in parallel with the inequalities generated by a regime that rejected the distribution of wealth through social policies such as those that the welfare states began to implement after World War II. In a context of exposure to innumerable vital risks, gambling became a social practice on which to rely in order to

Fables of Chance 119

overcome the effects of a poverty for which it was necessary to take individual responsibility. Therefore, hope in gambling must be analysed in parallel to the crisis generated by both the autarchic model and the transformations of a Liberalization Plan that did not include the creation of a welfare state among its objectives. The conception of this Plan was partly inspired by the literature elaborated by some of the economists gathered in the Mont Pèlerin Society, an organization founded in 1947 with the aim of acting against state interventionism and against the social welfare state (Mirowski and Plehwe ix–xxi). In 1949, Friedrich Hayek met in Barcelona with Joan Sardà, the future architect of the Stabilization Plan, and with other Catalan economists such as Salvador Millet and Lucas Beltrán, the only Spanish economist present at the annual sessions of the Mont Pèlerin Society. In an article entitled "Hayek in Barcelona", published in *La Vanguardia*, Salvador Millet spread among the readers the economist's ideas and insisted on the importance of the principles of "impersonality" and "spontaneity" that should govern the laws of the free market. In their opinion these principles, similar to the logics that defined the contingency of playful chance, should be the backbone of economic processes. The Catalan economist also highlighted for his readers the influence of Adam Smith as a precursor of a "Christian individualism" and described how the allegory of the "invisible hand" of the market served as an emblem to illustrate the functioning of the plans of divine providence, which transferred its action to the labyrinths of the economic field.

This defence of "impersonality" and "spontaneity" as principles regulating free competition in the market was part of the discourse that inspired the design of some of the new technocratic policies. It was a discourse based on the sanction of the welfare state as a supposed disincentive to the freedom of participants in the economic game, and on the defence of individual responsibility and charity as forms of wealth distribution. Faced with this lack of state alternatives to precariousness, hope in chance was perceived as a possible economic safeguard, so gambling became a popular practice of the period. Despite the fact that the Francoist government had sanctioned from the beginning of the dictatorship the private business of "las Casas de juego de suerte, envite o azar" [Gambling houses for games of luck or chance] (Pino 205), state lotteries and betting games proliferated during the 1950s and 1960s along with all kinds of raffles, drawings and tombolas managed by civil and ecclesiastical organizations.[2] Francoist press and newsreels capitalized on the

---

2 An emblem of the social importance of these games can be found in the title of one of the most successful films of the period, *Tómbola* (1962), starring the child star Marisol (Pepa Flores). As she stated in the song that gave the film its title, games of chance were inextricably linked to the idea of happiness: "La vida es una tómbola

120 *Fables of Development*

social hope generated by the raffles, as well as on the enthusiasm expressed by the winning citizens after the distribution of prizes. As recorded by the voice-over narrating the NO-DO at the beginning of Juan Antonio Bardem's film *Felices Pascuas* (1955), the National Lottery became in these stories a modern Wheel of Fortune, and a compendium of the theological virtues: a "fiesta de la paz" [celebration of peace] that embodied "la fe, la esperanza y la caridad de todos los españoles" [the faith, hope and charity of all Spaniards]. In parallel to these narratives, anti-Francoist cultural producers presented in their fictions a defiance based on their reflection on the living conditions of the working classes. In their works, games were recreated as the opposite of what they were supposed to be, transforming prizes into losses, and economic losses into political and moral victories, so that the logics of profit were completely dislocated. By displacing both the notion of "providence", grounded on theological grounds, and the idea of "randomness", implicit in the logic of the free market, these "fables of chance" recreated by anti-Francoist cultural producers offered the public an alternative political and aesthetic imagination of gambling through the representation of networks of solidarity among the most vulnerable and precarious members of society.

The National Lottery, a Game in Company

In 1951, *El Ciervo* began to be published, a Catholic magazine that emerged as a publication critical of the role that the Church should play under the dictatorship. One of its first issues included an opinion column entitled "Lotería y caridad" [Lottery and Charity], in which the writer Jesús Ruiz explained the relationship between the two social practices. The author argued how the capital investment with which players hoped to obtain the prizes of the National Lottery served at the same time to exercise charity, since the amount of the tickets purchased included a surplus in the form of a surcharge that the organizations that sold the participations used to carry out charitable works:

> Millones y millones salen de los bolsillos españoles para invertir en el Juego nacional. Nada tendríamos que objetar . . . si año tras año la lotería no se fuera confundiendo poco a poco con la caridad . . . Hacer bien pretendiendo lucrarse - y lo que es peor, materialmente- es contradecir en su más íntimo sentido la dulce virtud de la caridad. (2)

de luz y de color" [Life is a raffle of light and color]. In this way, the social ascent of Marisol's character in scripts constructed from the "rags-to-riches" formula was shared with spectators who received vicariously through these "fables of chance" the success achieved by the protagonist.

Fables of Chance

[Millions and millions come out of Spanish pockets to invest in the National Lottery. We would have nothing to object...if year after year the lottery were not being confused little by little with charity...to do good while pretending to profit —and what is worse, in a material way— is to contradict in its most intimate sense the sweet virtue of charity.]

Throughout the 1950s and 1960s, other Spanish authors reflected on this use of the lottery for charitable purposes. In 1963, the writer Ignacio Agustí considered the investment of players in the National Lottery as part of a providential plan in which luck would be predetermined by divine intervention:

Esta es la gran fábrica de sueños española, la creadora de los fabulosos mitos de la opulencia en la mente del ciudadano medio, del hombre de la calle. Ahora empieza a asediarnos la lotería desde todos lados, en forma de pequeños boletos y participaciones que vienen a ofrecernos, desde hace semanas, las gentes más diversas y desconocidas. . . La mayoría de esos boletos son estratagemas de entidades benéficas para el acopio de un suplemento de los fondos caritativos. La mayoría de ellos llevan una sobrecarga modesta, pero clarísima, que es aquella parte del premio que no nos va a tocar, pero que damos gustosos por creer que, en porcentaje de buena acción, puede mover a la Providencia a elegir, entre todas las cifras posibles, precisamente aquella en que el cálculo y la benemérita intención van tan íntimamente grabados . . . en cierto modo, hemos contribuido a esparcir la caridad y nos hemos prestado, a conciencia, al enorme juego de la rueda de la fortuna. (58)

[This is the great Spanish dream factory, the creator of the fabulous myths of opulence in the mind of the average citizen, the man in the street. Now the lottery begins to besiege us from all sides, in the form of small tickets and participations that the most diverse and unknown people come to offer us, week after week. . . Most of these tickets are stratagems of charitable organizations for the collection of a supplement of charitable funds. Most of them carry a modest but very clear surcharge, which is that part of the prize that we will not win, but which we gladly give because we believe that, as a percentage of good deed, it may move Providence to choose, among all the possible figures, precisely the one in which the calculation and the benevolent intention are so intimately engraved . . . In a certain way, we have contributed to the spreading of charity, and we have consciously lent ourselves to the enormous game of the wheel of fortune.]

Fables of Development

According to this system, the National Lottery tickets distributed the capital collected in a triple way. First, the prizes allowed players unexpected access to consumption, the backbone of the "dreams" mentioned by Agustí in his text. Secondly, the surcharge on the participations contributed to the financing of charitable activities. Finally, the money collected by the state in this game-tribute would be destined to various budgetary items including, among others, the construction of the Valley of the Fallen, financed by the annual lottery draws held from 1952 (Sueiro 200). This relationship between the lottery and the financing of state and charitable policies was part of a long-standing tradition in Spain, a country in which the organization of the sale and distribution of the game has always been (and still remains) a state monopoly. The game called "Renta de la lotería" [Lottery Revenue] was established by Charles III in 1763, as part of a tax reform to alleviate the public debt (Altabella 42–44), and the first "National Lottery", named after the draws held between Cadiz and Madrid in 1811, was intended to finance the War of Independence (Garvía "Historia" 72). From the reign of Charles IV, the state began to use this game-tax as a mechanism of wealth distribution, donating part of the income obtained to hospitals, charity centres and hospices. In its legislation on gambling, the Francoist State never considered the National Lottery as a tax but as a service exploited by the administration. In this sense, the lottery became a profitable regressive tax that meant a proportionally higher tax burden for the most disadvantaged citizens (Garvía, "Loterías" 102).

In addition to the National Lottery, other games of chance contributed to the subsidization of social assistance policies during the dictatorship. This was the case of the so-called *quinielas* [football pools], the popular betting game based on the results of the National Soccer League Championship. In 1946 the Patronato de Apuestas Mutuas Deportivo-Benéficas [Sports-Benefit Parimutuel Betting Board] was created for this purpose, which allocated 45% of its proceeds to the Dirección General de Beneficencia y Obras Sociales [General Directorate of Charities and Social Works] (Adelantado 354). Another game that was very popular at the time was the *Cupón Pro-Ciegos* ["Pro-blind" ticket], a type of lottery that allowed the financing of jobs for the blind created by the Organización Nacional de Ciegos [National Organization of Spanish Blind People], whose founding decree had been signed by Franco's government in Burgos in 1938 (Garvía Organizing 21–22). As in the case of the National Lottery, these betting games encouraged a distribution of capital that benefited the state and other welfare organizations in their collection efforts.

The popular game of the *quinielas* [football pools] was part of the theme of several literary and cinematographic works of the period. Thus, in contrast

Fables of Chance 123

to the friendly vision of the game recreated in films such as *La quiniela* (1959 [The Soccer Pool]) by Ana Mariscal or *Sucedió en mi aldea* (1956 [It Happened In My Village]) by Antonio de Santillán, the novel by the Falangist writer Juan Antonio de Zunzunegui *El mundo sigue* (1960 [Life Goes On]), later adapted for the cinema in 1963 by Fernando Fernán Gómez, offered a representation of the game from the perspective of a gambling addict, a disorder that destroyed the lives of the protagonists. In this sense, the novel accused the media of the time of "adoctrinar a las masas" [indoctrinating the masses] and of giving "más importancia a un partido de fútbol que a un certamen científico" [more importance to a soccer game than to a scientific contest] (337). On the basis of the characterization of gambling as a pathology, the novel and the film recreated this game as an instrument of alienation that provoked devastating effects among the working classes. The fondness for this popular gambling game also reached General Franco, who in May 1967 was one of the top ten winners with a betting pool of twelve results for which he won almost one million pesetas (Preston 731).

The participation of the popular classes in lotteries and gambling games has been analysed from a functionalist perspective by sociologists such as Edward C. Devereux, who defined these games as a "safety valve" (191) to channel in a socially acceptable way the tensions and frustrations derived from economic inequality. In a complementary way, the institution of the lottery has been interpreted from the Marxist critique as a form of access to an alternative economy that enjoys its own set of rules and its own measures of success. Within this theoretical framework, critics from different disciplines have interpreted this social practice as a device that contributes to reinforce a system in which the state, as the entrepreneur of the game, disregards the social inequalities on which it acts while collecting dividends.[3] With respect to the specificity of Spanish lotteries, sociologist Roberto Garvía has explained the continued success of this institution by describing the practice as a "juego en compañía" [game in company], which is expressed in the division of tickets and shares among friends, relatives, co-workers or members of an organization ("Historia" 96; "Loterías" 102–113). This practice, which emerged as a strategic response by gamblers to the increase in the price of bets during the nineteenth century, spread to all strata of society and followed a process of social institutionalization that continues to this day. The game in company is based on cooperation and interpersonal trust among the participants, who hand over their money to the managers of the different fractions of the ticket. Even today, three quarters of the country's population participates in this practice in work,

---

3 See Nibert and Peppard.

124   *Fables of Development*

neighbourhood and family environments during the Christmas period. Paradoxically, this process minimizes the prizes by maximizing the number of beneficiaries, so that the effect of this mode of play is inseparable from the idea of interdependent community that is expressed and defined in these exchanges of lottery ticket fractions. In this sense, the "game in company" serves to negotiate the social status of the participants within the social network to which they belong, so that the tickets would cease to be purely economic goods to become symbols of interpersonal ties. In the following pages I will analyse two works of fiction that offer an alternative political imagination of chance based on the recreation of communities that disrupt the economic and social logics governing the rules of the lottery game: Juan Antonio Bardem's film *Felices Pascuas* (1955 [Merry Christmas]) and Antonio Buero Vallejo's play *Hoy es fiesta* (1956 [Today's a Holiday]).

Felices Pascuas (Bardem, 1955) and *Hoy es fiesta* (1956) by Antonio Buero Vallejo: Interdependence and Randomness of Encounters

Juan Antonio Bardem, filmmaker and militant in the Spanish Communist Party, premiered *Felices Pascuas* in 1955, his first comedy directed alone. The plot of the film revolved around the Christmas Eve problems of Juan's family, a barber who has invested his savings in buying lottery tickets shared with friends and neighbours. The protagonist discovers at the beginning of the film that he is one of the winners of "El Gordo" [the Jackpot] of the Extraordinary Christmas Draw and decides to say goodbye to his job. However, the disappointment comes fast, as soon as he discovers that the winning ticket no longer belongs to him because his wife has been exchanging tickets and participations in different games of chance with her neighbours for months. Juan discovers that the ticket with the winning number was exchanged for a ticket corresponding to another raffle, in which the prize is nothing less than a suckling lamb. On the eve of Christmas, with no job and no money, the protagonist couple sees no other alternative for the celebration of their Christmas feast than to sacrifice "Bolita", the name with which their children have baptized the lamb.

From the opening credits at the beginning of the film, designed after drawings by Alfonso Paso, the references to the Easter lamb and the celebration of the birth of Christ are clear. In addition to the Christmas motifs, symbolized in the drawings of lambs and lottery tickets, the relationship between the two is visually complemented by a representation of the Catholic Monarchs and the conquest of America. These references, icons of the mythical imperial past on which Franco's historiography was

Fables of Chance   125

based, serve in the context of Bardem's film as emblems of the foundational violence of the National-Catholic state. While the lottery was associated in these images with the process of primitive capital accumulation in the history of the Spanish Empire, the representation of the figure of the lamb becomes the symbol of the evangelization that accompanied the military conquest. The images of the lambs in these captions made visible the violence of conquest while expressing, as a Christological emblem, the promise of solidarity and renewal of the bonds between the dispossessed that Christmas as a rite also celebrates.

In the course of the film, Juan and his wife are unable to kill the lamb to eat it for Christmas Eve dinner, even though, as he says, he had "to kill men in war". Not knowing what to do with his prize, the barber keeps asking aloud what a living lamb is good for. The future of an animal destined to be slaughtered for human consumption will be progressively linked to a process of anthropomorphization. This process intensifies as the protagonists experience, after the disappearance of the lamb, a sense of vulnerability that makes them equal to it, to such an extent that the protagonist denounces the animal's disappearance at the police station as that of another member of the family. The spectators thus witness the conflict between two moral and political logics: one that justifies the sacrificial violence of the animal, and one that is based on the recognition of the interdependence between the living beings of a community. The loss of the lottery ticket represents, in short, more than an economic loss. Juan and Pilar will not receive the 15,000 pesetas that would have given them access to the consumerism that the regime promoted in its utopian representations of gambling. In exchange, the couple places the hopes of their immediate future in the salvation of a missing lamb, an event in which their friends and neighbours are also involved.

Bardem's Christmas fable thus proposes an alternative imaginary about chance as a mechanism capable of generating events in which new forms of solidarity are activated. The Madrilenian director tells the story of the lamb's eventful journey and the neighbours' search for the animal, through which the spectators have access to spaces such as a nun's convent, a barracks and a cattle slaughterhouse. In this parable of life under dictatorship, the members of two institutions that supported the exercise of the Francoist biopower, the army and the Church, will try to catch the lamb to eat it as Christmas dinner. The director is especially ironic with respect to the voracity of these institutions, taking into account that the lamb is the animal that represents the sacred symbol of Christ's sacrifice. Bolita is finally saved and will spend Christmas Eve in the company of the family, who have decided not to carry out the predictable action that fate had in store for them, which was the

126   *Fables of Development*

seemingly unavoidable fact of having to end the life of an animal with their own hands. The happy ending of the film thus responded to a decision on the part of the protagonists, which is resolved with the renunciation of exercising the sovereign violence that crossed the whole of the social body over the body of the animal. Their decision thus implied the choice of a moral and political order that placed at the centre the interdependence of lives based on the recognition of a shared vulnerability.

A year after the premiere of *Felices Pascuas*, playwright Antonio Buero Vallejo received the National Theatre Award for his play *Hoy es fiesta*, first performed in September of the same year. The play revolved around a swindle perpetrated by a widow, who distributes fake shares of a winning national lottery ticket among her neighbours. The situation described by Buero Vallejo, in which the person who manages the division and sale of the numbers transgresses the trust granted by the rest of the participants in the practice of the game in company, was very similar to that of other swindles that flooded the press of the time. These news items, which included the fraudulent sale of lottery tickets or the organization of fake lotteries, occupied dozens of news items, reports, accounts of events and even became a topic that served to illustrate advertisements. In this way, the figure of the swindler, whose victims were usually citizens who had recently arrived in the city during the massive rural exodus, was disseminated in mass culture. The advertising of these scams encouraged the representation of a state of insecurity in which distrust was presented as the moral principle that should underpin relations between strangers. The media thus enhanced the ubiquitous presence of the swindler, presented as a social type whose criminalization displaced the real causes of the structural violence lying behind the processes of migration to urban areas. In this sense, a lottery-related swindle was also the central theme of Rafael Azcona's short story "Pobre" (1960), in which a beggar distributes false shares of a winning ticket among the inhabitants of a suburb of Madrid. The story makes visible the material conditions of existence of a community to which the media come for the first time, interested in telling the story of the supervening wealth, along with the representatives of banking institutions who take advantage of the occasion to recruit new clients. When the fraud is discovered, the "poor" swindler protagonist of the story is blamed by the media, and the poverty of the residents of the Madrid suburbs becomes once again invisible to the state and its ideological apparatuses.

In the context of the media's criminalization of swindlers, Buero Vallejo proposes in *Hoy es fiesta* a political interpretation of the phenomenon of the scam. In this play, the media's construction of the figure of the swindler takes on a different meaning when the spectators learn the real motives that have

Fables of Chance 127

led Doña Balbina to deceive her neighbours in her desperate desire to escape poverty. Her deceit destroys the expectations that the affected neighbours had raised after considering themselves winners of a prize that would have radically changed their lives. In this sense, the play shows the construction of the popular classes' desires to have access to capital through two practices in which the idea of the future was inscribed in everyday life: lottery and cartomancy. Indeed, spectators gain insight into the precariousness of these players through the questions that the neighbours direct to the character of the fortune-teller Doña Nieves, who feeds the hopes of those who consult her by interpreting omens with her deck of cards, as well as through the neighbours' conversations about their expectations of winning the National Lottery's extraordinary prize. In these conversations, dedicated to sharing their hopes and desires, the neighbours manage to escape from the private experience of suffering for a few moments. In their stories, the description of the effects of the war and the post-war period on the working classes has an impact on the fantasies of consumerism that the economy of the game proposes. In the play's denouement, good luck turns to catastrophe when the neighbours are informed of the deceit. The players, who expected everything from the lottery, affirm that "todo se ha perdido" [all is lost] (176) when the possibility of winning the prize vanishes before their eyes. This disaster is described by one of the neighbours as the culmination of an ongoing experience of deprivation in which they have been "toda la vida corriendo como perros tras las cosas sin conseguirlas nunca" [all their lives running like dogs after things without ever getting them] (176).

The scam tests the limits of the relationships between the members of the neighbourhood community by representing the conflict between two models of subjectivity constructed from two identitary logics such as those of the gambler-citizen model and that of the community of equals represented by the neighbourhood collective. As soon as they learn of the deceit, the neighbours try to take revenge by exercising physical violence on the swindler. However, the intervention of the character of the painter Silverio stops the collective rampage and encourages the neighbours to make a thoughtful decision about the future of the widow and her daughter, who have perpetrated the fraud out of sheer necessity, in order to be able to eat. Above the state law, which would qualify the action as a crime, and above the neighbours' frustration, who denounce that not only the "dinero de los pobres" [money of the poor] (175) has been gambled with, but "también con sus ilusiones" [also with their illusions] (175), Silverio suggests to those affected that they urgently think about the condition of poverty that equals them: "Es preferible la piedad. ¡Todos ustedes son pobres! ¿Y no van a tener compasión de la más pobre de todas?" [Pity is preferable. You

128   *Fables of Development*

are all poor! And won't you have compassion for the poorest of all?] (175). The decision-making power of the neighbours highlights their capacity to completely overturn the social order. The power to surrender two lives to the violence of the state machinery or to forgive those who have deceived them is in their hands.

The political, as understood by the philosopher Jacques Rancière as the articulation of dissent between a concrete problem and the general logics of domination, bursts then in the encounter between the established order and the possible emancipation in the handling of a wrong (59). As the character of Silverio —described as a "Quixote" by the neighbours— recalls, the sacrifice of two lives to calm the desire for revenge would only increase the losses already accumulated in their own lives: "Si la denuncian no van a sacar nada en limpio y sólo conseguirán perjudicar a estas dos mujeres. Una desgracia más aparte de las de ustedes" [If you denounce her, you will not get anything out of it, and you will only harm these two women. One more misfortune besides yours] (173). The neighbours finally decide to forgive the widow and her daughter and defend the value of their lives. The spectators witness this complex process of collective decision-making in which there is a distribution of roles that activate the power of the community, which requires the cooperation of the entire neighbourhood to vindicate a justice that defies the laws. Thus, in the face of the sovereign violence exercised by the Francoist state —and which they, as individuals under its laws, could also exercise— the renewal of the bonds of community interdependence through the salvation of the most vulnerable finally triumphs. In Walter Benjamin's words, the emancipatory energy latent in gambling would be sustained in the capacity to transcend the pre-concerted linear temporality of capitalism each time the possibilities of gambling take place: "This process of continually starting over again is the regulative idea of gambling, as it is of work for wages" ("Selected" 331). In connection with this reasoning on the emancipatory possibilities offered by games, Buero Vallejo proposes in his work a reflection on the redemptive impact of chance as a mechanism capable of generating a particular experience of temporality, seeing it as an experience that allows players to interrupt the hollow time of dictatorial life and provide life in common with new meanings based on solidarity.

Contest Time

A young couple walks the streets of Madrid as winners of a contest called "La pareja feliz" [The Happy Couple]. A scientist disguised as an Eskimo collects three thousand pesetas given by the popular announcer Bobby Deglané in the "Busque, corra y llegue usted primero" [Search, run, and get there first] contest. The old teacher of a rural school hopes to get from the radio programme "Doble o nada" [Double or nothing] the money needed for a sick child to be operated on in Sweden, and a teenager —thanks to the raffle of a brand of chocolate— hopes to travel to Italy to see her father who disappeared after the Civil War. An analysis of these scenes —which belong to the films *Esa pareja feliz* (1951 [That Happy Couple]) by Luis García Berlanga and Juan Antonio Bardem, *Historias de la radio* (1955 [Radio Stories]) by José Luis Sáenz de Heredia, and the novel *Fiestas* (1958) by Juan Goytisolo— will provide a literary and cinematographic itinerary that will explain why these productions, despite their creators' different political beliefs (José Luis Sáenz de Heredia was committed to the Franco regime but the other three were dissidents), placed at the centre of their plots the complex relationship between contests, competition, consumerism and solidarity. In these works, radio occupied a central place as a space in which the spectacular staging of games of chance articulated a particular connection between the state, the companies sponsoring the contests and the listeners. The broadcasting over the airwaves of an inventory of lexicons and lifestyles made possible the representation of different social identities in which radio listeners could act as contestants, stars for a day, donors or aid seekers assisted by their fellow citizens.

In his essay *Man, Play and Games* (1958), Roger Caillois analysed games using a classification based on four categories: *agon* (competition), *alea* (chance), *ilinx* (vertigo), and *mimicry* (simulacrum). Games belonging to the *ilinx* group would be related to the creation of vertigo or disorientation, while those deemed a simulacrum would imply the experience of illusory experiences for the players. Games based on competition presuppose previous training, skill or discipline on the part of the participants, while games of chance represent the result of an impersonal choice rather than a triumph over an opponent. On the basis of this analysis, Caillois classified social formations according to their relationship with the games predominant at a given time. The triumph of the virtues of merit (*agon*) and choice (*alea*) in modern societies would be, in his opinion, a sign of the advance of civilization. In the Spain of the 50s and 60s, all kinds of sweepstakes and contests proliferated, sponsored by commercial brands that found in these games the best way to advertise and sell their products. These contests were governed either by the rules of chance, by the competitiveness present in the contests that required the exhibition of some kind of skill, or by a combination of both types of games.

In this sense, the incursion of the radio into Spaniards' domestic sphere was decisive in bringing the public together around a schedule that functioned, according to Manuel Vázquez Montalbán, as "un campo

130 *Fables of Development*

experimental de nuevas técnicas publicitarias y como detonador de la mecánica mental consumista propuesta al pueblo español como la nueva panacea colectiva" [an experimental field of new advertising techniques and as a detonator of the consumerist mental mechanics proposed to the Spanish people as the new collective panacea] ("Medios" 160). The mass media thus contributed to the production of a "panorama mítico de lo cotidiano" [mythical panorama of the everyday] ("Medios" 161), which highlighted the gap between an image of abundance and the material conditions of "una sociedad en situación objetiva de preconsumo, a la que, sin embargo, se le trata de convencer de que vive el cuento de hadas del mundo convertido en un drugstore casi gratuito" [a society in an objective situation of pre-consumption, which, nevertheless, is trying to be persuaded that it is living the fairy tale of the world turned into an almost free drugstore] ("Medios" 163). The advertising displayed in the commercials broadcasted during the screening of movies and the commercial propaganda on the radio encouraged the massive proliferation of numerous sweepstakes and contests sponsored by commercial brands. These games of chance made it possible to preconfigure a society of potential consumers who expected to be able to obtain "un muestrario de objetos-mitos situados en el escaparate de la prosperidad: frigorífico, lavadora, televisor, coche utilitario" [a sampler of mythical objects placed in the showcase of prosperity: fridge, washing machine, television, utility car] ("Medios" 162). These were goods that were part of the Fordist "working class norm of consumption" (Aglietta 130), a model that Spain joined with delay in comparison to other European countries, sustained by what Raymond Williams called the "magic system" of advertising (170).

The increase of radio sets in Spanish households in the 1950s coincided with the transformations of a medium that depended on commercial promotion in order to reach larger audiences. Due to the new funding policies of radio stations, both radio formats and programme content had to adapt to the incorporation of advertising as the main source of income. Some of these changes included sponsorship by commercial brands, the distribution of prizes as a mechanism to attract new listeners, or the national broadcasting of highly successful local programs (Balsebre 154–164). These advertising practices were described by Vázquez Montalbán using a concrete example such as the popular variety programme entitled "Cabalgata Fin de Semana", presented by the Chilean announcer Bobby Deglané:

"Cabalgata Fin de Semana" marcó los primeros hitos en la España consumista. Un coñac y una fábrica de caldo concentrado se dedicaron a regalar una oncur parte de los excedentes de sus beneficios a través

Fables of Chance

de oncursus radiofónicos. Cada noche, la renta de los concursantes iba en aumento, y también la expectación del público presente y ausente, estimulada por los gritos entusiasmados de Bobby. Era la materialización del mito de Jauja. (Crónica 121)

["Cabalgata Fin de Semana" marked the first milestones in consumerist Spain. A cognac and a concentrated broth factory dedicated themselves to giving away a small part of their surplus profits through radio contests. Each night, the income of the contestants increased, and so did the expectation of the audience present and absent, stimulated by Bobby's enthusiastic shouts. It was the materialization of the myth of Jauja.]

Radio thus became a donor agent that exhibited the capacity to have a seemingly unlimited amount of merchandise and capital at the disposal of the consuming public. These awards were part of a commercial apparatus directed by businessmen who were involved both in the management of the media and in decision-making in the country's economy. This was the case of the lawyer Antonio Garrigues, chairman of the Board of Directors of Cadena SER and intermediary agent of the North American interests present in the network, and indeed of a significant part of the foreign investments that took place in Spain from 1951 onwards (Balsebre 16). The figure of this businessman was key in the foreign financing of the state in the early 1950s, at a time when a good relationship was forged between the Garrigues family and the Rockefeller family, "propietarios del imperio petrolífero de la Standard Oil y del Chase Manhattan Bank, uno de los primeros bancos que interviene en la concesión del crédito de 86.5 millones de dólares que recibe Franco en 1951" [owners of the Standard Oil empire and of the Chase Manhattan Bank, one of the first banks to intervene in the concession of the 86.5 million dollar loan received by Franco in 1951] (Balsebre 21). This relationship between Franco's government, businessmen and media owners, as well as the resulting confusion between public and private capital, can be analysed on the basis of a popular joke of the time. The dialogue contained in this joke expressed the intersection between General Franco's promises in the new cycle of economic liberalization and the famous radio contest "Un millón con casa y coche" [One million with house and car], sponsored by *Avecrem*, a popular brand of bouillon cubes:

Franco ha salido a cazar. Junto a un barranco, tropieza y cae al vacío. Consigue agarrarse a unas matas y pide auxilio. Providencialmente pasa un pastor, y lo rescata. El Generalísimo está tan agradecido que dice:

132 *Fables of Development*

– Por haberme salvado voy a hacerte un regalo muy importante. Te voy a
dar un millón de pesetas y una vivienda. ¿Te figuras quién puedo ser?
– ¡Claro, hombre! ¡Usted es el del Avecrem! (Vigara 20)

[Franco is out hunting. Next to a ravine, he stumbles, and falls into
the void. He manages to grab hold of some bushes and calls for help.
Providentially a shepherd passes by and rescues him. The Generalissimo
is so grateful that he says:
– For having saved me I am going to give you a very important gift. I
am going to give you a million pesetas and a house. Can you figure
out who I must be?
– Of course, man! You are the *Avecrem* guy!]

The joke expressed the convergence of agents in the construction of the
new consumer fantasies. Together with the government's plans —it had
announced in 1957 its housing policies under the slogan "We want a country
of proprietors, not proletarians"— the desire for access to property and
consumption was articulated under the imaginary coordinates proposed by
the media, the advertising industry and the companies that manufactured
mass consumer products such as those of the commercial brand that served as
support for the joke. The role of radio as a donor of capital and merchandise,
the expansion of advertising and the figure of Franco as a "benefactor" thus
overlapped in some representations of the new model of mass consumerism.

Esa pareja feliz (1951): Contests and Dreams of Consumerism in Times of Rationing

In 1951, Luis García Berlanga and Juan Antonio Bardem, two young graduates
of the IIEC (Instituto de Investigaciones y Experiencias Cinematográficas)
shot their first comedy, *Esa pareja feliz*, released in 1953 after the success of
¡Bienvenido, Mr. Marshall! (1952). The film, which broke into a film panorama
dominated by historical and religious cinema, focused on the daily life of a
young working-class couple. Due to their lack of resources, the protagonist,
Carmen, places her hopes in the luck present in sweepstakes and advertising
contests. In her opinion, the prizes would allow them to alleviate their
precarious situation and satisfy their desires for consumerism in a context
in which rationing cards still regulated access to food and other products
until their definitive elimination in May 1952. Bardem thus recalled other
films that he had taken as references when writing the script:

Las películas clave de *Esa pareja feliz* las tengo muy claras. Nace de
Navidades en julio de Preston Sturges; *Antoine et Antoinette* (*Se escapó*

Fables of Chance

la suerte) de Jacques Becker; *Soledad* de Paul Fejos y *De hoy en adelante* (*Own words*) de John Berry . . . Era un tipo de cine que se hacía en los años treinta sobre todo en Europa, en el que aparecían con frecuencia los problemas de los trabajadores . . . que tienen apuros económicos. (Cañeque y Grau 199–200)

[The key films for *That Happy Couple* are very clear to me. It was born out of Preston Sturges's *Christmas in July*; Jacques Becker's *Antoine et Antoinette*; Paul Fejos's *Lonesome* and John Berry's *Own words* . . . It was a type of cinema that was made in the 1930s, especially in Europe, and frequently featured the problems of workers . . . who are in financial straits.]

Chance is the main theme of the films mentioned by Bardem, as is the case of the radio contests in *Christmas in July* (Sturges, 1949) or the lottery in *Antoine et Antoinette* (Becker, 1947). Like the working protagonists of these films, Juan and Carmen are a young married couple living in a rented room in a *corrala* [courtyard] in Madrid. Juan works as an electrician in a film studio while he tries to improve his education by taking a correspondence course to become a specialized radio technician. Carmen, for her part, is a seamstress convinced that she can change her luck by participating in all the contests and lotteries she knows about. In one of the evening cinema sessions that the couple regularly attends, Carmen feels directly appealed to by the message launched by a host advertising a raffle sponsored by the soap brand "Florit": "Usted puede ser feliz" [You can be happy]. This promotional campaign intensifies the fetishism of a commodity such as a bar of soap, associating its purchase with the experience of happiness. For the philosopher Michel de Certeau, the "fables constituted by our advertising and informational media" (186) would be based on a providential type of thinking that directed the spectators' desires. These fictions promoted a new way of relating to the marvellous, in which the idea of predestination was once again inscribed in everyday life through consumerism: "Even more than the God told about by the theologians of earlier days, these stories have a providential and predestining function: they organize in advance our work, our celebrations, and even our dreams" (186).

After becoming the winners of the contest called "The Happy Couple", Juan and Carmen are informed of the prizes they will receive, which include gifts, invitations and promotions in several commercial establishments and entertainment venues in Madrid. On their journey through stores, restaurants and nightclubs, the characters gain access to leisure and consumer spaces reserved for a social minority. The format of this contest, of which numerous examples can be found in the press of the period, was

134 *Fables of Development*

based on an advertising strategy in which the sponsoring establishments offered participants a consumer experience that, as in the case of the film, was associated with the idea of happiness.[4] As Bishop Vicente Enrique y Tarancón had pointed out in his pastoral "El pan nuestro de cada día" [Our Daily Bread] (1950), those who benefited from the existence of the black market that had arisen as a consequence of the rationing policies exhibited ostentatious consumption practices: "para quien tiene dinero abundante, y no son pocos los que se han enriquecido desaforadamente en estos últimos años, no existen privaciones" [for those who have abundant money, and there are many who have become unbridledly rich in recent years, there are no privations] (quoted in Sinova 251).

Unlike these nouveau riche, Juan and Carmen belong to a social class whose expectations of material well-being were cut short during the war and the post-war period, and their situation is similar to that of other workers that Tarancón describes as being in a position of absolute precariousness at the beginning of the 1950s: "También los obreros que trabajan y que tienen un jornal objetivamente bastante remunerador, no pueden tener todo el pan que necesitan ni pueden comprar los alimentos indispensables" [Even the workers who labour and who have an objectively fairly profitable wage cannot have all the bread they need, nor can they buy the indispensable food] (quoted in Sinova 252). The protagonists of *Esa pareja feliz* reproach each other for the fantasies that sustain their respective aspirations of access to capital. Juan criticizes Carmen for spending a surplus of their salaries on gambling. For her, however, gambling is not an expense, but an investment, since in the past luck helped her to win in a raffle the sewing machine with which she can earn an income by working at home:

> – Carmen: Probar la suerte no es tirar el dinero
> – Juan: Que va, es meterlo en el banco. La quiniela, la lotería, los ciegos, el jabón Florit, la sopa . . . Tú crees en la suerte como un angelito que va a decir: "Mira qué parejita tan simpática" y ¡pum!, un coche a la puerta.

> [– Carmen: Trying your luck is not throwing your money away.
> – Juan: No, it's putting it in the bank. The football pool, the lottery, the pro-blind ticket, the Florit soap, the soup ...you believe in luck like a little angel who is going to say: "Look what a nice couple" and just like that, a car at the door.]

---

4 See Ríos Carratalá.

Fables of Chance

For her part, Carmen thinks that Juan's vision of capitalism as a system in which anyone can get rich through a stroke of luck is very similar to her own beliefs in gambling. Paraphrasing her husband's reasoning, Carmen responds by arguing that all his projects, based on the myth of the self-made entrepreneur, always fail: "Todos los millonarios empezaron vendiendo periódicos, hay que tener vista, y... ¡te metes en cada lío!" [You say that all millionaires started by selling newspapers, that you have to have vision, and...you get into trouble!]. Both fantasies of access to capital are ultimately based on a belief in chance as a mechanism that allows for the fortuitous attainment of profits. Thus, some of the projects in which Juan invests his money are geared towards his professional training as a radio technician by correspondence. At the beginning of the 1950s, coinciding with the regime's hydroelectric modernization project, in the country there was an increase in the number of radio sets such as the one that the protagonist acquires in instalments by receiving on his courses the necessary parts to build his own receiver.[5]

Slogans such as "The future belongs to electricity" or "Success through practice", which illustrated the advertising of this type of distance education, are also parodied in the catchphrase used in the film by the course seller: "¡A la felicidad por la electrónica!" [Happiness through electronics!]. Both the

---

5 As Vázquez Montalbán explains:

La radio tenía una envergadura considerable y estaba en condiciones de dictar la sentimentalidad popular, y así lo hizo entre 1950 y 1960. La cosa tuvo su prehistoria infraestructural: la intensa electrificación del país, la definitiva comercialización de los receptores. Se llegó a estimular las más variadas formas crediticias para comprar una radio. Por ejemplo; la de la radio hucha que funcionaba a base de ir metiendo monedas por una ranura. Periódicamente pasaba un empleado de la empresa vendedora y se llevaba la recaudación del mes. ¡Qué papel tan activo tenía el ciudadano en la búsqueda de su propia alegría! Es una fórmula no explotada lo suficiente y que tiene una interesante implicación educativa. (Vázquez Montalbán, "Crónica" 105)

[Radio had a considerable reach and was in a position to dictate popular sentimentality, and it did so between 1950 and 1960. The thing had its infrastructural prehistory: the intense electrification of the country, the definitive commercialization of the receivers. The most varied forms of credit to buy a radio were encouraged. For example, the radio-piggy bank that worked by inserting coins through a slot. Periodically an employee of the selling company would pass by and take away the monthly earnings. What an active role the citizen had in the search for his own happiness! It is a formula that has not been sufficiently exploited and has an interesting educational implication.]

radio set and the sewing machine found in the home of "the happy couple" were also a regular part of the repertoire of merchandise given away in raffles and contests. In a context in which the acquisition and commercial distribution of these goods was complicated for a social majority, prizes consisting of machines for sewing or writing, and even tractors or animals such as oxen or cows in rural areas, were highly appreciated. When Juan and Carmen win the contest, the situation of the so-called "happy couple" is beset by a series of misfortunes: Juan is fired from his job and swindled by the partner of one of his businesses. In the midst of constant arguments, the couple follows the itinerary in which they should find the promised happiness but only receive useless gifts such as a speargun for underwater fishing or a pair of high heels that break as soon as Carmen puts them on.

After an argument in a banquet hall where they are celebrating the end of their "happy day", the couple's journey ends at the police station and the courthouse, from where they are finally dismissed with a warning from the judge: ""Déjense de concursos y de pamplinas, ¡a trabajar!" [Forget all these contests and balderdash, and get back to work!]. Such exhortation on behalf of the authorities about the value of work is in stark contrast to the employment situation of the protagonists, who could barely subsist on their salaries before Juan's sacking. But it contrasts mainly with the final image of the film. At dawn, when they have ceased to be "the happy couple", Juan and Carmen abandon the parcels with the gifts next to the benches of a Madrid street, still taken up by the homeless people who have spent the night there.

The winnings of the contest were insignificant and the dreams of luxury promised by advertising that spoke to them "in the name of happiness" cannot change the situation of a married couple who recognize that their lives are nothing like those of the Hollywood movies that Carmen likes so much. The final film sequence is a perfect example of the mismatch between the fables of abundance publicized by the media and the reality of the homeless in Madrid at that time. According to figures mentioned by historian Antonio Cazorla, in 1950 "unas 50.000 personas vivían en cuevas y en chabolas en los alrededores de la capital, expuestos a la desnutrición y la tuberculosis" [some 50,000 people were living in caves and shacks on the outskirts of the capital, exposed to malnutrition and tuberculosis] ("Políticas" 95–96). The couple gets rid of the gifts and what they symbolically represent: signs of distinction in a luxury economy circuit accessible exclusively to those who have used poverty management to enrich themselves in the post-war period. The fantasies of consumerism that had been taken apart throughout the film —while the material conditions of existence of this working couple were revealed—show their cruellest reality in the final scene, with the image of the extreme misery and helplessness of the homeless on the streets of Madrid.

Fables of Chance 137

Contests and Providential Narratives in
Historias de la radio (Sáenz de Heredia, 1955)

In 1955 *Historias de la radio* was released, a comedy by José Luis Sáenz de Heredia that revolved around a radio station's programming. The director of *Raza* (1942), a film based on the novel of the same name written by Francisco Franco, had used in much of his previous cinematographic production a set of providential narratives in which the fantastic was mixed with a Catholic discourse recreated in a wondrous key. This was the case of *El destino se disculpa* (1945 [Fate Apologises]), where chance appeared incarnated in the character of "El Destino" (Fate), a figure depicted as a counsellor and spiritual guide who encourages the audience to resolve conflicts in accordance with "la moral cristiana y el sentido común" [Christian morality and common sense]. In the 1950s, films such as *Todo es posible en Granada* (1954), the musical comedy that portrayed Spain's agreements with the United States, or *Faustina* (1957), a contemporary version of the Faust myth, also developed their plots with the use of fantastic elements that were integrated into a National-Catholic imaginary.

Historias de la radio was made up of three chapters in which the radio contests of a broadcasting station in Madrid appeared as a space in which divine providence intervened in the lives of the characters through the principles of chance (*alea*) and competition (*agon*). The film included three contests that were part of the regular programming of a radio station. In these games, the participants are citizens in urgent need of money due to the lack of other sources of financing. The protagonists of these stories are two scientists seeking capital to patent an invention, a man about to be evicted who needs to pay off his debts, and a rural teacher chosen by his community to try and win the money with which to pay for the treatment of a child with a serious illness. In the first of the contests, based on the Cadena SER programme "Busque, corra y llegue usted primero" [Search, run and get there first], a cookie brand offers 3,000 pesetas to the listener who arrives first at the radio station dressed as an Eskimo. The second episode is based on a raffle sponsored by an insecticide in which money is given to a listener who has been randomly contacted through the telephone directory. In this case, the requirement to receive the prize is to show up on the live programme after receiving the call. In the last chapter, a quiz based on the Radio Madrid programme "Doble o nada" [Double or nothing], the participants' knowledge is tested through a series of general culture questions that can be used to win important prizes.

The credit promises of radio raffles and contests were presented as opportunities to be seized in a limited time. As one of the characters in

138   *Fables of Development*

Historias de la radio stated, if the opportunity to win the prize is not taken, "los billetes vuelven al éter, se evaporan" [the tickets go back into ether, they evaporate]. Through the contests, players and audiences were involved in a sort of "pedagogy" about the logic of the capitalist system itself. In this sense, the contests gave anyone the opportunity to learn how to manage the consequences of the risks of financial capitalism. Thus, in the case of contests based on the "double or nothing" mechanism, participants could use the money they had earned to become accumulators of capital or to speculate on their future earnings. As Caillois explains, spectators also participate vicariously in this process through experiencing the success of others, namely, the winners in the games: "One chooses to be a winner by third parties, by delegation, which is the only way for everyone to triumph at the same time and to triumph without effort or risk of failure. Hence the cult of modern society, of the star or the champion" (202).

In the case of *Historias de la radio* (1955), chance must be understood from the Catholic providentialist framework that shapes the social imaginaries recreated in the film. The film begins with a reflection by Father Venancio Marcos, who directed a religious consultation on Radio Nacional de España, on a parable from the New Testament. In his analysis of the parable, the priest reminds us that all the creatures of creation "pueden enseñarnos a confiar en la providencia de Dios" [can teach us to trust in God's providence]. In the first of the episodes, a scientist (José Isbert) who has travelled through the city in a tough competition to reach the radio station in his Eskimo costume, realizes upon arriving at the studio that he has lost the prize because another contestant has beaten him to it. In an open-microphone monologue, he explains to his partner that perhaps God's plan was not to give them the 3,000 pesetas they needed to patent their invention: "Todo ha sido inútil. Pero estoy contento por haber luchado por su ilusión y por la mía. ¡Que patenten los de la aeronáutica su pistón! y tire usted el nuestro a la basura, será que Dios lo quiere así" [It was all in vain, but I'm happy to have fought for your illusion and mine. Let the aeronautics people patent their piston, and let's throw ours in the trash, maybe God wants it that way]. However, an unexpected intervention will change the course of events. The broadcaster Bobby Deglané, moved by the engineer's speech, decides to finance the patent with his own money in exchange for becoming a capitalist partner in the project. The presenter thus provides the necessary funds so that the research can be put at the service of all Spaniards, since, according to the scientist, "un invento siempre es algo de interés nacional" [an invention is always something of national interest]. In this case, chance, guided by divine intervention, ends up favouring the loser of a contest marked by extreme competition,

Fables of Chance 139

in which even violence among the contestants has marked the way to the entrance to the radio station.

In the second episode of *Historias de la radio*, a man is interrupted in an attempted robbery by a phone call. While he is in the apartment of his landlord, to whom he owes money to pay the rent, he answers a call from the studios of Radio Madrid, where they have randomly selected a number from the city's telephone directory. The requirement of the contest is apparently simple: show up at the station within half an hour and prove that he is the owner of the phone line. Faced with the possibility of losing the 2,000 pesetas, the thief decides to go to the parish where his landlord is and share the prize with him, without mentioning the circumstances of the attempted robbery that led to this eventful situation. The homily that the priest is giving at that moment revolves around a reflection on the vanity of material goods and on the debt acquired by the parishioners with God. It is God who, as the true and only creditor of the believers, will ask them to account for their actions at the Last Judgment: "Será más rico el que más haya dado y más pobre el que se enterró con sus riquezas. El dinero representa los bienes materiales del mundo y estos no son propiedad de nadie, pertenecen a Dios y él es quien nos pide cuenta de lo que nos prestó y de lo que dimos" [He who has given more will be richer and he who has buried himself with his riches will be poorer. Money represents the material goods of the world and these are not the property of anyone, they belong to God and it is He who asks us to account for what we borrowed and what we donated].

From this moment on, the story revolves around the priest's reflections on the destiny of the money obtained in the prize, which is inserted in a moral economy where debts are interpreted on the basis of the logic of sin and forgiveness. For the parish priest, divine intervention is always present in the actions of the protagonists, whom he asks: "¿Qué quiso Dios evitar? ¿Qué usted fuera ladrón o que usted no fuera robado?" [What did God want to prevent: that you should be a thief or that you should not be robbed?]. Finally, the landlord and the thief decide to share the prize and make a donation to a second "thief", whom the priest allows to take the money from the parish collection box at night in order to make him become one of his parishioners. The Catholic moral economy of the film thus converted the prizes obtained by chance into spiritual "earnings" and donations to assist those in need of ecclesiastical charity.

In the last episode of the film, the people of a small village in the mountains of Madrid decide that they must raise money to be able to send a sick child to Stockholm, where a doctor has offered to perform an operation that could save his life. At first, the authorities are not clear that it is their responsibility to obtain the funds. They think that the Church does not have access to this capital in the form of donations; and they also believe that it is not the role of the government to manage health care, since "para eso está el Estado, para hacernos caminos y pantanos y para rascarnos los bolsillos, pero no para suministrarnos el amor propio que debe tener cada uno" [this is what the State is for, to make roads and swamps for us, and dig deep into our pockets, but not to provide us with the self-respect that everyone should have]. In the end, they decide to take up a public collection; it is their contention that if a foreign doctor is willing to help the child then the neighbours, being Spaniards, cannot stand idly by when it comes to helping a fellow countryman: "Por humanidad y por patriotismo. Para salvar la vida a esa criatura y para que no se nos caiga la cara de vergüenza" [Out of humanity and patriotism. To save the child's life and to keep our faces from falling in shame].

Solidarity, therefore, is not conceived in the film as a practice to achieve political and social rights, but as a feeling that operates through charity understood as a social bond based on patriotism. Once the amount of money that has been raised proves insufficient to cover the expenses of the trip, the radio is revealed as the only means available to obtain capital on the spot. Under the invocation of Saint Nicholas, patron saint of the town, the public school teacher is chosen by his neighbours to participate in the contest "Double or nothing", a quiz on general culture. In the essay *El sadismo de nuestra infancia*, Terenci Moix reflects on this sterile idea of "culture" that the Francoist school and the media promoted:

> Se recuerda, especialmente, *Lo toma o lo deja*, de Radio Barcelona, cuyos concursantes necesitaban de un cierto cargamento cultural ... La gama de preguntas era tan amplia – desde dónde se encuentran las pirámides de Gizeh hasta en qué año se fundó la orden del Císter o ... qué heroína de Alejandro Dumas interpretó en el cine Greta Garbo ... Es esa misma idea de cultura que daba la Historia de España explicada e interpretada en las películas de Cifesa ... es la cultura administrada para los niños en las secciones de pasatiempos de nuestros tebeos de entonces; es, en resumen, una de tantas facetas del verdadero sadismo de nuestra infancia. (102–3)

> [One remembers, especially, "Take it or leave it" (Lo toma o lo deja), of Radio Barcelona, whose contestants needed a certain cultural load ... The range of questions was so wide —from where the pyramids of Giza are located to what year the Cistercian order was founded or ... which heroine of Alexandre Dumas did Greta Garbo interpret in the cinema ... It is that same idea of culture given in the Cifesa films when explaining

Fables of Chance

and interpreting the history of Spain. It is the culture administered to children in the hobby sections of our comics of the time; it is, in short, one of the many facets of the true sadism of our childhood.]

In the three episodes of the film, access to capital is always presented as a service to the homeland, whether through the financing of an invention of "national interest", the conversion to Catholicism of people in need, or neighbourhood solidarity. The pursuit of individual profit was thus embedded in narratives about the distribution of wealth in which the notion of chance was "sacralized" through constant references to divine intervention in the circulation of capital. Expectations about the future were linked to the trust in the "Providence of God" with which the film began, which operates as an "invisible hand" guiding the logics of chance managed by the entertainment and mass consumer industries.

Raffles, Tombolas and Politics of Dispossession in *Fiestas* (1958) by Juan Goytisolo

In 1955, Juan Goytisolo finished writing his novel *Fiestas*, published in 1958 in Buenos Aires and Barcelona after undergoing a major revision by the censors. The story took place in Barcelona during the celebration of the International Eucharistic Congress of 1952, an event converted by Franco's government into an ideal occasion for the display of propaganda exalting National-Catholicism; thus, the regime exhibited its commitment to the Church on the eve of the agreements with the Holy See that were to take place a year later. In the novel, the ubiquitous presence of radio discourses heard in the houses and public spaces of an area of the city in which an old residential neighbourhood borders a recently built shantytown will serve as a guiding thread of the plot. These discourses include, as in the case of *Historias de la radio*, the presence of commercial advertising aimed at an audience that, according to the narrator's voice, "le daba igual oír el último capítulo del serial radiofónico 'Pilar, la princesa desventurada', que la emisión deportiva patrocinada por los Almacenes Modernos" [could not care less about listening to the last chapter of the radio serial "Pilar, the hapless princess" or the sports broadcast sponsored by Almacenes Modernos] (783). In the course of the narration, the voices of the radio also reproduce the speeches proclaimed in the events of the Eucharistic Congress, through the recreation of the broadcasts that burst into different passages of the novel:

En el interior de la habitación, la radio transmitía el discurso de un hombre de voz suave, dulcísima, '...con lo que, hijos míos, al acercarse

142 *Fables of Development*

a este gran acontecimiento, resuenen en la ciudad los himnos de amor y de ternura, flameen los gallardetes y las banderas, luzcan su indescriptible belleza las luminarias, como símbolo de la alegría que debe anidar en vuestros corazones por estos maravillosos días de paz, días de unión, días de... (786)

[Inside the room, the radio transmitted the speech of a man with a soft, very sweet voice, '...so, my children, as this great event approaches, let the hymns of love and tenderness resound in the city, let the pennants and flags fly, let the luminaries shine their indescribable beauty, as a symbol of the joy that should nest in your hearts for these wonderful days of peace, days of union, days of...]

In the midst of the multitudinous celebration of the Eucharistic Congress, the body of a murdered girl appears. The body belongs to an adolescent girl named Pira, an orphan who hoped that the chance present in the contests could change her destiny. At the beginning of the novel, the workers of a chocolate company come to the neighbourhood where Pira lives to hand out tickets to participate in a draw for a trip to Italy. Pira decides to participate in the contest motivated by the desire to win a prize that would allow her to be reunited with her father, a Republican army officer who disappeared at the end of the war and whom the girl imagines living abroad: "Boleto mil trescientos quince. El número lo he elegido yo misma. Anoche soñé precisamente en él y supe que sería premiado. Por fin el viaje a Italia, el encuentro con el padre, la vida común en el castillo" [Ticket one thousand three hundred and fifteen. I chose the number myself. Last night I dreamed about it and I knew it would be a winner. Finally the trip to Italy, the meeting with the father, the common life in the castle] (648). The girl lives with her relatives in an area of the city where the shacks or shanties built by recently arrived migrants from the south of the country are gradually spreading. As we know from the experiences of the shanty-dwellers in Barcelona, both the proximity between neighbours and their organization in procuring some of the basic needs in their neighbourhoods —such as access to goods and services for shared use— had generated in these spaces a tension with state control and with the logics of the market. In this sense, the daily practices of solidarity and mutual aid generated personal ties among the neighbours, for whom the street became the agglutinating space of social life. The presence of the state propaganda discourses and those of commercial advertising in the urban space are inscribed in Goytisolo's novel in the representation of graffiti located on the border of the space built by the shantytown neighbours: "Al final de la guerra habían inscrito una leyenda: 'Por el

Fables of Chance 143

Imperio hacia Dios', en gruesos caracteres negros, pero el calor y las lluvias la habían desfigurado. Ahora lucía un cartel flamante: 'Beba Coca-Cola', que anunciaba una hermosa mujer de pelo rubio y cara sonrosada" [At the end of the war they had inscribed a legend: 'For the Empire towards God', in thick black characters, but the heat and the rains had disfigured it. Now there was a brand new billboard: 'Drink Coca-Cola', announced by a beautiful woman with blond hair and a rosy face] (654).

At the end of *Fiestas*, the narrator describes the murder of Pira, which takes place when the girl begins the longed-for trip to Italy after losing the contest prize. Following the reasoning learned in her catechism classes that a "milagro puede ocurrir en cualquier sitio" [miracle may happen anywhere] (780), Pira trusts in divine intervention to make the trip on her own, so she sets off alone on a journey whose end is tragic for the young girl. In addition to the murder of Pira, the beginning of the Eucharistic Congress brings other misfortunes to the slum dwellers in the novel. The narrator recalls how, in the manner of an oracle, the advertisement for the contest sponsored by "Chocolate el Gato" stated: "Ustedes recibirán algo inesperado el mes de junio" [You will receive something unexpected in the month of June] (793). This statement will end up becoming, towards the close of the novel, a prophecy for the neighbours, who will receive the news of their eviction without prior warning:

> En el suelo, junto al banco, había unos papeles amarillos manchados por el polvo y la lluvia: "Gran rifa de "Chocolates El Gato", "Ustedes recibirán algo inesperado el mes de junio." Casi a pesar de él levantó la cabeza y observó la comitiva de murcianos. Verdaderamente la casa anunciadora había cumplido su promesa: nadie, en el barrio, había previsto aquella expulsion. (793)

> [On the floor, next to the bench, there were some yellow papers stained by dust and rain: "Great raffle of 'Chocolates El Gato", "You will receive something unexpected in the month of June". Almost in spite of himself he raised his head and looked at the retinue of Murcians. Truly the announcing house had kept its promise: no one in the neighbourhood had foreseen that expulsion.]

The urban space that they themselves had built is to be demolished in order to build a new church on the land. Goytisolo's argument may seem convoluted, but it referred harshly to the evictions of shanty dwellers that had taken place in Barcelona in 1952. Faced with the arrival of more than half a million people in the city, the city council demolished the

144 *Fables of Development*

shantytowns near the Diagonal, where the main events were to be held, and the inhabitants were relocated in record time. As one of the characters in the novel comments, persuaded by media propaganda, "Si los sacan es porque los alojan en otro sitio. Y los alojaban, sin duda. Por algo lo decían los diarios" [If they take them out, it is because they are housed elsewhere. And they were, no doubt. The newspapers said so for a reason] (839). Those "whereabouts" to which the character refers included the precariously built dwellings known as the "governor's houses", built 28 days before the Congress in the neighbourhood of Verdún. Another of these places was the Indigent Classification Centre, where they tried to return immigrants to their place of origin, or the Olympic Stadium of Montjuic, where families lived in overcrowded conditions for several months (Marín 77–78). It was a process of expropriation of urban space through which the state regained control of the emerging shantytowns, which grew at the same pace as migrations from the countryside to the city. It was a biopolitical project aimed at disciplining and socially framing the proliferation of neighbourhood bodies in the post-war period. In the development of this process, citizens were dispossessed of the spaces of autonomy in which they had managed to activate their own defence mechanisms as well as of the collective management of coexistence outside the state, while the virtues of the housing built by the state were promoted. The conditions of these dwellings and the urban environment in which they were built generated new problems for the neighbours, who endured both the lack of community services and the population control policies imposed by the regime in these spaces.

With respect to this housing problem brought up in *Fiestas*, the Catholic Church also used the chance involved in tombolas and raffles with the aim of raising funds for the construction of houses for workers without resources. This is the case of the Charitable Construction Company "Nuestra Señora de la Almudena" of Madrid, which between 1952 and 1954 raised nine million pesetas through the Diocesan Housing Tombola. Its programmatic objectives for the construction of two housing colonies leave no doubt about the process of biopolitical framing and indoctrination to which its tenants would be subjected. Some of the maxims of this construction company were "Todos propietarios" [All owners], "No habrá viviendas 'Malthusianas'" [There will be no 'Malthusian' housing] or "Queremos que nuestras colonias sean hermandades cristianas" [We want our colonies to be Christian Brotherhoods] (Secretariado 428–430). In the case of the Construction Company "Nuestra Señora de los Desamparados" of Valencia, the paper presented at the Social Week of Housing held in 1954 stated that in the realization of this real estate work "La Providencia actúa a través de los ingresos de la Tómbola Valenciana de Caridad" [Providence acts through the income of the Valencian Charity Tombola] (Secretariado 474). In this sense, the whole project was conceived as a great offering to God while at the same time serving to subject the tenants to the social control of the religious organizations that built parishes and Catholic schools next to the houses. In their own words, this real estate activity "es nuestro oro, la única moneda con que podemos pagar; es ese nuestro vehemente deseo de servir a nuestros hermanos; de servir a la Iglesia; de hacer bien a nuestra Patria, de sostener y restaurar la familia Española" [is our gold, the only currency with which we can pay; it is our vehement desire to serve our brothers; to serve the Church; to do good to our country, to sustain and restore the Spanish family] (481). For his part, in 1957 Ignacio María Aragó published an article in the magazine *El Ciervo* "Té-Bridge para obras de apostolado" [Tea-Bridge for apostolic works], in which he criticized charitable practices, such as charity raffles, linked to the leisure activities of the bourgeoisie:

> Otra fórmula que ocupa todos los años a millares de personas piadosas, es todo el sistema de tómbolas-loterías-rifas benéficas o té-bridge. Hay provincias en España en las que parece que todo el esfuerzo de la caridad diocesana se centra alrededor de una tómbola monumental, a cuya inauguración asisten elevadas autoridades civiles y eclesiásticas. ¡Qué lejos quedan hoy estos ambientes cuando se les juzga y se les relaciona con las ingentes masas de personas necesitadas! ¡Qué lejos queda todo esto del espíritu de comunidad parroquial! (3)

> [Another formula that occupies thousands of pious people every year is the whole system of tombolas, lotteries, charity raffles or tea-bridge. There are provinces in Spain where it seems that the whole effort of diocesan charity is centred around a monumental raffle, whose inauguration is attended by high civil and ecclesiastical authorities. How far away these environments are today when they are judged and related to the huge masses of needy people! How far away all this is from the spirit of the parish community!]

The charity raffles were praised by Falangist writers such as Tomás Salvador, who thought that "el deber de sostener a los hospitales, los centros de beneficencia, corresponde a los ciudadanos, no al Estado" [the duty of supporting hospitals and charitable centres corresponds to the citizens, not to the state] ("La tómbola" 7). For this author, the raffles were a success because they offered the taxpayer "algo, en su enorme mayoría de veces con un valor superior al medio duro que ofrece" [something, in the vast majority of cases with a value superior to the hard coin that he offers]. In his opinion,

146 *Fables of Development*

"llevar el comercio a la caridad es un gran acierto, es una sublimación del comercio... tiene el espíritu moderno que exigen los tiempos, lo que permite al caritativo incorporarse, sin darse cuenta, al negocio de Dios" [taking business to charity is a great success, it is a sublimation of commerce . . . it has the modern spirit demanded by the times, which allows the charitable person to join, without realizing it, God's business]. Based on the idea — recurrent in the media of the time— that the distribution of wealth was not an exclusive function of the state, chance was used as an instrument in which gamblers had the opportunity to bet on what these real estate developers called "el negocio de Dios" [the business of God] (Secretariat 474). In the so-called "bancos de Dios" [banks of God], as is the case of the Bank of Our Lady of the Forsaken in Valencia, the Church itself was in charge of administering the capital collected through the diocesan raffles: "No habrá Banco —decía— de mayor simpatía ni que reparta mayores dividendos... El que aporta al Banco de los Desamparados da a los pobres, pero le presta a Dios" [There will be no Bank —he said— of greater sympathy or that distributes greater dividends ... He who contributes to the Bank of the Forsaken gives to the poor, but lends to God] (quoted in Sánchez Jiménez 63). According to the promoters of the charitable construction business, divine providence would thus intervene in the management of the housing problem, since, as argued by the Constructora Benéfica "Viviendas del Congreso" of Barcelona, the "redistribución de la riqueza no puede ser función exclusiva del Estado, sino que lo es también de todos y cada uno de los ciudadanos" [redistribution of wealth cannot be the exclusive function of the state, but also of each and every citizen] (Secretariat of the National Board 456).

Goytisolo's novel offers a sceptical look at the leeway for action of those who refuse to participate in the regime's "parties". In opposition to those members of the community who fail in the practice of their daily resistance, the end of the novel poses the apparent triumph of violence and the propaganda apparatus of the state. This triumph is revealed in the dialogue between one of the neighbours and a Republican teacher, whose project of a school for the children of the shantytowns has been closed down:

> – Según decía el periódico, el Ayuntamiento construye para ellos un bloque de viviendas modernas y cómodas.
> – Los periódicos no dicen más que mentiras – le interrumpió el profesor.
> – La prensa está dirigida, desde luego –repuso, algo molesto, don Paco–, pero tal vez sea preferible esta limitación a los excesos de hace unos años. Porque usted mismo tendrá que reconocer que aquel desorden... (796)

Fables of Chance 147

[– According to the newspaper, the City Hall is building a block of
  modern and comfortable housing for them.
  – The newspapers tell nothing but lies – the teacher interrupted him.
  – The press is certainly guided – don Paco replied, somewhat annoyed
  – but perhaps this limitation is preferable to the excesses of a few
  years ago. Because you yourself will have to admit that the disorder...]

The discourse on the consolidation of "public order" and social peace seems
to be easily accepted by a good part of the neighbours who live in the most
affluent area of the neighbourhood and who look on with indifference at
the evictions while hundreds of citizens take to the streets to celebrate
the beginning of the Eucharistic Congress. In contrast to the opinion of
those who think that "la mejor solución es que cada uno tire por su lado,
sin preocuparse de lo que ocurre a su vecino" [the best solution is for
everyone to go their own way, without worrying about what happens to their
neighbours] (797), the teacher bitterly denounces how in the Francoist state,
"las fiestas de algunos no son las fiestas de todos" [the festivities of some
are not the festivities of all] (797). This lack of unity will be what, in his
opinion, will make it impossible to articulate a collective resistance capable
of putting an end to the dictatorship: "hemos perdido la capacidad de
rebelión. Estamos embrutecidos, como animales . . . desunidos . . . seremos
siempre un rebaño de esclavos" [we have lost the capacity for rebellion. We
are brutalized, like animals ... disunited ... we will always be a herd of slaves]
(797–798). In *Fiestas*, the violence of the regime's policies permeates all social
practices. The novel shows how the elites finally intervene by manipulating
the chance that supposedly made everyone equal. In the raffle of "Chocolate
El Gato" it was impossible for there to be winners, since the prize had been
awarded beforehand to the delegate of the mayor of Barcelona. In this
sense, Goytisolo's novel was not so far from a reality in which even General
Franco won in 1967 a million pesetas betting on a football pool. As in the
work of other anti-Franco creators, the myths about the games of chance
are questioned in order to ask new questions about structural poverty
or the social uses of gambling. Through the representation of collective
games, these fictions reflected on the need for social hope and solidarity
when articulating ethical and political alternatives to those proposed by the
dictatorship's fables of chance.

4

Fables of Grace

In 1962, historian Antoni Jutglar denounced in the Catholic magazine *El Ciervo* the strategies used by some institutions to encourage citizens to exercise charity. According to his analysis, some campaigns included advertising tactics in which charitable practices were described as a profitable "investment" for believers. The exercise of charity as a relational virtue based on the bond that unites men with divinity thus reproduced the inequality between donors and those assisted in the context of Franco's dictatorship:

> No creo sea muy positivo incitar a las personas para que entreguen alguna cosa como limosna, organizando campeonatos de la caridad y modalidades de concursos para ver si se rebasan tales o cuales "records"; pero menos lo puede ser todavía el que imitando ciertos slogans publicitarios se pretenda fomentar la "caridad" mediante frases, que muy bien podrían servir para respaldar determinadas inversiones financieras, pero que muy poco sirven a la causa de Dios: invierta en el Banco de Dios, es el más seguro, está fabricado a prueba de ladrones, no puede quebrar y además siempre paga el 100 por 1. (2)

> [I do not think it is very positive to incite people to give something as alms, organizing charity championships and contests to see if such and such "records" are surpassed; but it is even less positive to try to promote "charity" by imitating certain advertising slogans with phrases that could very well serve to support certain financial investments, but that serve very little to the cause of God: invest in the Bank of God, it is the safest, it is thief-proof, it cannot go bankrupt and it always pays 100 per 1.]

During the 1950s and 1960s, charity was an important guiding principle in the distribution of wealth and resources in Spain. Charity, understood as a social bond, reinforced in daily life the hierarchy of unequal and arbitrary power relations, while at the same time it presupposed on the part of those who exercised it the submission of the assisted, who would be obliged to correspond with their obedience or gratitude. For the Francoist biopolitical project, citizens were not considered subjects of social rights, but rather members of a National-Catholic community in which beneficence became the basis of the gratifiable nature of social assistance. This was a very particular "economy of grace" that operated in an arbitrary manner, as a code opposed to that of social justice obtained from recognized rights. In this sense, charity became a main vector articulating this model of wealth and resource distribution in this particular intersection between theology and economics that characterized the transition from autarchy to developmentalist capitalism.

Bartolomé Clavero studied the historical trajectory of the notion of charity as a social relationship in which persons who receive a benefit must reciprocate to their donors in some way. Clavero found a name for this relationship which recurs in theological treatises: "antidora", a term from Greek which literally means "counter-gift" (15–34). The code of "antidora", as it was configured in Europe since the Middle Ages, established that individuals in a higher position should relate to those at a lower level through liberality, magnificence and charity, virtues to which the benefited parties were obliged to reciprocate with gratitude or service. Thus, in societies that maintained the Catholic creed after the Protestant Reformation, the exercise of charity as a virtue gave rise to what Clavero calls "Antropología católica de la economía moderna" [Catholic anthropology of the modern economy]. This was a model that established "the priority of generous and charitable relations over contractual and legal relations; the priority of proportional and distributive equality over strict commutative equality; [and] the priority of the order of family and friends over public and administrative authorities" (Hennaf 317). In this way, charity has historically consolidated the exclusion of large social majorities from the decision-making process regarding their destiny; it has also contributed to the absence of social policies that are based on the recognition that the situation of poverty of those assisted corresponds to a need resulting from systemic social inequality (Reich 65–105; Raventós and Wark 29–50).

From the beginning of the New State under Franco, nothing existed in Spain that could be assimilated to a general and universal social security system with recognized rights for all citizens; the latter depended on the beneficence of the Catholic Church and the welfare works of Falangism, which operated as vehicles for propaganda, the disciplining of citizens and political loyalty. Social security during the Francoist regime had its first design in the so-called Law of Bases of Social Security of 1963, a year after the 1962 great strikes, and was ratified by a General Social Security Act in 1966. Its development responded to a situation in which the model of compulsory social insurance proved insufficient for a country that needed to respond to the demands of Fordist production with measures that would help the management and reproduction of the labour force (Rodríguez López 71–73; Cayuela 235–248). Both laws unified almost all partial mandatory insurances such as old age, sickness, maternity, unemployment and accident benefits. However, its coverage was not universal, since those who were not contributing workers, their dependents, or pensioners were left out of the system (González y Ortiz 375). Many citizens were thus excluded from the assistance system and continued to depend on the charitable institutions managed by the Obras Sindicales [Union Works] or the Catholic Church (Moreno and Sarasa 17). As Antonio Cazorla recalls, the need to accept official assistance resources often entailed the imposition of a series of degrading conditions, as well as the additional burden of stigma: "reliance on Catholic charities was considered a humiliation because it always came with conditions attached, or, worse, because it was a sign of being a bad son, daughter, or sibling" (Cazorla, "Fear" 71). In this sense, the Catholic Church's welfare action was not subsidiary to the shortcomings of the state, but rather it was the social areas that belonged to its apostolate by right. Throughout the 1950s and 1960s, the social doctrine of the Church burst forth through organizations such as Caritas and Acción Católica [Catholic Action], which were in competition with the "totalitarismo estatista" [statist totalitarianism] of the Falange (Sánchez Jiménez 176).

More than forty years after the end of the Francoist dictatorship, part of Spanish society identifies the dictatorial regime as a driving force behind the welfare state in Spain (González Madrid and Ortiz Heras 361–388). As critical studies on this period have shown, successive governments during the dictatorship limited themselves to maintaining and reinforcing the welfare policy of the early twentieth century with the aim of building, but above all of imagining, a cohesive and disciplined national community. In the Francoist social security model that began in the 1960s, there was nothing like a levying State with budgetary and fiscal involvement in its financing, nor a redistributive state that guaranteed the extension of this social policy. The basis of the social security budget during Franco's regime was financed by 90%, with the contributions of salaried workers, and its function corresponded to a model of social engineering in which the low salaries received by men had a connection with the domestic work carried out by women who did not receive a salary. The state budget did not finance the social security system; furthermore, paradoxically, the contributions system was used by the dictatorship to finance works and projects outside the protection system —such as INI projects, infrastructure and even bank liabilities— so that it eventually became "an adjuvant mechanism in the process of capital accumulation" (Moreno and Sarasa 19).

During the first fifteen years of the dictatorship, the weakest sectors of society were exposed to poverty, and so the regime used their needs to act politically and try to gain acceptance among the beneficiaries (Del Arco Blanco and Anderson 1–18; Richards "Fear" 57–94). The basic needs of the population were instrumentalized by the New State by investing charitable assistance with a clear political function that was accompanied by a vocation of social control and vigilance over the population. Over the years, and especially in rural areas, access to any aid, subsidy or assistance also meant submitting to the periodic inspection of Falange members or state officials, which implied the establishment of some types of dependency or clientelistic relationships (González Madrid and Ortiz Heras 369; Molinero 127–157). In the absence of a state policies that promoted equality and social justice, a large part of the population was socialized in a banal and everyday Francoism that fed the myth of the dictatorship as an authoritarian welfare regime.

The Francoist regime did not need civil consensus to maintain social peace, and thus the system of general and redistributive social security that was part of the European welfare state model did not take place in Spain. Economists who promoted the Development Plans, such as Mariano Navarro Rubio, Minister of Finance between 1957 and 1965, explicitly rejected the welfare state, considering that it was a system "implacable con los ciudadanos laboriosos" [implacable with hard-working citizens], against whom it launched "todo un ejército de inspectores" [a whole army of inspectors] while reserving "todas sus ternuras para con una larga serie de parásitos derrochadores" [all its tenderness for a long series of wasteful parasites] (71); it was his belief that it constituted a limit to the generation of wealth since it slowed down "las iniciativas creativas de los industriales y comerciantes" [the creative initiatives of industrialists and traders] (71). Navarro Rubio, like other promoters of the new economic plans, followed the ideas of ordoliberal economists such as Wilhelm Röpke, a disseminator of so-called "Christian capitalism" and a guest at the Instituto de Análisis Económico (Institute for Economic Analysis) in 1949 (Beltrán 231–233). It was a model based on the contiguity between liberalism and Christianity, where individual responsibility and charity in its different forms became the only solutions to the problems derived from poverty and inequality. As Vicenç Navarro pointed out, public spending policies during Franco's regime were always insufficient: in 1960, "los gastos militares en España representaban el 126 % (más del doble) de la totalidad de gastos públicos en

Fables of Grace 153

sanidad y educación" [military spending in Spain represented 126% (more than double) of total public spending on health and education] (254); and by the dictator's death in 1975, public spending on social protection was only 14% of GDP, while in Western Europe it reached 22.9% (110).

In addition to the redistribution of resources by means of public and private charity, the Francoist State delegated the punctual distribution of social assistance in urban areas to some companies. Both Miguel Siguán, in his book *Del campo al suburbio* (1959), and Francisco Candel, in his essay *Ser obrero no es ninguna ganga* (1976), explained that the provision of services by some companies is key to understanding the processes of emigration to the cities during the 1950s and 1960s. In the so-called "labour cities", such as the housing colony Ciudad Pegaso in Madrid, the policies of what is known as "industrial paternalism" (Babiano) were used by many companies to provide their employees with social benefits such as housing, company stores, schools, leisure facilities and bonuses (Nielfa 237). With regards to the role of religious organizations in the management of charitable assistance, it should be noted that the intervention of the Catholic Church in this field was at the heart of a debate that spread throughout the 1950s and reached its climax with the celebration of the Second Vatican Council (1962–1965).

Since the early 1950s, the country's continuing misery had attracted the interest of a new generation of Catholics who took increasingly critical positions against the regime and its policies. In this sense, both the Hermandad Obrera de Acción Católica [HOAC, Catholic Action Workers' Brotherhood] and the Juventud Obrera Católica [JOC, Catholic Worker Youth] —the youth branch of Acción Católica [Catholic Action]— became platforms of militancy that used a political discourse that pointed out the obvious differences between the official rhetoric and the reality of inequality in the country, thus warning about the social consequences of the new economic policy while still legitimizing it.[1] These organizations played an important role in the shift towards the so-called "compromiso temporal" [temporary commitment] method, in which the growing influence of Marxism as a method of analysing reality produced a drift whereby numerous Christian militants began to collaborate with the workers' and neighbourhood movements in the new developmentalist cycle. In the mid-1960s these movements went hand in hand with the amendment of the agreements signed by the Spanish government with the Holy See in 1953. Such agreements began to be questioned after a Council which led to documents such as the encyclical *Gaudium et Spes* (1965), which inclined the action of the Church to a clear separation from the State; or the so-called *Christus Dominus* (1965), where

1 See Fernández de Castro and Moreno Seco.

154   *Fables of Development*

states such as Spain were asked to review the legal, political and economic privileges that the Church had obtained while the Francoist regime benefited from this alliance to obtain international recognition.

The first part of this chapter examines the role of the Catholic Church as an agent responsible for charitable policies in relation to children; a social group on whom, after the war, the Francoist regime largely targeted its biopolitics for the inclusion of the defeated into the new National-Catholic community. These ecclesiastical charity policies were publicized in the context of the Concordat with the Holy See (1953) in films like *Cerca de la ciudad* (Luis Lucia, 1952 [Close to the City]) and *Marcelino Pan y Vino* (Ladislao Vajda, 1954 [Marcelino Bread and Wine]); and later on in a developmentalist comedy like *Sor Citroën* (1967 [Sister Citroën]), where such practices are fully shaped by the new technocratic imaginaries in which charity is driven and oriented by the market and technological advances. The second section analyses the representation of charity in two films released in 1961, *Viridiana* (Luis Buñuel) and *Plácido* (Luis García Berlanga), both of which explore the effects of this Christian virtue on its recipients. These effects unfold in situations where there is an interaction between benefactors and donors, dramatized in the form of banquets attended by both poor and rich. Finally, this chapter closes by looking at Juan Marsé's novel *La oscura historia de la prima Montse* (1970 [The Dark Story of Cousin Montse]) with the purpose of analysing the evolution in the rationale and practices of charitable organizations of the lay apostolate in the context of the Second Vatican Council's *aggiornamento*.

Childhood, Charity and Pastoral Power

In 1975, the year of General Franco's death, the cartoonist Carlos Giménez published the first instalment of his comic book series *Paracuellos*, in which he recounted his experience as a child taken in one of the homes of the Spanish Falange Social Aid during the 1950s. In these comics, Giménez portrayed this children's asylum as one of the spaces that Ricard Vinyes calls "concentration camps for children" in his documentary *Els nens perduts del franquisme* (The Stolen Children of the Franco Dictatorship) (2002). During the long post-war period, thousands of children like Giménez were under the guardianship of institutions that depended on the Dirección General de Beneficencia y Obras Sociales [Department of Assistance and Social Welfare] (Aragüés 164); this was the governing through which the New State had since 1940 validated the competency of those organizations entrusted with "la guarda y dirección de los huérfanos" [the care and direction of orphans], and which acquired the character of legal guardians "por el simple hecho de poner los

Fables of Grace

menores bajo su cuidado directo" [by the simple fact of placing the minors under their direct care] (Aragüés 166). For the families of the foster children who belonged to the Republican side, this model of assistance implied the possibility of losing legal guardianship of their offspring, since this could only be obtained by persons "irreprochables desde el triple punto de vista religioso, ético y nacional" [irreproachable from the triple religious, ethical and national point of view] (quoted in Domingo 284). The government thus sought to eradicate the lineages and families of which the children of the defeated were a part, promoting policies that ensured the suppression of their offspring, both in a biological and moral sense (Sánchez León, "Tan solo" 36–37). In parallel, up to 30,000 children were stolen from their families throughout the dictatorship, in a process in which religious networks and civil institutions were actively involved (Duva and Junquera 12).

In the Spanish cinema of the 1950s, orphaned or abandoned children became the protagonists of stories in which priests, friars and nuns took the minors under their tutelage. Films such as *Cerca de la ciudad* (Luis Lucia, 1952) or *Marcelino Pan y Vino* (Ladislao Vajda, 1955) were shot in the context of the government's Concordat with the Holy See, and showed Spanish religious figures creating guardianship communities in which the orphans assisted were incorporated into the Catholic Church and, therefore, into the national community. As Jo Labanyi noted, at a time when the Catholic Church as an institution was gaining political ascendancy over the Falangist sector, religious cinema played an essential role in helping men make a transition "from the military values of wartime" to "a privatized domestic model of masculinity appropriate to peacetime under dictatorial rule" (Labanyi, "Feminizing" 181). The protagonist of *Cerca de la ciudad* is Father José (Adolfo Marsillach), a priest assigned to a parish located in a shantytown in the suburbs of Madrid where he finds a group of homeless children whom he takes to live in his parish house. At the end of the film, Father José gets a rich landlady to donate a building to set up a children's home project in the slum, and also, thanks to a charity campaign launched by the press, to finance a school and workshops for vocational training where the children can become "men fit for work".

The journalists in charge of developing this campaign insist on the interclass nature of a charitable action in which all Madrilenians can feel involved: "Todas las clases sociales acudirán en su ayuda. El espíritu caritativo de Madrid se volcará sobre el suburbio" [All social classes will come to their aid. The charitable spirit of Madrid will be poured on the suburbs]. This campaign corresponded to the usual fundraising actions for the new neighbourhoods that arose in the main cities as a result of the rural exodus during the 1950s, and which were known as "Semana del Suburbio"

156 *Fables of Development*

[Suburb Week]. In the 1955 campaign, the Bishop of Madrid, Dr Elijo Garay, made a public appeal with the aim of promoting charity as the instrument capable of "redeeming" citizens from their material and spiritual poverty through a hygienist discourse:

> El suburbio es a la manera de una ventosa que absorbe cuánto hay de pobre, mísero y malsano en la ciudad. No es una calamidad exclusivamente nuestra, sino de todas las capitales inevitablemente cercadas por un conglomerado cochambroso y triste, donde la corrupción y la falta de sentido moral tienen clima propicio . . . Es una obra de saneamiento a la que nadie debe negar su cooperación, incluso por egoísmo, para cegar cuanto antes el foco de la miseria que enrarece el aire de la ciudad. (9)

> [The suburb is like a suction pad that absorbs all that is poor, miserable and unhealthy in the city. It is not a calamity exclusively ours, but of all the capitals inevitably surrounded by a filthy and sad conglomerate, where corruption and lack of moral sense have a propitious climate ... It is a work of sanitation with which no one should refuse to cooperate with, even out of selfishness, in order to seal off as soon as possible the source of the misery that is poisoning the air of the city.]

In this context, the so-called Francoist "missionary cinema" of the 1950s moved the action of its films from the exotic colonial settings of the religious cinema of the late 1940s to the suburbs of the Spanish metropolis, whose inhabitants were imagined as "'savages' to be pacified" (Labanyi "Internalisations" 31). In Lucia's film, the shanty dwellers are referred to as "Koreans" by the former inhabitants of the neighbourhood, who consider them a population reluctant to religious and political "conversion". As one of the sanctimonious women living in the diocese warns Father José, "aquella es tierra de infieles, no trate de convertirlos" [this is a land of infidels, don't try to convert them]. In order to achieve success in the conversion of these "infidels", the priest follows the advice of one of his superiors: "Los niños son buena tierra para sembrar. Los mayores tienen cabeza dura" [Children are good soil for sowing. The older ones are hard-headed]. Thus, his first action will be to shelter in his house a group of brothers who live alone in a shack because their father is serving a prison sentence, while at the same time gaining the trust of other children in the neighbourhood, whom he introduces to catechesis.

At a time when the Church wanted to transmit values in line with the claim of "social peace" in Spain, the cinematographic representation of the

Fables of Grace   157

priest thus distanced itself from the paradigm of masculinity of Falangist cinema, shifting towards values and practices considered feminine, such as the care of children. As Jo Labanyi points out, in *Cerca de la ciudad* this appropriation of feminine values reaches such extreme heights that all social relations are of exclusively male filiation and affiliation: "in appropriating the maternal role, Father José eliminates both gender and class difference. The feminised man functions as a brilliant strategy for imposing the law of the Father" ("Internalisations" 37). After his release from prison, the priest convinces the father of the foster brothers to attend the Midnight Mass together with other neighbours who had renounced Catholicism, thus achieving the father's gratitude for his work in assisting and educating the minors as well as his "conversion". With the final "redeeming" mass attendance of the children and their parents, this biopolitical model based on charity was presented in Spanish cinemas as an example of the regime's success in completing its project of re-education, redemption and integration of both the members of the so-called "Anti-Spain" and their descendants into the national community.

After the Concordat with the Holy See, the representation of ecclesiastical charity in relation to children became an international cinematic success thanks to one of the most famous films of the period, *Marcelino Pan y Vino* (Vajda, 1954), awarded at the Cannes, Venice and Berlin festivals. The director Ladislao Vajda worked with the Falangist writer José María Sánchez Silva in the adaptation of the screenplay of his homonymous story, which narrates the miraculous death of an orphan boy who lives in a monastery during the period of national reconstruction after the War of Independence (1808–1814). In the film, which takes place in a time contemporary to that of the viewers, it is a friar who narrates the life and passing away of Marcelino to a girl in the throes of death, thus bringing to mind the exemplary story that gives rise to the miracle. It so happens that the same story is being commemorated in the annual pilgrimage held at that time in the village, a ritual celebration of the child's death in sanctity that represents a triumphant experience for the martyr while reaffirming the collective values of the community.

The story of Marcelino begins when a community of Franciscan friars finds a newborn baby at the door of their monastery. In the absence of information about the child's parents, the friars venture that it was probably an "avergonzada y desgraciada" [ashamed and unhappy] mother who had decided to abandon her child. In the Spain of the 1950s, this description was in keeping with the way single mothers were looked upon, as socially stigmatized women whose children were often part of the so-called "lost children of Franco's regime". In Vajda's film, the Franciscans decide that

158   *Fables of Development*

none of the families in the area is qualified to raise the child as a Christian and that they will raise the child themselves, with each of the friars being "su padre y su madre" [his father and mother]. When Marcelino turns five years old, he transgresses the most important order he must obey, which is the prohibition to go up to the attic of the monastery where the friars keep the statue of a crucified Christ; as a result of the discovery of the child, who brings him bread and wine as a work of charity, the statue comes to life. At the end of the film, the statue asks Marcelino what his greatest wish would be, and he answers that he would like to see his mother and also Christ's mother, since he has been told by the friars that both are "in Heaven". After formulating his wish, the friars find the boy dead next to the statue.

Vajda's cinematographic fiction turns the death of the orphan into a mass spectacle destined for the global entertainment industry. It was a religious fable that made it possible to erase the presence of the real families of the children fostered by ecclesiastical institutions at different moments in the history of Spain. As in the miracle of the bread and wine of the Eucharist that gives the film its title, in this cinematic fiction there is an authentic exercise of transubstantiation regarding the meaning of the sacrifice of a child's life, which, like that of Christ, is offered to viewers all over the world as an example of holiness. The life of Marcelino is interpreted through the miracle that causes his death, becoming the exemplary story of a life redeemed thanks to the work of a group of friars. It is a story in which those families excluded from the national community, such as the children assisted by the charitable institutions of the Francoist regime, are eliminated from the historical narrative. As Justin Crumbaugh recalls in his analysis of the film, the return of Marcelino's story as both sacrificial victim and spectre of the past raises a silent indictment of these absences: "Spectacular acts of victim enshrinement are precisely what produce, through attempted erasure, the ghosts of the unrecognized dead ... who return to a time to which they do not belong, and promise to return again and again in the future, as a result of an unresolved injustice" (347–348). In this way, the Spanish cinema of the 1950s showed the world that it was capable of achieving an enormous box-office success through the spectacularization of the death of an orphaned child who could only be incorporated into the National-Catholic community through a redemption that had taken place thanks to the charitable work of the religious orders and the sacrifice of his own life.

Some young anti-Francoist writers reacted to this propaganda on charity policies and recreated in their works the conditions in which Spanish children, the main victims of poverty and lack of health care, often lived. Sick children and boys were the protagonists of the stories "Chico de Madrid" [The Kid from Madrid], "Quería dormir en paz" [He Only Wanted

Fables of Grace

to Rest in Peace] or "Vísperas del silencio" [The Eve of Silence] by Ignacio Aldecoa; of "La conciencia tranquila" [A Clear Conscience] by Carmen Martín Gaite; or of "Niño fuerte" [Strong Kid] by Rafael Sánchez Ferlosio. In Jesús Fernández Santos's short story "Cabeza rapada" [Shaved Head], a homeless boy's account of the situation in which a ten-year-old friend, sick with pulmonary tuberculosis, finds himself, leaves no doubt about the ineffectiveness of charity when there is no social assistance to save the lives of these boys. Writers such as Juan Goytisolo or Ana María Matute also recreated in their works the voices of the orphans, of the street children who showed their contempt, their rebellion and their mockery towards the charitable institutions. In her *Libro de juegos para los niños de otros* (1961 [Book of Games for the Children of Others]), Matute draws up a particular catalogue of the different strategies of resistance used by these children to defend themselves from the pastoral and ecclesiastical power that sought to discipline them through charity. The protagonists of Juan Goytisolo's *La resaca* (1958 [The Undertow]) are also children and adolescents, minors who live on the streets, surviving in their own community and sharing the benefits they obtain from stealing or begging. In the pages of the novel there are children without families and parents who have lost their children and adopt those of others in exchange for money. All this in a context in which, as the narrative voice recalls, the trafficking and trade of children affected families without resources: "Muchas familias pobres, cargadas de hijos, se desprendían de alguno a cambio de unas pesetas. De tapadillo, el hecho se repetía todos los días y hacía correr mucha tinta en los diarios" [Many poor families, loaded with children, got rid of some of them in exchange for a few pesetas. Out of sight, this was a regular occurrence, a fact that caused much ink to be spilled in the newspapers] (926). Posing as collaborators in the collection of donations given to the so-called "Cruzada Cordimariana" [Crusade of the Immaculate Heart of Mary], a movement that spread the message of the Virgin of Fatima, the boys get the money they need by appealing to charitable purposes. In this way, the protagonists of Goytisolo's novel escape the control of the institutions and manage, by means of a swindle, to appropriate the same charitable practices put into practice by the religious organizations.

The charitable policies that the Catholic Church exerted in the area of child welfare would be transformed in parallel to the implementation of the Development Plans. In 1967 and 1968, almost two million spectators went to Spanish cinemas to see the developmental comedy *Sor Citroën* (1967), directed by Pedro Lazaga. The film featured Sister Tomasa (Gracita Morales), a young nun who decides to expand her duties at the girls' orphanage where she works by learning to drive. The nun will be known by drivers in Madrid as

160 *Fables of Development*

"Sister Citroën" for her reckless way of driving the vehicle that the mother superior of the convent has bought following her advice. According to Sister Tomasa, the purchase of a Citroën 2CV would maximize the collection of alms and donations. Appropriating the technocratic language that had permeated society, the nun manages to persuade the religious order of the opportunities for raising capital that the vehicle will provide the sisters: "Andando todo un día pedimos en veinte casas, con el coche pediremos en cien. Así, aumentaremos la productividad, ¡hay que motorizarse!" [Walking all day we ask in twenty houses, with the car we will ask in a hundred. Thus, we will increase productivity, we must motorize!]. Due to the constant fines and repairs, the vehicle ends up becoming an enormous source of expenses; however, again using an economistic discourse, Sister Tomasa opposes its sale by highlighting the long-term benefits that the use of the car can bring to the orphanage: "Es una inversión y se amortizará, madre, verá usted cómo se amortiza" [It is an investment and it will pay off, Mother, you will see how it will pay off].

Viewers learn about the work of the nuns when two orphaned children, Nando and Luisa, whose parents have died in a traffic accident, arrive at the convent. At various points in the film, the vehicle driven by Sister Citroën will be an indispensable element for the nun to care for and protect these children, and also proves to be a providential instrument in saving the life of little Luisa, who is taken to La Paz Hospital in time to undergo an urgent operation. As Jorge Pérez has pointed out, the cinematographic montage that juxtaposes images of the girl's surgery with scenes of the orphanage community praying for her serves as an emblem of the synergy between technological and scientific progress and divine intervention: "the dexterous camera work, editing, and lighting in *Sor Citroën* contribute to emphasize the coalescence of the adept effort of the doctors and Sor Tomasa resorting to the latest developments in medicine and mechanical engineering combined with holy protection" (14). The combination of scientific and technological achievements and human endeavour with the salvation project of Catholicism thus reinforced the idea that the "miracle" of developmentalism counted on the intervention of providence in this cinematographic fable in which the values of mobility and modernization were placed at the service of the traditional creed.

However, in the film, the advantages of technical progress are not without their drawbacks for the religious community. These problems become apparent when Sister Citroën discovers that she has received a fine and that her car is about to be taken away by the police for being improperly parked. After spending a whole morning begging for alms door-to-door in the company of Sister Rafaela and two girls from the orphanage, Sister Tomasa discovers that she has to pay in order to avoid having her car towed

Fables of Grace 161

away. In an attempt to cancel her debt, the nun appeals to the charitable sentiments of the policeman and the passers-by gathered around the vehicle, claiming that the demand for payment from the nuns is an "abuse of authority". To persuade the police, Sister Tomasa and Sister Rafaela appeal to the importance of their charitable work, arguing that the whole of society should take responsibility for helping them in their task of protecting and assisting minors. Sister Citroën thus challenges the police authority by appealing to the importance of the missionary work of the clergy, a task aimed at achieving social justice, one of the objectives promoted by the Church after the Second Vatican Council (1962–1965). The emotionally charged scene in front of the police, reinforced by the close-up of the nun's face bathed in tears as she thanks the passers-by for their donations to pay the fine, contributes to sublimate the role of the charity of religious institutions in the new post-conciliar developmentalism.

Although the money received by Sister Citroën is a proof of the increase in purchasing power among the working classes, the logic of charity as a social bond that reproduces inequality remains despite the fact that charitable practices have apparently been modernized. The scene helps to make invisible the darker side of the charity carried out by the ecclesiastical orders in practices in which they use the minors in their care to appeal to the donors' compassion, as in the case of the orphans who accompany the nuns in their home visits. The instrumentalization of the children, for whom the nuns are legally responsible, will reach its climax at the end of the film when Nando escapes from the orphanage where he lives in order to find his sister. Once again, it will be Sister Tomasa on board her vehicle who finds the child and decides that the two brothers can be together by going to live with her own father, a widowed railwayman who lives in the small town of La Roda (León). This denouement is profoundly significant considering how at the beginning of the film the viewers have watched a flashback which shows the nun abandoning her father's house in order to give her life to God. Sister Tomasa thus manages to repay the debt contracted with her father by giving him the two little orphans as putative children. The nun belongs to the young post-conciliar clergy, more concerned with social transformation than compliance with ecclesiastical norms. At the end of the film, the mother superior reminds her that charity must be practised "with order" and informs her that they have decided to transfer her to Bilbao as a disciplinary measure. The sublimation of the nun's social commitment operates as a moral alibi that legitimizes the authority that the nun attributes to herself to make decisions about the lives of minors.

By linking the modernization of the clergy with aspects such as automobile mobility, one of the symbols of Spanish developmentalism,

162   *Fables of Development*

the film reinforces the more superficial aspects of the *aggiornamento* of the post-conciliar Church. In this sense, the representation of the lower clergy through the character of Sister Citroën diverted attention from the reality of many Spanish religious workers in a context in which, at the time of 1969, the National Clergy Survey indicated that "among young priests, 47% were in favor of socialism" (Díaz-Salazar 39). It was a reality of political commitment and active militancy in which change was unstoppable since, as Antonio Cazorla points out, "some of the best minds of the Catholic Church began to embrace 'subversive' ideologies and made it difficult, at times, to distinguish Catholic enterprises from the initiatives of illegal opposition groups" (136). Pedro Lazaga's film claimed an updating of the old practices of National-Catholic charity through the new discourses of modernization theory at the end of the cycle of the First Development Plan (1964–1967), at a time when discussing social problems and the political role of the Church had already become a normal practice for many Catholics.

Charity and Redistribution Banquets: *Viridiana* (Buñuel, 1961) and *Plácido* (García Berlanga, 1961)

Two films were released in 1961 that changed the history of Spanish cinema: *Plácido*, a comedy directed by Luis García Berlanga, and *Viridiana*, a Spanish-Mexican co-production by exiled Aragonese filmmaker Luis Buñuel. Both posed a profound critique of charity in Franco's Spain and coincided in their representation of this Christian virtue through a staging that included the celebration of banquets in which the recipients of the charity participated. According to Rosa Luxemburg, the image of the banquet corresponded to a vision of charity that in the times of primitive Christianity had been shaped by the creation of communities of consumption of goods distributed by the state (103). For Raymond Williams, the image was one that continued to express itself historically through the emblem of the communal banquet with "the Christian board and breaking of bread as its natural images, and the feast as its social consummation" (31). It was an idea of communal redistribution that inevitably became a mystification that assumed that any existing inequality could be redeemed "by the charity of the consequent feast" (31).

Although the banquets recreated in *Viridiana* and *Plácido* are very different, both represent an allegory about charity as an *antidoral* relationship that generates different reactions among the poor who would be obliged to correspond with gratitude and obedience to their donors. In this sense, the image of the banquet was used during Franco's regime as an allegory of charity in all kinds of representations related especially to Christmas celebrations, as part of the staging of the fraternization between rich and poor that should take place in this annual rite. Thus, in Juan Marsé's novel *Esta cara de la luna* (1962 [This Side of the Moon]), a character of the Barcelona bourgeoisie recalls one of the campaigns called "Navidad del Pobre" [Christmas of the Poor] and his participation in the allegorical banquet held in a parish theatre performance: "Uno de ellos tenía que ser hijo de una familia rica, representaba al rico e iba vestido de niño rico. El otro tenía que pertenecer a una familia pobre, representaba el papel de pobre e iba de niño pobre. El rico estaba a la izquierda y el pobre a la derecha. Un detalle espeluznante del director escénico" [One of them had to be the son of a rich family, he represented the rich and was dressed as a rich boy. The other had to belong to a poor family, he played the role of the poor and was dressed as a poor child. The rich one was on the left and the poor one on the right. A creepy detail of the stage director] (158).

In May 1961, the General Director of Cinematography, José Muñoz Fontán, collected the Palme d'Or at the Cannes Film Festival for a Spanish film. The award had been granted to the Spanish-Mexican co-production *Viridiana*, the first film directed by Luis Buñuel in his country of origin after the Civil War. His film *Nazarín* (1959) had received the festival's International Award two years earlier and was also on the verge of winning a Catholic Office Award. However, on this occasion, the newspaper *L'Osservatore Romano* described *Viridiana* as a "sacrilegious and blasphematory" film (Buache 119). Julio Alejandro, co-scriptwriter of *Viridiana*, recalls how Buñuel's initial project was based on an adaptation of Benito Pérez Galdós' novel *Ángel Guerra* (1890), which the director thought of combining with the novel *Halma* (1895), a continuation of the adventures of the cleric Nazario Zaharín, protagonist of *Nazarín* (1895) (Alejandro 45). Several narrative elements of these three novels, each revolving around a reflection on charity, were present in the plot of *Viridiana*, whose protagonist was described by Buñuel as a "Quixote with skirts" (Fuentes 158). As in the case of *Nazarín*, a film in which the Aragonese director set the action of the novel in Mexico during the Porfiriato, in *Viridiana* Buñuel transferred to contemporary Spain the reflections on charity and beneficence that Galdós had developed in several of his *Novelas Contemporáneas* belonging to the so-called "spiritual" or "spiritualist" cycle.

The protagonist of *Viridiana* is a novice who is about to take her first vows and receives a request from her uncle Jaime (Fernando Rey) to leave the convent for a few days and visit him. During her stay, Don Jaime explains to Viridiana (Silvia Pinal) the resemblance she bears to his deceased wife and tries to persuade her to accept his marriage proposal. Viridiana decides to return to the convent and her uncle replies that she no longer needs to do so, since she was drugged and abused by him the night before. After the rejection

164 *Fables of Development*

of his wedding proposal, Don Jaime decides to rewrite his will before ending his days by hanging himself in one of the trees of his estate. From that moment on, Viridiana becomes the new owner of the place together with her cousin Jorge (Francisco Rabal), Don Jaime's illegitimate son, who has also been acknowledged as heir. The novice moves into the house and decides to decline the Mother Superior's request to return to the convent, motivated by the decision to run her own charitable organization without depending on the interference of religious and civil institutions. Like the protagonists of the novels *Halma* and *Angel Guerra*, Viridiana decides to set up a private asylum for the poor, exercising her evangelizing work through charity. To begin her mission, she contacts the mayor of the nearest town to send to his estate some vagrants who, according to the historical context of the film, would be part of one of the social groups persecuted by the 1954 *Ley de Vagos y Maleantes* [Law of Vagrants and Thugs]. The group is made up of individuals excluded from the world of work and from the welfare rights associated with work: the elderly, single mothers, the disabled and the sick, all of whom are under Viridiana's care instead of being under the control of the immense network of hospices, asylums, schools, work colonies and alms houses that are spread throughout the national territory —a network of institutions in which collaborated members of the lay apostolate, like Viridiana, would have professed the vows of chastity, poverty and obedience. After listening to the homeless, we realize that they are unable to join the labour market due to various reasons that have to do with their illnesses and disabilities, with poor access to education or vocational training, or with social stigmatization, as in the case of single mothers.

Under the tutelage of the former novice, the group of beggars come under a new type of disciplinary control. While residing on the estate, which is owned by the one they call their "Santa protectora" [saintly protector], she manages their schedules, oversees the distribution of space ("los hombres dormirán separados de las mujeres" [the men will sleep separately from the women]), provides over their food and even over the distribution of tobacco. Viridiana finds that the servants who work in her service do not share her idea of Christian fraternity, and she also realizes that not all the poor are willing to participate in the proposed model of authority. Faced with the protests of one of the beggars, Viridiana poses the conditions under which they can access the asylum: "Si quiere quedarse tendrá que soportar cierta disciplina. Eso y tener más humildad con todos" [If you want to stay you will have to endure a certain discipline. That and be more humble with everyone]. Viridiana exerts pastoral power over a community whose organization is based on the practices of conventual life. She organizes the life of the vagabonds and proposes their contribution to the running of the farm's economy, with requirements that the assisted persons did not expect when they were welcomed: "Desde mañana, todos van a trabajar. Todo será a la medida de sus fuerzas y en lo que cada uno prefiera. Lo que quiero es que se distraigan y que hagan un poco de ejercicio" [From tomorrow, everyone will work. Everything will be to the extent of one's strength and in what each one prefers. What I want is for all of you to be distracted and to get some exercise]. Not only does the former novice assume the role of Mother Superior in this space, but, as owner of the hacienda, she establishes a relationship with the guests based on the traditional Catholic patronage in which the owner promises the protection of the laborers and tenants of the land in exchange for their gratitude, loyalty and submission.

In addition to the activities assigned to each of them, participation in the daily prayer cycles at the estate is mandatory, as evidenced in the scene in which Viridiana, accompanied by the beggars kneeling at her feet, leads the Angelus prayer. The scene is presented through a cinematographic montage that intersperses images of collective prayer with images of the construction work carried out for the house renovation by a team of masons led by Jorge (Richardson 163–164). In this way, the montage expresses the dialectic between the two economic anthropologies that coexist in the same space: the model of charity based on the Catholic economy of grace and the model of modernization, understood as productivist development. Viridiana's use of the property she has inherited clashes with the management carried out by her cousin Jorge. Viridiana pursues the creation of a space of personal autonomy where, outside the intervention of ecclesiastical and administrative institutions, she can provide "techo, comida y un poco de calor humano" [shelter, food and a little human warmth] to those who ask for her help. This project will abruptly clash with the economic plans of Jorge, who decides to transform the property into a farm by adding infrastructures such as access to electricity in order to stop living "como en la Edad Media" [like in the Middle Ages]. While the beggars pray and work so as to stay on the farm, the architect criticizes his cousin's decisions, arguing that "socorrer a esos pocos entre tantos miles no arregla nada" [helping those few among so many thousands doesn't fix anything].

In the second part of the film, the implementation of these economic regimes unfolds reflections on the effects of the violence that both models generate. In the absence of Jorge and Viridiana, the vagabonds decide to enter the house and discover an opportunity to enjoy an experience of luxury that was forbidden to them. The beggars, whom Viridiana imagined as submissive subjects in her fantasy of domination based on the exercise of pastoral power, enjoy an orgiastic banquet that in no way resembles their usual dinner in the stables of the estate. In the film's most famous

166   *Fables of Development*

scene, the beggars take the place of Christ and the apostles, emulating the distribution of the figures in Leonardo da Vinci's *The Last Supper*. Although the iconoclastic representation of the painting has usually been analysed in relation to the practice of surrealist *detournement* (Scarlett 40; Egea 69–70), in the context of Franco's Spain the staging of this scene could also remind viewers of the *tableaux vivants* staged by Republican militiamen, who were photographed posing with works of sacred art in their incursions into religious spaces —iconoclastic practices in which, among other motives, the mechanisms of intervention of the Spanish Church in the social and political life of these workers' communities were denounced (Thomas 100–121; Delgado 179–202). Similarly, the celebration of the banquet in the halls of Viridiana and Jorge's mansion recalled common scenes of the collectivization processes of the wealthier classes' luxury spaces during the Civil War, which included places such as hotels and aristocratic residences (Ealham 161).

The scene is crucial to understand the reflection on the scope of charity that the film poses. Up to this point, Viridiana has offered her help to the beggars on condition that it remains at the level of satisfying basic needs, which she herself establishes and regulates. The ancient novice thus asserts her power and her superior rank vis-à-vis the poor, establishing the conditions under which they should enjoy the assistance received on the terms of her own desire as a donor and provider agent. In this sense, Viridiana's ascetic practices in the first part of the film can be mistaken for a kind of masochistic paraphernalia, in which both the renunciation of pleasure and the asceticism imposed on herself and her protégés can become a perverse source of jouissance. As Elizabeth Scarlett recalls, "Buñuel teases out the extreme of ascetic self-denial as it blends into perversion, in an ironic commentary on the practices of Opus Dei" (38). As happens in *Viridiana*, the use of the cilice and corporal mortifications were practices that Opus encouraged among its followers as a means of reinforcing the institution's image of Catholic orthodoxy (Walsh 117–124). For the organization, these practices allowed it to curb criticism of the heterodoxy of its neo-capitalist project, whose roots were clearly Protestant in its promotion of professional life as a formula for Christian sanctification. In the same way that Opus Dei made the distinction between religious and lay vocations unnecessary, as well as clerical and sacramental mediations, Viridiana, as a laywoman who chooses to sanctify herself through the exercise of charity, imposes on her assistants an asceticism in the practices of life that she herself exerts, an asceticism that the beggars defy in the famous scene of their "last supper" in the house of their benefactress.

The vision of charity developed by the protagonist can be analysed in the light of Jacques Lacan's reflections on charity from the legend of Saint Martin, whose action of splitting his cloak to share it with a beggar has become an emblematic representation of this Christian virtue. Jacques-Alain Miller delved into these reflections of Lacan with the aim of exploring the violent counterparts of charity through the implications of the principle of pleasure and jouissance. According to this argument, which takes into account the reaction of the assisted person, "perhaps the beggar asked, or would have wanted, desired, longed, for St. Martin to kiss him or kill him" (132). It is, in short, an exchange that implies a response from the other "beyond necessity". In his opinion, the enunciation of need in moral and utilitarian terms eliminates reflection on desire and enjoyment, experiences that would go beyond the satisfaction of basic needs. The beggars react to Viridiana's charitable treatment by "desecrating" her property and demanding access to luxury they had never been able to enjoy before. At the end of the dinner, two of them will go further in trying to satisfy their desire by attempting to sexually abuse her, only to be rescued by her cousin's intervention.

Once her asylum plan has failed, the protagonist decides to abandon the project around which she had tried to build a space of personal autonomy through the exercise of charity and destroys the religious objects she used in her ascetic practices. At the close of the film, Viridiana ends up visiting the bedroom of her cousin, who invites her to share a game of cards with him and Ramona, the maid of the house. The film thus concludes with the suggestion of a possible intimate relationship between the three of them to the rhythm of the rockabilly song "Shimmy Doll". Viridiana's body remains impassive in the transition to new forms of biopolitical subjection while the song —with the suggestive line "Shake your cares away"— invites her to abandon her fears to the rhythm of rock. At that moment, the protagonist seems to settle into a fantasy of acceptance of the new social order within the house, which reproduces the one that her uncle intended to establish in his sentimental relationship with the two women who should be economically and morally indebted to him: Ramona, single mother of a girl whom Jaime took into his home, and the novice.

Once out of the convent and her charitable project cancelled, Viridiana approaches the new head of the family, lord and master of the house, who tells her how to behave in this new situation. The new domestic order is restored in such a way that the monetary and libidinal economy of the estate will now be managed by the patriarchal line, which is reinstated without anything threatening both the reproduction of the old latifundist order and the idea of charity practised by the new owner of the estate. This idea does not imply any rebellion on the part of those who receive it, as happens in the film in the famous scene of the so-called "parable of the dog", in which Jorge frees one of these animals that runs tied to a cart while the spectators

168 *Fables of Development*

see immediately approaching another one that he is not going to untie. It is a sense of charity that remains under the control of the benefactor, which can be deployed as long as the paternalism of the actions performed maintains the silence and submission of those on whom it is exercised.

The relationship between charity and banquets was also explored in the film *Plácido*, a peculiar "Christmas story" by José Luis García Berlanga that revolves around the involvement of a Spanish provincial town's inhabitants in a charity campaign. Launched under the slogan "Siente a un pobre en su mesa" [Sit a pauper at your table], the purpose of the campaign is the celebration of banquets in which families with resources invite a poor person to dine at their homes on Christmas Eve.[2] The campaign uses as a means of promotion the celebration of a parade that includes a carriage pulled by a motorcycle cart that Plácido, the protagonist who owns the vehicle, rents to the organizers. His motorcycle cart hauls a rudimentary platform on which the so-called "Cuadro plástico del Pobre y el Rico" [Plastic Picture of the Poor and the Rich] is staged, a performance where two costumed beggars recreate the banquet that will take place that night in the homes of those neighbours who invite other people without resources to share their table. The campaign is sponsored by local organizations and by a stainless steel cookware company that incorporates its commercial advertising with the ad "Cocinex practica la caridad" [Cocinex practises charity]. On the radio programme organized by the local radio station, the distribution of the poor among the participating families is done through a public auction in which the benefactor families "bid" to choose the diners to be invited. The depiction of this type of practice merely reflected the charity events of Spain in the 1960s, such as the festivals called "La Navidad del pobre" [The pauper's Christmas]. These were charitable events in which politicians, sportsmen and showbusiness stars promoted their image while exercising philanthropy. The radio, press and news programmes of the dictatorship used these activities as another means to promote the regime's large fortunes, and also the firms of the incipient consumer industry, like Cocinex, the brand of pots and pans that Berlanga parodied in his film.

Rafael Azcona, co-screenwriter of *Plácido*, also actively participated in the criticism of these charitable practices through his collaborations as a writer in the illustrated magazine *La Codorniz*. Satire was the mechanism employed by the writer to make visible the motives of the "benefactors" to exercise charity, especially by parodying different literary genres, whether it was the manifesto "Defensa de la mendicidad" [Defence of begging], the epistolary genre in "Carta a un pariente pobre" [Letter to a poor relative], the journalistic report "Congreso de benefactores" [Congress of benefactors] or

2 See Marsh 122–144.

Fables of Grace

the philosophical essays ("Se pueden aprovechar los niños enfermos graves?" [Can seriously ill children be used?], "Consejos a los mendicantes" [Advice to mendicants], "¿Pueden utilizarse los pobres para el bien común?" [Can the poor be used for the common good?], and "Sobre la explotación de los huérfanos" [On the exploitation of orphans]). In these texts, Azcona used as a narrative voice that of the rich "benefactors", who justified the existence of charity as a means to reaffirm their need to reproduce hierarchical relations that legitimize social inequality, since the inferior have the obligation to reciprocate, but they can never achieve equivalence:

> Las personas de orden, que pagamos nuestros impuestos y conocemos y cumplimos mejor que nadie nuestros deberes cívicos, tenemos el derecho a ejercer la caridad . . . No veo ninguna razón para que los pobres de pedir limosna sean retirados de la circulación. Los pobres dan una nota de color a la ciudad, tocan el corazón de los duros de ídem, facilitan a las personas de orden su derecho a ejercer la caridad y, por si esto fuera poco, dan continuidad a las tradiciones. (411)

> [We people of order, who pay our taxes and know and fulfil our civic duties better than anyone else, have the right to engage in charity...I see no reason why the poor beggars should be taken out of circulation. The poor give a note of colour to the city, touch the hearts of the hard-hearted, make it easier for us, orderly people, to practise charity and, as if this were not enough, give continuity to traditions.]

In *Placido*, the whole city participates in the show of charity through the radio, the device used to broadcast the events of the campaign for propaganda purposes. The so-called "radio-beneficence" acted during the Francoist regime as an intermediary in the public sphere between donors and the beneficiaries, and covered all kinds of actions ranging from the holding of annual campaigns in favour of sick children to the appeals made on an individual basis on programmes such as "Cuéntenos su caso" (Radio Juventud [Tell us about your case]), "El rincón de la caridad" (RNE Sevilla [The Corner of Charity]), "El caso del Sábado" (Radio Barcelona [Saturday's Case]) or "Llamad y se os abrirá, pedid y se os dará" [Knock and you will be opened, ask and you will be given], presented by Father Vicente Mena on RNE Madrid. The radio also served to organize relief operations for the victims of disasters and natural catastrophes such as the floods that occurred in Valencia (1957), Sevilla (1961) or El Vallés (1962), in which the intervention of celebrities participating in these campaigns constituted an institutional image of the radio station and the stars of great social and economic profitability (Balsebre 305).

170 *Fables of Development*

In *Plácido*, the poor are obliged to participate in the campaign's activities. After being classified and distributed according to categories such as "pobre del asilo" [asylum pauper] or "pobre de la calle" [street pauper], their needs are also identified and met through charity vouchers redeemable for clothes or food. Emilia, Plácido's wife, also accepts the vouchers offered by the organizers, showing viewers how the most basic needs were also widespread among the working classes. As it becomes clear, even workers like Placido and his wife live in situations of extreme poverty, trying to subsist while paying off the debts of their bank loans. When the radio-beneficence show ends, the whole family must help the widow of one of the beggars who has died during dinner at the home of their hosts, making it clear that the poor only count on the solidarity of other poor people and that charity ends when it has ceased to serve the interests of the benefactors. The film ends with viewers listening to a popular Christmas carol that underlines the similarity between the poverty and helplessness of the holy family at the birth of Christ and the precariousness and vulnerability of working families like Plácido's in Spain in the early 1960s:

Madre en la puerta hay un niño
más hermoso que el sol bello
tiritando está de frío
porque viene medio en cueros
Anda, dile que entre
se calentará
porque en esta tierra ya no hay caridad
ni nunca la habido
ni nunca la habrá.

[Mother at the door there is a child
more beautiful than the beautiful sun
shivering with cold
because he comes half in the buff
go on, tell him to come in
he will warm up
because in this land there is no more charity
nor has there ever been
nor ever will be.]

For the calculations of the sovereign power and the economic powers, it is a "disposable" population, a punctual recipient of charitable practices in which the recipients are impotent and designed to remain impotent.

Fables of Grace

Memories of Charity in the 50s and 60s:
Juan Marsé's *La oscura historia de la prima Montse*
(The Dark Story of Cousin Montse)

At the beginning of Juan Marsé's novel *La oscura historia de la prima Montse* (1970 [The Dark Story of Cousin Montse]), one of the characters mentions a private screening of the film *Viridiana* organized by a group of religious in Barcelona: "Hace poco pude ver *Viridiana* en una sesión especial con coloquio organizado por sacerdotes. Las cosas han cambiado mucho por aquí ... ¿No has probado esta mostaza? Es francesa. Y europeando sobre la mesa, su mano posibilista y vernácula alcanzó la transpirenaica y democrática *moutarde*" [Recently I was able to watch *Viridiana* in a special session followed by a colloquium organized by priests. Things have changed a lot around here ... Haven't you tried this mustard? It's French. And travelling over the table as if it were Europe, his vernacular and possibilist hand reached out to the trans-Pyrenean and democratic *moutarde*] (38). The narrator of this scene is Francisco Bodegas, cousin of Montserrat Claramunt, the protagonist of the "dark story" that gives the novel its title. Paco reproduces in this conversation the voice of Salvador Vilella, Montse's brother-in-law and former companion of the protagonist in the Juventudes Obreras de Acción Católica (Catholic Action Workers' Youth, JOC) at the end of the 1950s. The narrator's reflection dismantles the heroic story that Villella is trying to construct about himself as a young political leader within the Catalan Christian Democrat movement. For Salvador, both the viewing of Buñuel's film with progressive priests and the consumption of imported mustard are signs of distinction and development for new elites whose project is the future incorporation of the country into the group of European liberal democracies. In the course of this conversation, readers have access to more information about the lives of Montserrat and Salvador, who coincided a decade ago while carrying out activities related to the lay apostolate in a parish in Barcelona located in "una vieja zona residencial devorada por la expansión de Gracia y por la foránea invasión de la posguerra que nutrió de charnegos el Guinardó y el Carmelo" [an old residential area devoured by the expansion of Gracia and by the foreign invasion of the post-war period that nourished (the neighbourhoods of) Guinardó and Carmel with charnegos] (104). At the beginning of the novel, the apostolate work that Montse carried out during her youth is described at a JOC conference for parish visitors like her:

> Apostolado . . . entre niños de los parvularios y guarderías, centros para obreros y estudiantes, ancianos, enfermos y presos sin familia,

172   *Fables of Development*

y en chozas de suburbio o ambientes selectos de parroquias urbanas, siempre en estrecha colaboración con la Asistenta Social y la joven Divulgadora . . . siempre interesadas por el bien ajeno, sembrando serenidad y paz en los hogares. (21)

[Apostolate...among children in kindergartens and nurseries, centres for workers and students, the elderly, the sick and prisoners without families, and in slum huts or select environments of urban parishes, always in close collaboration with the Social Assistant and the young Advocate...always interested in the good of others, sowing serenity and peace in their homes.]

Marsé's novel deployed a wide repertoire of discourses on Catholicism at the crossroads between the Concordat of 1953 and the convening of the Second Vatican Council with the aim, according to the author, of "ilustrar las contradicciones y la hipocresía de un sector de la sociedad tradicional católica" [illustrating the contradictions and hypocrisy of a sector of traditional Catholic society" and of "poner en evidencia la falsedad de su sistema educativo y moral" [exposing the falsity of its educational and moral system] (Rodríguez). The writing of the novel would reveal itself as an operation of memory linked to Marsé's childhood and adolescent experiences. In this way, the author is involved in the construction of a story through which a genealogy of the relationships between ecclesiastical power, the exercise of charity and the political field at the end of the 1960s can be established: "Se trata de una historia muy vinculada a una etapa de mi vida, en la adolescencia. Los muchachos pobres del barrio hacían entonces lo que podríamos llamar vida de parroquia, o de centro parroquial, y eran objeto de actividades diocesanas y de apostolado o catequísticas" [It is a story closely linked to a stage of my life, when I was an adolescent. The poor boys of the neighbourhood were then involved in what we could call parish life, or the parish centre, and were the object of diocesan and apostolic or catechetical activities] (Rodriguez).

Secular apostolate organizations such as the Hermandad Obreras de Acción Católica [Catholic Action Workers' Brotherhood, HOAC] and its youth branch, Juventudes Obreras Católicas [Catholic Workers' Youth, JOC], had spread in the 1950s with the aim of promoting the social doctrine of the Church, and by the end of the decade they had between "60 y 80.000 afiliados, entre militantes y adherentes" [60 and 80,000 members, including both militants and adherents] (Tello 175). These organizations underwent a working-class drift that resulted both in the promotion of a pastoral work of a "missionary" type and in the direct or indirect defence of a trade

Fables of Grace 173

unionism that was both vindictive and authentically representative. Thus, the social turn of Catholic Action materialized in a self-criticism of welfarist paternalism as well as in a proposal closer to a social justice commitment and sociological research of the structural causes of poverty. Taking up the criticisms of the 1959 Economic Stabilization Plan previously denounced by JOC and HOAC, in January 1960 the Spanish episcopate drafted a document entitled "Declaración sobre actitud cristiana ante los problemas morales de la estabilización y el desarrollo económico" (Declaration on Christian attitude towards the moral problems of stabilization and economic development), which pointed out that the working class "era la más perjudicada por las consecuencias del Plan de Estabilización y que "los 'pudientes' persistían en su actitud egoísta e insolidaria" [was the most harmed by the consequences of the Stabilization Plan" and that "the 'well-to-do' persisted in their selfish and unsupportive attitude] (quoted in Berzal 179).

Marsé dissects the different entries into adulthood of the characters of the Claramunt family taking into account precisely their experiences as subjects socialized into these charitable practices during their childhood and adolescence. The new model of parish action experienced by Montse involved the discovery of the so-called "compromiso temporal" [temporal commitment], a social and political awareness that was critical of social injustice. The method of formation and action developed by Catholic Action was called "Revisión de vida" [Life Review], and it was based on the participants' ongoing reflection through the dialectic concatenation of three actions: "Ver, juzgar, y actuar" [See, judge, and act]. As the people who mentor Montse in the parish argue, by putting this sequence into practice, activists like her could delve into problems in order to bring about social transformation:

> Los tiempos exigen planificar, utilicemos las armas del enemigo...
> ¿cómo captarse a un preso orgulloso de su soledad, amargado? me
> preguntaba nuestra compañera Montse el otro día. Pues interesándonos
> por lo que a él le interesa, por sus preocupaciones, compartiendo
> sus sufrimientos y logrando serle útil, en una palabra, y termino,
> procurando ser más humanos. (22)

> [These times demand planning, let us use the enemy's weapons ... How
> can we recruit a prisoner who is proud of his loneliness and bitter? Our
> colleague Montse asked me the other day. Well, by taking an interest in
> what interests him, in his concerns, by sharing his sufferings and being
> useful to him, in a word, and I conclude, by trying to be more human.]

174   *Fables of Development*

In the instructions that Montserrat receives during her period of training, references to the "Review of Life" are combined with the planned and rational approach to the practice of charity. Along with the implementation of administrative efficiency, this model of apostolate fostered a relationship between benefactors and assisted persons based on empathy and understanding, affections that will lead the protagonist to fall in love with Manuel Reyes, a prisoner she meets in the Modelo prison during her work as a parish visitor and with whom she is ready to start a new life after discovering that she is pregnant. Manuel Reyes, known as Pijoaparte, is the protagonist of Marsé's novel *Últimas tardes con Teresa* (1966 [Last Afternoons with Teresa]), a character who had already failed to have an affair with a girl from the Catalan bourgeoisie. For her cousin Paco, Montse was not only a pioneer in assuming religious practices that would later be socially recognized as part of the dogma of the post-conciliar Church, but also in facing a process of declassing that questioned the moral order of the "benefactora y limosnera burguesía" [beneficent and almsgiving bourgeoisie] (99) to which she belonged. In this sense, Montse's character has a vision of charity that clashes head-on with the work her mother performs from her executive positions in Caritas and the World Union of Catholic Women's Organizations, institutions from which she controls and directs "su vasto y palpitante mundo de necesitados" [her vast and throbbing world of the needy] (79).

In contrast to Montserrat's ethical commitment to her charitable work, the character of Salvador Villela is presented as a careerist who uses his experience in the JOC to achieve social advancement. His entry into the political field from the parochial world is described by Juan Marsé as a process of social mobility that turns out to be "an equivalent of Opus" (quoted in Clark, "Catholic" 98). Vilella, a boy of humble origins, marries Nuria Claramunt after acquiring a deep knowledge of the relationships between social classes, structured around the practice of charity in the diocese where he meets his wife. He thus becomes an example of the new developmentalist subject who alternates his work as an advertising technician with his work as a catechist, and whose backpack contains "textos encíclicos en estudio, informes de ventas y de mercados" [encyclical texts under study (as well as) sales and market reports] (247). As Paco argues, Salvador is the palpable proof that adherence to the new political and economic forces has opened up the possibility of social ascent for those who know how to adapt to the social game of the elites in the new economic cycle: "El hecho de que el catequista oscuramente parroquial y suburbano que fuiste tú ocupe hoy . . . un cargo en la Diputación y se codee con el cardenal Acquaviva. . . debe de ser una prueba del desarrollo del país" [The fact that

Fables of Grace

the obscurely parochial and suburban catechist that you were occupies today
... a position in the Deputation and rubs shoulders with Cardinal Acquaviva
... must be evidence of the development of the country] (37). The narrator
thus describes an emerging political class of technocratic Catholics, of which
Vilella will not be the only exponent in the novel, as evidenced in the lecture
given by a businessman at a retreat for Catholic workers:

> La manera de alcanzar la igualdad social . . . debéis concebirla en
> términos de la más característica ideología cristiana: una mayor
> laboriosidad, la capacitación profesional, la perseverancia, la honradez
> y el comportamiento que inspire confianza en vuestros superiores,
> eso os abrirá el camino hacia los bienes materiales y los bienes de
> la cultura. Muchos trabajadores de mi padre me preguntan: señorito
> Fernando, ¿qué quiere decir Marketing? Y yo les digo: Noi, t'has de
> fer una cultureta, no basta con ser honrado. ¡Debemos hacernos una
> cultureta, sí, pero sobre la roca firme de la fe! (206)

> [The way to achieve social equality...you must conceive it in terms of
> the most characteristic Christian ideology: greater industriousness,
> professional training, perseverance, honesty and behaviour that
> inspires confidence in your superiors, that will open the way to both
> material and cultural goods. Many of my father's workers ask me: Mr
> Fernando, what does marketing mean? And I tell them: "Noi, t'has de
> fer una cultureta": it is not enough to be honest, one must become a
> person of culture, yes, but on the firm rock of faith!]

Paco describes these new elites who were "navegando en aquellas encharcadas
y pestilentes aguas del posibilismo político" [sailing in those stagnant and
pestilent waters of political possibilism] (306) and trusts that their political
project will fail as soon as the workers become aware of the economic and
social model that these "mandarines" [mandarins] (52) promote: "Por cada
obrero que lográis que descubra a Dios, hay diez que descubren vuestros
ingresos. Corren malos tiempos. Estáis perdidos" [For every worker you
manage to get to discover God, there are ten who discover your income.
These are bad times. You are lost] (306). In this way Paco was trying to
ward off other political prophecies of the time, which gave leaders like
Salvador Vilella a hegemonic role in the future of the country. This would
be the case of Jorge Semprún's analysis in 1965, when he stated that at that
time the only two organizations that would have a definitive role in the
political opposition after the death of the dictator would be the Communist
Party of Spain (PCE) and Christian Democracy (39–55). At the end of the

176   *Fables of Development*

1960s, Salvador has become part of the elite that will lead the transition to democracy after the death of the dictator; it is then that Paco reminds him how the same post-conciliar ideological current he now uses opportunistically was the one Montse was criticized for years ago: "Recuerdo que a Montse la llamabais borrega y tonta por situarse hace ocho años en esa línea que ahora, precisamente, los nuevos vientos ecuménicos os recomiendan" [I remember that you called Montse a simpleton and a fool for taking that line eight years ago that now, precisely, the new ecumenical winds are recommending to you] (40).

Montserrat takes her own life in the summer of 1960, throwing herself from the bridge of the Vallcarca neighbourhood, with her back turned "a las luces expiatorias del Tibidabo, con la gran imagen del Sagrado Corazón, siempre con los brazos abiertos a la ciudad" [to the atoning lights of Tibidabo, with the great image of the Sacred Heart, always with arms open to the city] (305). As Paco explains, the experience of social commitment had turned the young woman into an ethical reference in the face of the opportunism and hypocrisy of those around her. It was a life choice that "no presentaba ninguna relación directa con la estupidez y la flojera mental de las Hijas de María, sus compañeras del grupo parroquial" [had no direct relationship with the stupidity and mental laziness of the Daughters of Mary, her companions in the parish group] (315).

In this way, Marsé claimed a new reading in political terms of the work of women like Montse, who used the spaces of socialization of the secular apostolate to intervene in the public sphere. This vital attitude appeared in the early 1970s as "un viejo sueño de integridad, de ofrecimiento total, de solidaridad o como quiera llamarse eso que la había mantenido en pie . . . frente a miserables enfermos, presidiarios sin entrañas y huérfanos" [an old dream of integrity, of total offering, of solidarity or whatever you want to call that which had kept her on her feet...in the face of sick wretches, gutless convicts and orphans] (315). At the end of the cycle of the First Development Plan, Juan Marsé testified to the existence of a new critical vision of charity that was spreading among groups of Catholics who were beginning to work together with autonomous associations opposing the regime as well as with neighbourhood movements. Against the promotion of charity as a device that reproduced social inequality, these grassroots networks reflected on other possible meanings of solidarity and social justice. These were collective networks in which new political subjects and communities were formed, and which played an essential role in the re-emergence of a civic culture that permeated the social movements in the transition to democracy. Only in democracy would the institutionalization of social rights in the welfare state guarantee health care, public education and social security.

Fables of Grace

Gone were the decades when the most vulnerable members of society had to depend on the charity managed by the government, the Falange or the Catholic Church to have access to basic needs. In mid-twentieth century Spain, "43 percent of the Spanish population was still served by charity" (Delgado and De la Hoz 62), and, in 1965, "there were three million Spaniards in a situation of absolute poverty" (Odekon 1016) according to Caritas, a religious non-governmental organization. In this way, charity in Franco's Spain consolidated the exclusion of large social majorities from the decision-making process regarding their destiny; it also contributed to the absence of social policies that were based on the recognition that the situation of poverty of those assisted corresponded to a need resulting from systemic social inequality.

Afterword

"Each epoch not only dreams the next, but also in dreaming, strives toward the moment of waking."

Walter Benjamin, *Reflections* (162)

During the Christmas of 1961, the children of La Salle Bonanova —a school in Barcelona— posed in front of a rocket-shaped artifact containing a figure of the Christ Child. The image combined the celebration of the Christian epiphany with the desire for modernity harboured by the space race, a phenomenon essential to understanding mass utopia in both East and West during the twentieth century. The photograph that the children's families received connected technological enchantment with a representation of the school chapel and the star that guided the Magi to Bethlehem. The conquest of the *cielo* (sky) in which aerospace technology circulated —spacecraft, missiles and satellites that became emblems of Cold War development— converged in this image of Spain in the 1960s with the belief in *cielo* (Heaven) to which the technocrats in charge of the economic modernization project appealed. One of the children photographed, whose image appears on the cover of this book, was the poet, composer and painter Pepe Sales (1954–1994), a victim of the HIV/AIDS epidemic of the 1990s. Sales was one of the countercultural youth in the political transition to democracy and was part of the generation that lived through the economic transition from autarchy to developmentalism in his childhood. The first years of life of this generation took place in the long journey stretching from the end of the so-called "hunger years" to the 1970s, when many of these young people participated in emancipation projects against the dictatorship that sought to transform the world and change their own lives. The potential of their ideas to threaten the existing world and to imagine other worlds can be measured by the enormous

180 *Fables of Development*

violence with which the Francoist regime reacted against these young people, deploying prison and psychiatric repressive strategies.[1]

At the beginning of the twentieth century, Walter Benjamin was one of the authors who reflected in depth on the potential of the collective imagination and its relation to capitalism. In his analyses, the social imagination is embodied in cultural artifacts, which contain complex webs of memory and desires that "might enter into a revolutionary constellation with the present" (Buck-Morss 70). With the aim of understanding some of the fantasies that shape the economic and social model in recent history in Spain, this book has sought to shed light on some of the mythologies, everyday beliefs and aspirations that emerged in the 50s and 60s and still survive in a residual form in today's society. An emblematic example of the providential narratives that still today articulate some of the country's economic fantasies can be found in the construction in the twenty-first century of "ghost airports", airports without airplanes that have little or no use after public investments of millions of euros. These places, authentic ruins of contemporary development, have become a symbol of the Spanish real estate bubble that collapsed in the Great Recession that began in 2008. If one of the characters in the science-fiction literature featured in these pages were to visit one of these places, he or she would wonder what kind of collective fantasies sustain an economic model that believes that the construction of spaces with no real function is capable of attracting capital from tourism and commerce. It is a belief that was already present in the dream shipments launched by American airplanes in *¡Bienvenido, Mr. Marshall!* or in the belief in the existence of providential donor agents. These fantasies operating as collective rituals of wealth attraction have been analysed in the first part of this book, with the symbolic logic of the so-called cargo cult.

Some of the social imaginaries on the circulation and distribution of capital examined in these pages survive in today's Spain, including the country's integration into international economic and military circuits after the intervention of the United States and the utopian impulse of technoculture and science fiction —analysed in chapters one and two— or the social uses of charity and collective participation in games of chance, studied in the chapters three and four. To cite some recent examples, we can recall how in the spring of 2021 the measurement of radioactivity was resumed in the area surrounding Palomares (Almeria), showing since then higher levels of Americium 241, a derivative of the plutonium carried by the four thermonuclear bombs that were accidentally dropped in 1966; two of them, with a power 75 times more destructive than those of Hiroshima,

---

1 See Labrador Méndez.

Afterword 181

released about 9 kilos of radioactive material that is still present in the area, and whose clean-up by the US government is still pending. During the confinements due to the Covid-19 pandemic in 2020, the number of reports of aircraft sightings also increased in Spain, in a year in which the US Department of Defence released recordings of strange aircraft and announced the creation of a special unit, the Unidentified Aerial Phenomena Task Force (UAPTF).

The pandemic years have also seen the development of a new space race, this time starring a group of billionaires vying to open up the colonization of other planets and space tourism to the private sector. In the scenario of a future climate collapse, powerful corporations promote the idea that the conquest and exploitation of space represents a social hope, while obtaining large public and private profits for a project described as "extraterrestrial capitalism" (Lepore), driven by fantasies that come from science fiction. Since the beginning of the pandemic, some social agents in Spain proposed the practice of charity as a mechanism by which the distribution of some resources could be solved punctually, through actions that were publicized in the media to favour the image of the donors. In parallel, the media have also continued to promote the redistribution of wealth through state lotteries, as well as to advertise gambling games managed by private companies. For Christmas 2020, the National Lottery campaign presented under the slogan "Comparte como siempre, comparte como nunca" [Share as ever, share as never before] a series of ads featuring citizens exchanging lottery tickets in scenarios that recreated the continuity of this game from the post-war period to the confinements. The gambling sector, which accounts for 0.9% of annual GDP and an important source of revenue for the public coffers, has also increased its income in recent years thanks to the unstoppable growth of an industry that destroys the lives of young working-class people, who have seen the number of betting shops multiply in their neighbourhoods.[2] In Madrid alone, there has been a 636% growth of gambling houses in the last 5 years and the rates of juvenile gambling addiction have tripled.

Neoliberalism has recently been analysed as a true contemporary theodicy that uses the sacrificial logics of markets to justify exploitation, precarity and ecological devastation.[3] It is an ideology that was born to destroy social solidarity and the welfare state, and that intervenes in the creation of subjectivities and structures of salvation based on the capacity of subjects to compete economically, which absorb the meaning of the notion

2 See Barrial and del Amo.
3 See Vogl and McCarraher.

of citizenship.[4] As Margaret Thatcher explained when she stated "economics are the method; the object is to change heart and soul", late capitalism has as its goal the construction of new subjectivities and identities based on shared beliefs. Prior to the Thatcher and Ronald Reagan governments, neoliberal policies as a development strategy had already been introduced in the countries of the global South (Connell and Dados 122–124; Ban 101–115). In this sense, we can consider the so-called "Spanish economic miracle" as a laboratory that allowed for experimentation with new economic policies and the fantasies associated with them in the scenario of a dictatorship. It was an authoritarian and repressive regime already consolidated in which it was not necessary to provoke a coup d'état like those that were part of the "Neoliberal Shock Doctrine" (Klein) in the 1970s. As had already happened in the Spanish case, the capitalist bloc supported the military governments that implemented the neoliberal proposals in countries such as Chile, Argentina and Indonesia. After the collapse of Lehman Brothers in 2008, numerous reflections have been proposed on the anti-democratic component of the ideas of economists such as Wilhelm Röpke, Friedrich Hayek or Milton Friedman. All of them supported military coups, apartheid or dictatorial governments that replaced the notion of the citizen with that of the "sovereign consumer" (Olsen 19–64). According to neoliberal ideology, markets should take over state functions and the state should be strong — and even authoritarian— to protect them while destroying the mechanisms that articulate social solidarity and the welfare state. After the death of General Franco, Manuel Vázquez Montalbán reflected in his *Diccionario del Franquismo* (1977) on the term "Developmentalism", underlining precisely how, since the 1950s, the social integration of Spaniards had been promoted through consumption while they were kept away from the political sphere:

> El sistema capitalista de los años cincuenta generó esta doctrina sustitutiva de la del crecimiento económico, para estimular la producción y el consumo, garantizar el pleno empleo con su consecuente tranquilidad social y ofrecer así un modelo de prosperidad "para todos"

---

4 The main objectives of the neoliberal model policies since the second half of the twentieth century include "privatization of public assets and functions; de- and re-regulation resulting in greater upward distribution of profits and rents; liberalized trade; the insulation of market actors from democratic oversight; disinvestment in social services and re-investment in the punitive, policing, and military functions of the state; and the cultivation of market principles in an ever-widening ambit of human life" (Moreton 89). On the birth of neoliberalism, its global expansion and its implementation in different national models see Slobodian (2020), Ban (2016), and Moreton (2021).

Afterword

dentro del sistema capitalista. La paz y la democracia eran equivalentes a la integración social a través del bienestar y el consumo. (28)

[The capitalist system of the 1950s generated this doctrine as a substitute for that of economic growth, to stimulate production and consumption, guarantee full employment with its consequent social tranquillity and thus offer a model of prosperity "for all" within the capitalist system. Peace and democracy were equivalent to social integration through welfare and consumption.]

The dictatorship promoted a supposed "economic miracle" that was sustained by high social costs that included the exploitation of the working class, political repression, forced emigration and substandard housing in the big cities. However, the objective of a hypothetical balanced and harmonious development was a goal for both the Francoist government and some opposition economists, who accepted the framework of modernization theory in which the regime's managers moved. In 1976, José Manuel Naredo warned of the problems of this model by pointing out that "críticos progresistas" [progressive critics] established comparisons between "los niveles de producción o de consumo por habitante de acero, abonos químicos, Kw/H, automóviles, televisores o abrelatas eléctricos" [the levels of production or consumption per inhabitant of steel, chemical fertilizers, Kw/H, automobiles, televisions or electric can openers] to show "la 'enorme distancia que nos separa' de los países capitalistas más desarrollados y el consiguiente atraso histórico secular que hay que recuperar tomando como objetivo la imagen de 'modernidad' y 'progreso' que ofrecen los países de capitalismo 'maduro'" [the 'enormous distance that separates us' from the most developed capitalist countries and the consequent secular historical backwardness that must be recovered by taking as an objective the image of 'modernity' and 'progress' offered by countries of 'mature' capitalism] (25). Some of the progressive economists focused on pointing out the technocratic character of the reforms, without questioning a model which, according to Naredo, unfolded the vision of "un desarrollo capitalista ideal que haría las delicias del buen tecnócrata: un desarrollo 'fuerte', 'equilibrado', 'autosostenido', sin inflación ni problemas de balanzas de pago, sin paro y con salarios muy elevados" [an ideal capitalist development that would delight the good technocrat: a 'strong', 'balanced', 'self-sustained' development, without inflation or balance of payments problems, without unemployment and with very high wages] (1976, 28). For many social researchers, economic change in Spain was but another manifestation of a development that was becoming generalized on a global scale; a perception that would allow them

184   *Fables of Development*

to differentiate themselves from ideologues sympathetic to the regime by disseminating "the slogan that in Spain development was taking place 'in spite of Franco'" (Sánchez León, "Desclasamiento" 76).

By 1964, Spain had become the world's leading tourist destination and tourism accounted for nearly 9% of GDP by the end of the decade. Tourism reorganized the Spanish productive model, emphasizing the attraction of European consumption and demand, and the development of the real estate sector. The Ministry of Information and Tourism, directed by Manuel Fraga since 1962, was in charge of designing the master lines of the boom of a sector that has managed to secure for several decades a firm place for Spain in the global leisure industry. The boom in the tourism sector allowed Franco's government to continue imposing its agenda while attracting foreign investment and solidifying the illusion of consumption in the interior of the country. It was an "art of government" (Crumbaugh 23) in which the spectacle of tourism deployed a propaganda system to promote the ideas of development, welfare and order that marked late-Francoism, especially during the official "25 Years of Peace" campaign in 1964. After Franco's death, economic policies in times of democracy continued to depend on the tourism and real estate sectors.[5] Barely a month after the 1977 general elections, the Moncloa Pacts confirmed the readjustment of income policy, a central piece in the European neoliberal agenda that allowed the recovery of the rate of profit by capital as well as cuts in workers' wages. The implementation of these pacts occurred in parallel to the so-called "industrial restructuring" that contributed to a greater dependence on the real estate and financial sectors, which had their main pillar in the same middle classes that had been part of the legacy of developmentalism. Thus, the first governments in democracy consolidated a model of "embedded neoliberalism" (Ban 34–64), with a meagre welfare state and compensatory measures for those who lost out as a result of globalization and the dislocating effects of the market.

The macroeconomic figures of the "Spanish miracle" have led the historian Stanley Payne to consider General Franco "as the country's definitive modernizer, leader of the most successful of all would-be 'development dictatorships' of the twentieth century" (Payne and Palacios 515). This is an interpretation that leads certain social sectors today to elaborate a historical narrative in which the construction of the democratic rule of law, and the subsequent insertion of Spain into the framework of the European Union would emerge as a sort of "natural" consequence of the country's previous modernization. This narrative reinforces the relationship between economic development and a democracy in which the achievement of the "political

---

5 See González de Andrés and Etxezarreta.

miracle" would only be the corollary of the successes of the "economic miracle". The transition to democracy would be, according to this narrative, the "logical, expected, and almost predictable result of the social change of the sixties" (Pérez Picazo 263). This would deny the historical contingency of the political process of transition, as well as the role of broad sectors of the population in the struggles for social rights and in the expression of dissent against the persistence of elements of the dictatorship in times of democracy.

As this book has examined, during the 1950s and 1960s many cultural producers challenged the narratives about the "economic miracle" and the circulation and distribution of capital promoted by the Francoist regime. Writers, filmmakers and cartoonists who reflected on the situation of the country in the Cold War, and who imagined a life in outer space more just and supportive, as well as creators who invented fictions critical of the spectacle of gambling or against the privileges of those who exercised charity gave new meanings to ideas about development and the distribution of wealth. A careful analysis of cultural productions in the transition from autarchy to economic liberalism reveals the deep complexity of the uneven development of the economic, political and ideological instances of Spanish society at that historical juncture. In this sense, the providential narratives that characterized the fables of development in the cultural production of this period expressed these contradictions through the incorporation of supernatural, transcendent or extraordinary elements in the imaginaries of economic modernization, which progressively displaced the ideological scheme of the autarchic period. If, as Walter Benjamin stated, "each epoch dreams the next", the analysis of the fantasies that were part of the lives of the generations that preceded us can lead us to understand not only what their ideas about the "Spanish economic miracle" were, but also to preserve the memory of what their wishes were about the distribution of that "miracle". I hope this book has shed some light on the lives and voices that in times of dictatorship imagined a present and future that includes us, as well as on our own possibilities of imagining other potential futures.

Works Cited

Adamson, Matthew, Lino Camprubí, and Simone Turchetti. "From the Ground Up: Uranium Surveillance and Atomic Energy in Western Europe." *The Surveillance Imperative: Geosciences During the Cold War and Beyond*, edited by Simone Turchetti and Peder Roberts, Palgrave Macmillan, 2014, pp. 23–44.

Adelantado, José. *Cambios en el Estado del bienestar: políticas sociales y desigualdades en España*. Icaria; Universitat Autònoma de Barcelona, 2000.

"La administración Eisenhower significará la reacción contra el dirigismo demócrata con un ensayo de individualismo capitalista." *ABC. Edición de Andalucía*, 1 Jan. 1953, p. 58.

Adorno, Theodor. *Critical Models: Interventions and Catchwords*. Columbia UP, 2005.

Afinoguénova, Eugenia. "'Unity, Stability, Continuity': Heritage and the Renovation of Franco's Dictatorship in Spain, 1957–1969." *International Journal of Heritage Studies*, vol. 16, no. 6, 2010, pp. 417–433.

Agamben, George. *The Kingdom and the Glory: For a Theological Genealogy of Economy and Government*. Stanford UP, 2012.

Aglietta, Michel. *Regulación y crisis del capitalismo*. Siglo XXI, 1986.

Agustí, Ignacio. "El júbilo navideño." *Triunfo*, no. 80, 1963, p. 58.

"Ahora están de moda los globos fantasmas." *El liberal*, 25 Aug. 1909.

Alares, Gustavo. *Políticas del pasado en la España franquista (1939–1964)*. Marcial Pons, 2017.

Aldecoa, Ignacio. *Cuentos completos, Vol. 1*. Madrid: Alianza, 1978.

Aldiss, Brian W. *Non-Stop*. Orion, 2000.

Alejandro, Julio. "Colaborar con Buñuel." *Contracampo*, no. 16, pp. 3–45.

Alfaya, Javier. *Crónica de los años perdidos: la España del tardofranquismo*. Temas de Hoy, 2003.

Alonso, Luis Enrique, and Fernando Conde. *Historia del consumo en España: Una aproximación a sus orígenes y primer desarrollo*. Debate, 1994.

Altabella, José. *La lotería nacional de España (1763–1963)*. Dirección General de Tributos Especiales, 1962.

Althusser Louis. *For Marx*. Verso, 2005.

Álvarez-Buylla, Adolfo, and Enrique Jarnés. *2055: Recordando las aventuras de Diego Valor*. Universidad Internacional de Andalucía, 2014.

Anderson, Lara. *Control and Resistance: Food Discourse in Franco Spain*. Toronto: University of Toronto Press, 2020.

188   *Fables of Development*

Aragó, Ignacio María. "Té-Bridge para obras de apostolado." *El Ciervo*, no. 53, 1957, p. 2.

Aragüés Estragués, Rosa. *Las rojas y sus hijos, víctimas de la legislación franquista. El caso de la cárcel de Predicadores, 1939-1945.* Editorial Sanz y Torres, 2014.

Arbaiza, Diana. *The Spirit of Hispanism: Commerce, Culture, and Identity across the Atlantic, 1875-1936.* University of Notre Dame Press, 2020.

Armengou, Montse, and Ricard Belis. *Els nens perduts del franquisme.* Televisió de Catalunya, 2003.

¡Aquí hay petróleo! Directed by Rafael J. Salvia. Asturias Films, 1956.

Azcona, Rafael. "Pobre." *Pobre, Paralítico, y Muerto.* Ediciones Arión, 1960.

—. *¿Son de alguna utilidad los cuñados? Y otros textos (1956-1958).* Logroño: Pepitas de Calabaza: Fulgencio Pimentel, 2014.

Babiano Mora, José. *Emigrantes, cronómetros y huelgas: un estudio sobre el trabajo y los trabajadores durante el franquismo (Madrid, 1951-1977).* Siglo XXI, 1995.

Balibar, Etienne. "Elements for a Theory of Transition." *Reading Capital: The Complete Edition,* edited by L. Althusser and E. Balibar, Verso, 1979, pp. 273-308.

Ballester Olmos, Vicente-Juan. *Ovnis: el fenómeno aterrizaje.* Plaza & Janés, 1984.

Balsebre, Armand. *Historia de la radio en España (1939-1985).* Cátedra, 2002.

Balzac, Honoré de. *A Bachelor's Establishment.* Macmillan, 1896.

Ban, Cornel. *Ruling Ideas: How Global Neoliberalism Goes Local.* Oxford UP, 2016.

Banco Hispano-Americano. *La situación económica en 1962.* Banco Hispano-Americano,1963.

Barciela López, Carlos, editor. *Autarquía y mercado negro: el fracaso económico del primer franquismo, 1939-1959.* Crítica, 2003.

—. "Los años del hambre." *El País.* 5 Feb. 2012.

—. and Antonio Escudero. *Dos lecciones de historia.* Universidad de Alicante, 2007.

Barrial, Cristina, and Pepe del Amo. *La apuesta perdida. Ludopatía, ciudad y resistencia.* Bellaterra, 2021.

Barrios, Nuria. "La ambición del dibujante." *El País* (Babelia), 11 Dec. 2010, pp. 4-5.

Barthes, Roland. *Mythologies.* Noonday Press, 1972.

—. *The Eiffel Tower, and Other Mythologies,* University of California Press, 1997.

Bartholomew, Robert E., and George S. Howard. *UFOs & Alien Contact: Two Centuries of Mystery.* Prometheus Books, 1998.

Battaglia, Debbora, editor. *E.T. Culture: Anthropology in Outerspaces.* Duke UP, 2006.

Beltrán Lucas, editor. *Ensayos de Economía Política.* Unión Editorial, Madrid, 1996.

Benavente, Jacinto. "El asunto del día." *La Vanguardia,* 14 Apr. 1950, p. 5.

Benjamin, Walter. *Selected Writings,* edited by Marcus Bullock and Michael W. Jennings. Belknap Press, 1996.

—. *The Arcades Project,* edited by Rolf Tiedemann. Belknap Press, 2002.

Bennett, Jane. *The Enchantment of Modern Life: Attachments, Crossings, and Ethics.* Princeton UP, 2001.

Berzal de la Rosa, Enrique. *Del Nacionalsocialismo a la lucha antifranquista. La HOAC de Castilla y León entre 1946 y 1975.* Biblioteca Virtual Miguel de Cervantes, 2002.

¡Bienvenido, Míster Marshall! Directed by Luis García Berlanga. Uninci, 1953.

Bloch, Ernst. *The Principle of Hope.* MIT Press, 1986.

"Bombas atómicas a bordo de platillos volantes". *Imperio: Diario de Zamora de Falange Española de las J.O.N.S.,* 2 Jan. 1951, p. 1.

Works Cited

Botti, Alfonso. *Cielo y dinero: El nacionalismo en España, 1881–1975.* Alianza, 2008.

Bould, Mark and China Miéville. *Red Planets: Marxism and Science Fiction.* London: Pluto, 2009.

Bowen, Wayne H. *Truman, Franco's Spain and the Cold War.* University of Missouri Press, 2017.

Box, Zira. *España, año cero: la construcción simbólica del franquismo.* Alianza Editorial, 2010.

Bravo, Eduardo. *Ummo: Lo increíble es la verdad.* Autsaider Cómics, 2019.

Buache, Freddy. *The Cinema of Luis Buñuel.* Tantivy Press, 1973.

Buck-Morss, Susan. *Dreamworld and Catastrophe: The Passing of Mass Utopia in East and West.* The MIT Press, 2002.

Buero Vallejo, Antonio. "Del Quijotismo al 'mito' de los platillos volantes." *Primer Acto,* vol. 100–101, 1968, pp. 73–74.

—. *La doble historia del doctor Valmy; Mito.* Espasa-Calpe, 1976.

—. *Hoy es fiesta; El tragaluz.* Cátedra, 2011.

Cabria García. Ignacio. *Entre ufólogos, creyentes y contactados: una historia social de los OVNIs en España.* Cuadernos de Ufología, 1993.

"Cae un platillo volante en Madrid." *Imperio: Diario de Zamora de Falange Española de las J.O.N.S.,* 30 Dec. 1954: 3.

Caillois, Roger. *Man, Play and Games.* University of Illinois Press, 2001.

Calabuch. Directed by Luis García Berlanga. Águila Films, Films Costellazione, 2002.

Calvo Serer, Rafael. "Una nueva generación española." *Arbor,* no. 24, 1947, pp. 333–348.

—. *España, sin problema.* Ediciones Rialp, 1949.

—. *La aproximación de los neoliberales a la actitud tradicional.* Editora Nacional, 1956.

Camprubí, Lino. *Engineers and the Making of the Francoist Regime.* The MIT Press, 2014.

Canalda, José Carlos e Igor Cantero Uribe-Echeberria. "Escritores de novelas de a duro: los grandes desconocidos de la ciencia ficción española." *La ciencia ficción española,* edited by Fernando Martínez de la Hidalga. Ediciones Robel, 2002.

Candel, Francisco. *Ser obrero no es ninguna ganga.* Ariel, 1968.

Cañeque, Carlos, and Maite Grau. *¡Bienvenido, Mr. Berlanga!* Ediciones Destino, 1993.

Carr, Raymond. *España: de la Restauración a la democracia, 1875–1980.* Ariel, 1983.

—. *La época de Franco (1939–1975): Política, Ejército, Iglesia, Economía.* Espasa Calpe, 1996.

Carr, Raymond and Juan Pablo Fusi. *España, de la dictadura a la democracia.* Planeta, 1979.

Casanova, José. "The Opus Dei Ethic, the Technocrats and the Modernization of Spain." *Social Science Information/Sur les sciences sociales,* vol. 22, no. 1, 1983, pp. 27–50.

Casanova, Julián. *Cuarenta años con Franco.* Crítica, 2015.

Castoriadis, Cornelius. *The Imaginary Institution of Society.* MIT Press, 1987.

Catalán, Jordi. *La economía española y la segunda guerra mundial.* Ariel, 1995.

Cayuela Sánchez, Salvador. *Por la grandeza de la patria. La biopolítica en la España de Franco.* FCE, 2014.

190 *Fables of Development*

Cazorla, Antonio. *Políticas de la victoria: la consolidación del Nuevo Estado franquista (1938-1953)*. Marcial Pons, 2000.

—. *Fear and Progress: Ordinary Lives in Franco's Spain 1939-1975*. Chichester, 2010.

Cela, Camilo José. "Los platillos volantes o un mundo con astigmatismo." *Imperio: Diario de Zamora de Falange Española de las J.O.N.S.*, 26 Mar. 1950, p. 4.

—. "Tres hombrecillos de un metro." *La Vanguardia*, 18 May 1952, p. 7.

Celaya, Gabriel. *Entreacto*. Ágora, 1957.

Cerca de la ciudad. Directed by Luis Lucia. Goya Films, 1952.

Certeau, Michel de. *The Practice of Everyday Life*. University of California Press, 1984.

Chapman, James. *British Comics: A Cultural History*. Reaktion Books, 2011.

Christian, William A. Jr. "Religious Apparitions and the Cold War in Southern Europe." *Religion, Power and Protest in Local Communities*, edited by Eric Wolf, Mouton, 1984, pp. 239-266.

Clarasó, Noel. "Platillos volantes cruzan el sueño." *La Vanguardia*, 8 Apr. 1950, p. 7.

Clark, Jerome. *The UFO Encyclopedia*. Apogee Books, 1990.

Clark, Rosemary. *Catholic Iconography in the Novels of Juan Marsé*. Tamesis, 2003.

Clarke, David and Andy Roberts. *Out of the Shadows: UFOs the Establishment and Official Cover-Up*. Piatkus, 2002.

Clavero, Bartolomé. *Antidora. Antropología católica de la economía moderna*. Giuffrè, 1991.

Collado, Sergio. "En la muerte de Don Dacio Crespo". *Imperio. Diario de Zamora de Falange Española de las J.O.N.S*, 26 Oct. 1954, p. 1.

Cortes-Cavanillas, Julián. "Tierra-Marte-Venus-Tierra." *ABC*, 29 Dec. 1956, p. 45.

Crumbaugh, Justin. *Destination Dictatorship: The Spectacle of Spain's Tourist Boom and the Reinvention of Difference*. State University of New York Press, 2009.

—. "Spectacle as Spectralization, Untimely Timelessness: Marcelino Pan y Vino and Mid-1950s' Francoism." *Journal of Spanish Cultural Studies*, vol. 15, no. 3, 2015, pp. 1-14.

Dardot, Pierre and Christian Laval. *The New Way of the World: On Neoliberal Society*. Verso, 2013.

de Grazia, Victoria. *Irresistible Empire: America's Advance through Twentieth-Century Europe*. Harvard UP, 2005.

De la Torre, Joseba, and María del Mar Rubio-Varas. "Nuclear Power for a Dictatorship: State and Business Involvement in the Spanish Atomic Program, 1950-85." *Journal of Contemporary History*, vol. 51, no. 2, 2016, pp. 385-411.

Dean, Jodi. *Aliens in America: Conspiracy Cultures from Outerspace to Cyberspace*. Cornell UP, 1998.

"Defensa civil yanqui." *Imperio: Diario de Zamora de Falange Española de las J.O.N.S.*, 2 Jan. 1951, p. 1.

del Arco Blanco, Miguel Ángel. *Hambre de siglos: mundo rural y apoyos sociales del franquismo en Andalucía Oriental (1936-1951)*. Comares, 2007.

Deleuze, Gilles. "Postscript on Control Societies." *October*, vol. 59, 1992, pp. 3-7.

Delgado, Luisa Elena. *La nación singular: fantasías de la normalidad democrática española: 1996-2011. Siglo XXI*, España, 2014.

Delgado, Manuel. *La ira sagrada. Anticlericalismo, Iconoclasta y anti-ritualismo en la España contemporánea*. Editorial Humanidades, 1992.

Works Cited

Delgado Gómez-Escalonilla, Lorenzo. "Modernizadores y tecnócratas. Estados Unidos ante la política educativa y científica de la España del Desarrollo." *Historia y Política*, vol. 34, 2015, pp. 113–146.

Derrida, Jacques. *The Beast and the Sovereign, Volume 1*. University of Chicago Press, 2011.

Devereux, Edward. *Gambling and the Social Structure: A Sociological Study of Lotteries and Horse Racing in Contemporary America*, Arno, 1949.

Díaz-Salazar, Rafael. *Nuevo socialismo y cristianos de izquierda*. HOAC, 2001.

Domingo, Carmen. *Coser y cantar*. Lumen, 2007.

Duva, Jesús, and Natalia Junquera. *Vidas robadas*. Santillana, 2011.

Duvall, Raymond, and Alexander Wendt. "Sovereignty and the UFO." *Political Theory*, vol. 36, no. 4, 2008, pp. 607–633.

Ealham, Chris. *Class, Culture and Conflict in Barcelona, 1898–1937*, Routledge, 2004.

Egea, Juan. *Dark Laughter: Spanish Film, Comedy, and the Nation*. University of Wisconsin Press, 2013.

Eghigian, Greg. "'A Transatlantic Buzz': Flying Saucers, Extraterrestrials and America in Postwar Germany." *Journal of Transatlantic Studies,* vol. 12, no. 3, 2014, pp. 282–303.

—. "Making UFOs Make Sense: Ufology, Science, and the History of Their Mutual Misunderstanding." *Public Understanding of Science*, vol. 26, 2017, pp. 612–626.

Ekbladh, David. *The Great American Mission: Modernization and the Construction of an American World Order*. Princeton UP, 2011.

El astronauta. 1970. Dir. Javier Aguirre. Colmenar Viejo: Suevia, 2002. DVD.

"El avión misterioso." *Política*. 25 Nov. 1930, p. 5.

El destino se disculpa. Directed by José Luis Sáenz de Heredia. Estudios Ballesteros, Cibeles Film, 1944.

"El humor. Arma de lucha popular." *Cultura y democracia*, no. 5, 1 May 1950.

El mundo sigue. Directed by Fernando Fernán Gómez. Ada Films, 1963.

El tigre de Chamberí. Directed by Pedro L. Ramírez, Aspa, 1958.

Elijo Garay, Leopoldo. "El domingo, día del suburbio." *La Vanguardia*. 14 Dec.1955, p. 9.

Engelhardt, Tom. *The End of Victory Culture: Cold War America and the Disillusioning of a Generation*. University of Massachusetts Press, 2007.

Enguídanos, Pascual. *La abominable bestia gris*. Editora Valenciana,1974.

Esa pareja feliz. Directed by Juan Antonio Bardem, and Luis García Berlanga. Altamira, 1951.

Escobar, Arturo. *Encountering Development: The Making and Unmaking of the Third World*. Princeton UP, 1995.

Estapé, Fabián, and Mercè Amado. "Realidad y propaganda de la planificación indicativa en España." *España bajo el Franquismo*, edited by Josep Fontana, 1986, pp. 206–214.

Estefanía, Joaquín. "La larga marcha." *El País*, 3 May 1998.

Estruch, Juan. *Santos y pillos: el Opus Dei y sus paradojas*. Editorial Herder, 1994.

Etxezarreta, Miren. *La reestructuración del capitalismo en España, 1970–1990*. Crítica, 1986.

192 *Fables of Development*

Faustina. Directed by José Luis Sáenz de Heredia Chapalo Films, Suevia Films, 1957.

Federici, Silvia, and Peter Linebaugh. *Re-Enchanting the World: Feminism and the Politics of the Commons.* PM Press, 2019.

Feijoo, Benito Jerónimo. *Teatro critico universal: ó discursos varios en todo género de materias, para desengaño de errores comunes, Volumen 3.* Imprenta Real de la Gaceta, 1765.

Felices Pascuas. Directed by Juan Antonio Bardem. Floralva, 1954.

Fernández Clemente, Eloy, and Carlos Forcadell. "El bajo Ebro." *Andalán*, vol. 25, 1973, p. 7.

Fernández de Castro, Ignacio. *Del paternalismo a la justicia social.* Euramérica, 1956.

Fernández de la Mora, Gonzalo. *El crepúsculo de las ideologías.* Rialp, 1965.

Fernández Santos, Jesús. *Aunque no sé tu nombre.* Edhasa, 1991.

Flaherty, Robert Pearson. "UFOs, ETs, and the Millennial Imagination." *The Oxford Handbook of Millennialism*, edited by Catherine Wessinger. Oxford UP, 2016, pp. 587–610.

Fraga Iribarne, Manuel. *Horizonte español.* Editora Nacional, 1965.

—. *El desarrollo politico*, Bruguera, 1975.

Franco, Francisco. *Habla el Caudillo.* Editora Nacional, 1939.

—. *Palabras del Caudillo: 19 abril 1937 – 7 diciembre 1942.* Madrid: Ediciones de la Vicesecretaría de Educación Popular, 1943.

—. *Pensamiento social.* Organización Sindical de F.E.T. y de las J.O.N.S., 1959.

—. *Discursos y mensajes del Jefe del Estado, 1955-1959.* Dirección General de Información. Publicaciones Españolas, 1960.

—. *El Pequeño libro pardo del general.* Ruedo Ibérico, 1972.

Franco Fernández, Francisco José. "Franco y el extraño viaje a Cartagena." *Cuadernos Republicanos*, no. 9, pp. 77–84.

Fraser, Benjamin. "Feijóo on Mars: A Brief Note on the Literary Godfather of Spanish Science Fiction." *Dieciocho,* vol. 36, no. 1, 2013, pp. 37–50.

Foucault, Michel. *The Birth of Biopolitics: Lectures at the Collège de France 1978–1979,* Palgrave Macmillan, 2008.

Fuentes, Víctor. *Los mundos de Buñuel.* Ediciones Akal, 2000.

Fuertes, Gloria. *Historia de Gloria (amor, humor, desamor).* Cátedra, 2004.

Furtado, Celso. *El Mito del desarrollo económico y el futuro del Tercer Mundo.* Periferia, 1974.

Gabilliet, Jean-Paul. "Making a Homefront without a Battlefront: The Manufacturing of Domestic Enemies in the Early Cold War Culture." *European Journal of American Studies*, vol. 7, no. 2, 2012, pp. 1–9.

Gajić, Tatjana, *Paradoxes of Stasis: Literature, Politics, and Thought in Francoist Spain.* University of Nebraska Press, 2019.

Gallo, Max. *Spain Under Franco; A History.* Dutton, 1974.

Garcés, Joan. *Soberanos e intervenidos. Estrategias globales, americanos y españoles.* Siglo XXI, 1996.

García Bilbao, Pedro Alberto y Carlos Sáiz Cidoncha. *Viajes de los Aznar: Historia completa de la gran saga de George H. White.* Silente, 2002.

García Blanco, Javier. *Humanoides: encuentros con entidades desconocidas.* Edaf, 2003.

Works Cited

García-Donoso, Daniel. *Escrituras post-seculares: sedimentos de la religión en la narrativa española, 1950–2010*. Biblioteca Nueva, 2018.

García Escudero, José María. *Los españoles de la conciliación*. Espasa Calpe,1987.

Garvía, Roberto. *Historia ilustrada de las Loterías en España*. Loterías y Apuestas del Estado, 2007.

—. *Loterías. Un estudio desde la nueva sociología económica*. Centro de Investigaciones Sociológicas, 2008.

—. "Loterías, institucionalización y el juego en compañía." *Fortuna y virtud. Historia de las loterías públicas en España*, edited by Roberto Garvía. Sílex, 2009, pp. 13–65.

—. *Organizing the Blind: The Case of ONCE in Spain*. Routledge, 2019.

Geppert, Alexander C.T. "Extraterrestrial Encounters: UFOs, Science and the Quest for Transcendence, 1947–1972." *History and Technology*, vol. 28, no. 3, 2012, pp. 335–362.

Gilman, Nils. *Mandarins of the Future: Modernization Theory in Cold War America*. Johns Hopkins UP, 2007.

Giménez, Carlos. *Todo Paracuellos*. Ediciones Debolsillo, 2007.

Gindin, Sam, and Leo Panitch. *The Making of Global Capitalism: The Political Economy of American Empire*. Verso, 2013.

Gómez López-Quiñones, Antonio. "Sin perpetradores: crisis económica, publicidad televisiva y la ontología social del azar." *Perpetradores y memoria democrática en España, Hispanic Issues Online*, edited by Ana Luengo y Katherine Stafford, University of Minnesota Press, 2017, pp. 109–130.

González, Erika and Pedro Ramiro. *A dónde va el capitalismo español*. Traficantes de Sueños, 2019.

González Cuevas, Pedro Carlos. "La Derecha tecnocrática." *Historia y política: Ideas, procesos y movimientos sociales*, vol. 18, 2007, pp. 23–48.

González de Andrés, Enrique. *La economía franquista y su evolución (1939–1977): Los análisis económicos del Partido Comunista de España*. Libros de la Catarata, 2014.

González de Cardedal, Olegario. *La teología en España (1959–2009): Memoria y prospectiva*. Encuentro, 2010.

González Fernández, Ángeles. "La otra modernización: tecnocracia y 'mentalidad de desarrollo' en la península ibérica (1959–1974)." *Historia y política: Ideas, procesos y movimientos sociales*, vol. 35, 2016, pp. 313–339.

González González, Manuel Jesús. *La economía política del franquismo (1940–1970)*. Tecnos, 1979.

González Madrid, Damián, and Manuel Ortiz Heras, editors. *El Estado del Bienestar entre el Franquismo y la Transición*. Sílex, 2020.

Goux, Jean-Joseph. *Symbolic Economies: After Marx and Freud*. Ithaca, NY: Cornell UP, 1990.

Goytisolo, Juan. *Obras completas. 1, Novelas*. Aguilar, 1977.

Graeber, David. *En deuda: una historia alternativa de la economía*. Ariel, 2014.

Gramsci, Antonio. "Religion, the Lottery and the Opium of Poverty". *Further Selections from the Prison Notebooks*, edited by D. Boothman, Lawrence & Wishart, 1995.

Grego, Laura. *A History of Anti-Satellite Programs*, Union of Concerned Scientists, 2012.

194   *Fables of Development*

Grünschloß, Andreas. "Waiting for the 'Big Beam': UFO Religions and 'Ufological' Themes in New Religious Movements." *The Oxford Handbook of New Religious Movements*, edited by James R. Lewis. Oxford UP, 2008.

Guiral, Antoni. *Cuando los cómics se llamaban tebeos: la escuela Bruguera (1945–1963)*. Ediciones El Jueves, 2005.

—. *TBO: Edición coleccionista (1951–53): ¡Las mejores páginas de Benejam y Coll!* Salvat, 2011.

Guirao, Fernando. *Spain and the Reconstruction of Western Europe, 1945–57: Challenge and Response*. Palgrave Macmillan, 1998.

Halperin, David J. *Intimate Alien: The Hidden Story of the UFO*. Stanford: Stanford UP, 2020.

Harris, Marvin. *Cows, Pigs, Wars and Witches: The Riddles of Culture*. Random House, 1974.

Hendershot, Cyndy. *I Was a Cold War Monster: Horror Films, Eroticism, and the Cold War Imagination*. Bowling Green State University Popular Press, 2001.

—. *Anti-Communism and Popular Culture in Mid-Century America*. McFarland, 2002.

Hennaf, Marcel. "Religious Ethics, Gift Exchange and Capitalism." *European Journal of Sociology*, no. 44, 2003, pp. 293–324.

Herzberger, David. *Narrating the Past: Fiction and Historiography in Postwar Spain*. Duke UP, 1995.

Historias de la radio. Directed by José Luis Sáenz de Heredia. Chapalo Films, 1955.

Ilie, Paul. *Literature and Inner Exile: Authoritarian Spain, 1939–1975*. The Johns Hopkins University Press, 1980.

Jameson, Fredric. "The Vanishing Mediator: Narrative Structure in Max Weber." *New German Critique*, vol. 1, 1973, pp. 52–89.

—. *Archaeologies of the Future: The Desire Called Utopia and Other Science Fictions*. Verso, 2005.

—. "The Experiments of Time: Providence and Realism." *The Antinomies of Realism*. Verso, 2013, pp. 195–231.

Jiménez, Iker. *Encuentros: La Historia de los O.V.N.I. en España*. Edaf, 2008.

Jung, Carl G. *Flying Saucers: A Modern Myth of Things Seen in the Sky*. Harcourt, Brace, 1959.

—. *Collected Works of C. G. Jung, Volume 11: Psychology and Religion: West and East*, edited by Gerhard Adler and R. F.C. Hull, Princeton UP, 2014.

Juste, Rubén. *IBEX 35: Una historia herética del poder en España*. Capitán Swing, 2017.

Jutglar, Antoni. "Caridad y 'caridad'." *El Ciervo*, no. 102, 1962, p. 2.

Keller, Patricia. *Ghostly Landscapes: Film, Photography, and the Aesthetics of Haunting in Contemporary Spanish Culture*. University of Toronto Press, 2016.

Keyhoe, Donald. *The Flying Saucers Are Real*. New York: Fawcett Publications, 1950.

Kindelán, Alfredo. "Las preocupaciones extranjeras y las nacionales." *ABC*, 12 Dec. 1952, p. 3.

—. "Platillos volantes." *ABC de Sevilla*, 2 Dec. 1954, p. 3.

Klein, Naomi. *The Shock Doctrine*. Knopf, 2007.

La caza. Directed by Carlos Saura. Elías Querejeta, 1966.

"La ciencia yanki militarizada." *Cultura y democracia*, no. 5, May 1950, p. 95.

"La moda de los platillos volantes." *Imperio: Diario de Zamora de Falange Española de las J.O.N.S.*, 24 Nov. 1954, p. 1.

Works Cited

"La navegación aérea y los norteamericanos." *La Época*. 19 Apr. 1897, p. 2.

"La paz, salvación de España y de su cultura." *España y la paz*, 1 Sept. 1952.

La quiniela. Directed by Ana Mariscal. Bosco Films, 1960.

"La renta nacional." *Imperio: Diario de Zamora de Falange Española de las J.O.N.S.*, 26 Apr. 1962, p. 1.

"La VI Flota yanki visita España." *Imperio: Diario de Zamora de Falange Española de las J.O.N.S.*, 9 Jan. 1955, p.1.

Labanyi, Jo. *Myth and History in the Contemporary Spanish Novel*. Cambridge UP, 1989.

—. "Feminizing the Nation: Women, Subordination and Subversion in Post-Civil War Spanish Cinema." *Heroines without Heroes: Reconstructing Female and National Identities. 1945–51*, edited by Ulrike Sieglohr, Cassell, 2000, pp. 163–184.

—. "History and Hauntology; Or, What Does One Do with the Ghosts of the Past? Reflections on Spanish Film and Fiction of the Post-Franco Period." *Dismembering the Dictatorship: The Politics of Memory Since the Spanish Transition to Democracy*, edited by J. R. Resina, Rodopi, 2000, pp. 65–82.

—. "Internalisations of Empire: Colonial Ambivalence and the Early Francoist Missionary Film", *Discourse*, vol. 23, no. 1, 2001, pp. 25–42.

Labrador, Germán. *Culpables por la literatura. Imaginación política y contracultura en la transición española (1968–1986)*. Akal, 2017.

Lago Carballo, Antonio. *Eugenio d'Ors, anécdota y categoría*. Marcial Pons, 2004.

Lagrange, Pierre. "The Ghost in the Machine: How Sociology Tried to Explain (Away) American Flying Saucers and European Ghost Rockets, 1946–1947." *Imagining Outer Space: European Astroculture in the Twentieth Century*, edited by Alexander Geppert, Macmillan, 2012.

Landes, Richard. *Heaven on Earth: The Varieties of the Millennial Experience*. Oxford UP, 2011.

Lara, Antonio. "Los tebeos del franquismo." *Historietas, cómics y tebeos españoles*. Presses Universitaires du Mirail, 2002, pp. 44–74.

Latham, Michael E. *The Right Kind of Revolution: Modernization, Development, and U.S. Foreign Policy from the Cold War to the Present*. Cornell UP, 2011.

Lazo, Alfonso. *La Iglesia, la Falange y el fascismo: un estudio sobre la prensa española de Posguerra*. Universidad de Sevilla, 1995.

Lears, T. J. *Fables of Abundance: A Cultural History of Advertising in America*. Basic Books, 1994.

Lepore, Jill. "Elon Musk Is Building a Sci-Fi World, and the Rest of Us Are Trapped in It." *New York Times*, 4 Nov. 2021.

Lepselter, Susan. *The Resonance of Unseen Things: Poetics, Power, Captivity, and UFOs in the American Uncanny*. University of Michigan Press, 2016.

Lévi-Strauss, Claude. *El pensamiento salvaje*. Fondo de Cultura Económica, 1964.

Lieberman, Sima. *Growth and Crisis in the Spanish Economy: 1940–93*. Routledge, 2005.

Lindstrom, Lamont. *Cargo Cult: Strange Stories of Desire from Melanesia and Beyond*. University of Hawaii Press, 1993.

Longhurst, Alex. 2000. "Culture and Development: The Impact of 1960s 'Desarrollismo'." *Contemporary Spanish Cultural Studies*, edited by Barry Jordan and Rikki Morgan-Tamosunas, Oxford UP, pp. 17–28.

López Hernández, Isidro, and Emmanuel Rodríguez López. *Fin de ciclo: Financiarización, territorio y sociedad de propietarios en la onda larga del capitalismo hispano (1959-2010)*. Traficantes de Sueños, 2010.

López Rodó, Laureano. *Política y desarrollo*. Aguilar, 1970.

—. *Memorias*. Plaza & Janés, 1990.

Los jueves, milagro. Directed by Luis García Berlanga. Ariel; Continental Produzione Domiziana, 1957.

"Los platillos volantes proceden de los Estados Unidos." *Imperio. Diario de Zamora de Falange Española de las J.O.N.S.* 1 Apr. 1950, p. 1.

Löwith, Karl. *Meaning in History*. University of Chicago Press, 1957.

Lucanio, Patrick. *Them or Us: Archetypal Interpretations of Fifties Alien Invasion Films*. Indiana UP, 1987.

Luxemburg, Rosa. *Socialism and Churches: Marxism, Socialism and Religion*. Resistance Books, 2001.

Maeztu, Ramiro de. "El globo fantasma." *La Correspondencia de España*. 25 May 1909, p. 13.

Marcelino pan y vino. Directed by Ladislao Vajda. Falco Film, 1955.

Marín i Corbera, Martí. "Familiares pero desconocidas: Las migraciones interiores durante el régimen franquista" *El Franquismo y la Transición en España: Desmitificación y reconstrucción de la memoria de una época*, edited by Damián Alberto González, Libros de la Catarata, 2008.

Mars Aicart, Sergio. "Pascual Enguídanos: el universo visto desde Llíria." *Memoria de la novela popular: homenaje a la colección Luchadores del espacio*, edited by Pablo Herranz, Universitat de València, 2004.

Marsé, Juan. *Esta cara de la luna*. Seix Barral, 1962.

—. *La oscura historia de la prima Montse*. RBA, 1994.

Marsh, Steven. *Popular Spanish Film under Franco: Comedy and the Weakening of the State*. Palgrave MacMillan, 2006.

"Marte coloca en Madrid su primera piedra." *El Alcázar*. 8 Feb. 1955, p. 1.

Martín, Annabel. "¡Bienvenido, Mr. Marshall!: La identidad nacional como artificio." *The Cincinnati Romance Review*, vol. 15, 1996, pp. 73-80.

Martín Gaite, Carmen. *Cuentos completos*. Alianza, 1978.

—. *Esperando el porvenir: homenaje a Ignacio Aldecoa*. Ediciones Siruela, 1994.

Martín-Márquez, Susan. "Coloniality and the Trappings of Modernity in *Viridiana* and *The Hand in the Trap*." *Cinema Journal*, vol. 51, no. 1, 2011, pp. 96-114.

Martín Serrano, Manuel. *Publicidad y sociedad de consumo en España*. Edicusa, 1970.

Martínez de la Hidalga, Fernando. *La ciencia ficción española*. Ediciones Robel, 2002.

Martínez-Alier, Joan. "Notas sobre el franquismo." *Papers: Revista de Sociología*, vol. 8, 1978, pp. 27-51.

Marx, Karl. "A Contribution to the Critique of Hegel's Philosophy of Right." *Karl Marx: Early Political Writings*. Cambridge UP, 1994, pp. 1-27.

"Más aviones yankis que nunca en Occidente." *Imperio: Diario de Zamora de Falange Española de las J.O.N.S.*, 9 Jan. 1955, p. 1.

Matute, Ana María. *Libro de juegos para los niños de los otros*. Editorial Lumen, 1961.

McCarraher, Eugene. *The Enchantments of Mammon: How Capitalism Became the Religion of Modernity*. Harvard UP, 2019.

Works Cited

Medina, Alberto. *Exorcismos de la memoria: políticas y poéticas de la melancolía en la España de la transición.* Ediciones Libertarias, 2001.

Menéndez Chacón, Manuel. "Algunas opiniones de calidad sobre lo que puede haber de realidad y de fantasía en torno a los famosos discos volantes", *ABC de Sevilla,* 31 Mar. 1950, p. 9.

"Mensaje de Franco a los españoles." *Imperio: Diario de Zamora de Falange Española de las J.O.N.S.,* 2 Jan. 1951, pp. 1–3.

Mercer, Leigh. "The Games Men Play: The Stock Market and the Casino." *Urbanism and Urbanity: The Spanish Bourgeois Novel and Contemporary Customs (1845–1925).* Bucknell UP, 2013, pp. 105–138.

Mesa, Roberto. *Jaraneros y alborotadores: documentos sobre los sucesos estudiantiles de febrero de 1956 en la Universidad Complutense de Madrid.* Editorial de la Universidad Complutense, 1982.

Miller, Jacques-Alain. *El partenaire síntoma.* Paidós, 2008.

Millet, Salvador. "Hayek en Barcelona." *La Vanguardia.* 23 Aug. 1949, p. 11.

Milner, Andrew. *Locating Science Fiction.* Liverpool UP, 2014.

Miracolo a Milano. Directed by Vittorio de Sica. Produzioni di Sica, 1951.

Mirowski Philip, and Dieter Plehwe, editors. *The Road from Mont Pèlerin: The Making of the Neoliberal Thought Collective.* Harvard UP, 2009.

Moix, Terenci. *El sadismo de nuestra infancia.* Kairós, 1970.

—. *El peso de la paja: Memorias. El cine de los sábados.* Plaza & Janés, 1998.

—. *Historia social del comic.* Bruguera: Ediciones B, 2007.

Molinero, Carme. *La captación de las masas. Política social y propaganda en el régimen franquista.* Cátedra, 2005.

—. "El reclamo de la 'justicia social' en las políticas de consenso del Régimen franquista." *Historia Social,* vol. 56, 2006, pp. 93–110.

Montero, Feliciano. "El modelo educativo del movimiento social católico." *Génesis y Situación de la educación social en Europa.* UNED, 2003, pp. 153–173.

Moradiellos, Enrique. *Franco: Anatomy of a Dictator.* I. B. Tauris, 2018.

Morán, Gregorio. *El cura y los mandarines. Historia no oficial del Bosque de los Letrados. Cultura y política en España, 1962–1996.* Akal, 2014.

Moreno, Luis, and Sebastià Sarasa. "Génesis y desarrollo del Estado del Bienestar en España." *Revista Internacional de Sociología,* no. 6, 1993, pp. 27–69.

Moreno Seco, Mónica. "De la caridad al compromiso: las mujeres de Acción Católica (1958–1968)" *Historia Contemporánea* 26, 2003, pp. 239–265.

Moreton, Bethany. "Our Lady of Mont Pèlerin: The 'Navarra School' of Catholic Neoliberalism." *Capitalism: A Journal of History and Economics,* vol. 2, no. 1, 2021, pp. 88–153.

Moriente Díaz, David. *España, ¿me reciben? Astronáutica y cultura popular (1957–1989).* Ediciones de la Universidad de Castilla-La Mancha, 2019.

Naredo, José Manuel. *Por una oposición que se oponga.* Anagrama, 2001.

Navarro, Vicenç. *Neoliberalismo y Estado del bienestar.* Ariel, 1997.

Navarro Rubio, Mariano. *Mis memorias. Testimonio de una vida política truncada por el Caso Matesa.* Plaza y Janés, 1991.

Nibert, David. "State Lotteries and the Legitimization of Inequality." *The Sociology of Risk and Gambling Reader,* edited by James Cosgrave. Routledge, 2006, pp. 319–338.

Nielfa, Gloria. *Mujeres y hombres en la España franquista: sociedad, economía, política, cultura.* Editorial Complutense, 2003.

Núñez, Clara Eugenia, and Gabriel Tortella Casares. *El desarrollo de la España contemporánea. Historia económica de los siglos XIX y XX.* Alianza, 2014.

Odekon, Mehmet. *The SAGE Encyclopedia of World Poverty.* Sage, 2016.

Oliver, Joan, Joan Pagès, y Pelai Pagès. *La Prensa clandestina: 1939-1956.* Planeta, 1978.

Olsen, Niklas. *The Sovereign Consumer: A New Intellectual History of Neoliberalism.* Palgrave Macmillan, 2019.

"Opinión sobre los platillos volantes." *Hoja oficial de la provincia de Barcelona.* 30 Jan. 1950, p. 2.

Ordoñez, Javier, and José Manuel Sánchez-Ron. "Nuclear Energy in Spain: From Hiroshima to the Sixties." *National Military Establishments and the Advancement of Science and Technology: Studies in 20th Century History,* edited by Paul Forman and José M. Sánchez-Ron, pp. 185–213.

Ortiz-Echagüe, Javier. *Yuri Gagarin y el conde de Orgaz: Mística y estética de la era espacial (Jorge Oteiza, Yves Klein, José Val del Omar).* Fundación Museo Jorge Oteiza, 2014.

Oslington, Paul. "God and the Market: Adam Smith's *Invisible Hand.*" *Journal of Business Ethics,* vol. 108, no. 4, 2012, pp. 429–438.

"Otros dos platillos volantes 'vistos' en Orense." *Imperio: Diario de Zamora de Falange Española de las J.O.N.S.,* 9 Jan. 1955, p. 1.

Pack, Sasha D. *Tourism and Dictatorship: Europe's Peaceful Invasion of Franco's Spain.* Palgrave Macmillan, 2006.

"Parece que darán buen resultado las explotaciones petrolíferas de Granada." *Imperio: Diario de Zamora de Falange Española de las J.O.N.S.,* 9 Jan. 1955, p. 1.

Passport to Pimlico. Directed by Henry Cornelius. Ealing Studios, 1949.

Pasulka, Diana. *American Cosmic: UFOs, Religion, Technology.* Oxford UP, 2019.

Pavlović, Tatjana. "*¡Bienvenido, Mr Marshall!* and the Renewal of Spanish Cinema." *Cine-Lit: Essays on Peninsular Film and Fiction,* edited by George Cabello-Castellet, Jaume Martí-Olivella and Guy H. Wood. Portland State UP, 1995, pp. 169–174.

—. *The Mobile Nation. España cambia de piel (1954-1964).* Intellect, 2011.

Payne, Stanley G. *The Franco Regime, 1936-1975.* University of Wisconsin Press, 1987.

Payne, Stanley and Jesus Palacios. *Franco: A Personal and Political Biography.* The University of Wisconsin Press, 2014.

Peñarroya. "Pitagorín." *Pulgarcito,* no. 1837, 1966, pp. 5–6.

Peppard, Donald M. "Government as Bookie: Explaining the Rise of Lotteries for Revenue." *Review of Radical Political Economics,* vol. 19, no. 3, 1987, pp. 56–68.

Pérez, Dionisio. "El milagro del oro que podría salvar a España." *ABC.* 9 Dec. 1934, pp. 173–178.

Pérez, Jorge. *Confessional Cinema: Religion, Film, and Modernity in Spain's Development Years, 1960-1975.* University of Toronto Press, 2017.

Pérez Galdós, Benito. *Halma.* Impr. La Guirnalda, 1895.

Pérez Olivares, Alejandro. "Abastecer, racionar... y pasar hambre. Franquismo y control social en la posguerra." *Los "Años del hambre". Historia y memoria de la posguerra franquista,* edited by Miguel Ángel Del Arco, Marcial Pons, 2020, pp. 173–194.

Pérez Perucha, Julio. *Antología crítica del cine español. 1906–1995: Flor en la sombra*. Cátedra, 1997.

Pérez Picazo, María Teresa. *Historia de España del siglo XX*. Crítica, 1996.

Pilkington, Mark. *Mirage Men: A Journey into Disinformation, Paranoia and UFOs*. Constable, 2010.

Pino Abad, Miguel. *El delito de juegos prohibidos: análisis histórico-jurídico*. Dykinson, 2011.

Plácido. Directed by Luis Garcia Berlanga. Jet Films, 1960.

"Poema terrestre dedicado a los habitantes de la luna." *Solidaridad Obrera: A.I.T. Órgano del movimiento Libertario español en Francia*. 22 Jan. 1959, p. 3.

Pope Paul VI. *Encyclical Letter of His Holiness Pope Paul VI on the Development of Peoples [Populorum progressio]*. Paulist Press, 1967.

Portero, Florentino, and Rosa Pardo, "La *política exterior*." *La época de Franco (1939–1975): Política, Ejército, Iglesia, economía y administración*, edited by Raymond Carr, Espasa Calpe, 1996, pp. 193–299.

Prados de la Escosura, Leandro. *Spanish Economic Growth, 1850–2015*. Palgrave Macmillan, 2017.

Presas i Puig, Alberto. "Science on the Periphery. The Spanish Reception of Nuclear Energy: An Attempt at Modernity?" *Minerva*, no. 43, 2005, pp. 197–218.

Preston, Paul. *Franco: A Biography*. Fontana Press, 1995.

Rada, Juan S. *60 aniversario de El Caso: semanario de sucesos*. Grupo Editorial 33, 2011.

Rancière, Jacques. "Política, identificación y subjetivación." *El reverso de la diferencia. Identidad y política*, edited by B. Arditi, 2000, Nueva Sociedad, pp. 145–152.

Raventós, Daniel, and Julie Wark. *Against Charity*. AK Press, 2018.

Reich, Rob. *Just Giving: Why Philanthropy Is Failing Democracy and How It Can Do Better*. Princeton UP, 2018.

Reig Tapia, Alberto. *Franco: el César superlativo*. Tecnos, 2005.

Rejón, Raúl. "EEUU sacrificó la salud de soldados y vecinos para silenciar Palomares, aún contaminado con plutonio." *El diario.es*. 20 Jun. 2016.

Renau, Josep. "Dibujo." *España y la paz*, 28 Sep. 1954, p. 1.

Reyes, Luis. "Y vinieron los yanquis." *El País*. 24 Sep. 1978.

Richards, Michael. "'Terror and Progress': Industrialization, Modernity, and the Making of Francoism." *Spanish Cultural Studies: An Introduction*, edited by Helen Graham and Jo Labanyi, Oxford UP, 1995, pp. 173–182.

—. *After the Civil War: Making Memory and Re-Making Spain since 1936*. Cambridge UP, 2013.

Richardson, Nathan. *Constructing Spain: The Re-Imagination of Space and Place in Fiction and Film, 1953–2003*. Bucknell UP, 2011.

Rieder, John. *Colonialism and the Emergence of Science Fiction*. Wesleyan UP, 2008.

Rist, Gilbert. *The History of Development: From Western Origins to Global Faith*. Zed Books, 2014.

Roca, Paco. *El invierno del dibujante*. Astiberri, 2010.

Rodríguez, Fermín. *Mujer y sociedad: la novelística de Concha Alós*. Orígenes, 1985.

Roglá, Vicente. *Astronáutica y espíritu*. Dirección General de Enseñanza Media, 1962. Romero de Pablos, Ana and José Manuel Sánchez Ron, *Energía nuclear en España: De la JEN al CIEMAT*. CIEMAT, 2001.

Ros Hombravella, Jacint. *Trece economistas españoles ante la economía española.* Oikos-Tau, 1975.

—. *Política económica española (1959–1973).* Blume, 1979.

Rosendorf, Neal M. *Franco Sells Spain to America: Hollywood, Tourism and Public Relations as Postwar Spanish Soft Power.* Basingstoke, UK: Palgrave Macmillan Press, 2014.

Ross, Christopher J. *Spain Since 1812.* Routledge, 2015.

Rostow, W. W. *The Stages of Economic Growth: A Non-Communist Manifesto.* Cambridge UP, 1960.

Roth, Christopher. "Ufology as Anthropology: Race, Extraterrestrials, and the Occult." *E.T. Culture: Anthropology in Outerspaces,* edited by Debbora Battaglia. Duke UP, 2005.

Roush, Wade. *Extraterrestrials.* The MIT Press, 2020.

Ríos Carratalá, Juan Antonio. *Usted puede ser feliz: La felicidad en la cultura del franquismo.* Ariel, 2013.

Rodríguez, Emma. "Juan Marsé: Es una novela más atrevida de lo que creí en su día." *El Mundo.* 22 Feb. 2001.

Rodríguez López, Emmanuel. *Por qué fracasó la democracia en España. La Transición y el régimen del '78.* Traficantes de Sueños, 2015.

—. *El efecto clase media. Crítica y crisis de la paz social.* Traficantes de Sueños, 2022.

Röpke, Wilhelm. "Liberalism and Christianity." *Modern Age,* vol. 1, no. 2, 1957, pp. 128–134.

Ruiz, Jesús. "Lotería y caridad." *El Ciervo,* no. 3, 1951, p. 2.

Salinas, Pedro. *La bomba increíble: fabulación.* Aguilar, 1988.

Salvador, Tomás. *La nave.* Ediciones Destino, 1959.

—. "La tombola." *La Vanguardia.* 14 Oct. 1960, p. 7.

Sampedro, José Luis. "Le Plan de développement espagnol dans son cadre social." *Revue Tiers Monde,* vol. 8, no. 32, 1967, pp. 1033–1041.

Sánchez Ferlosio, Rafael. *El escudo de Jotán: Cuentos reunidos.* Debolsillo, 2015.

Sánchez Jiménez, José. *50 Años de acción social: Cáritas Española (1947–1997).* Cáritas Española, 1997.

—. "Conservadores en política y reformistas en lo social. La Acción Católica y la legitimación política del régimen de Franco (1940–1960)." *Ayer,* vol. 39, 2000, pp. 165–180.

Sánchez León, Pablo. "Desclasamiento y desencanto. La representación de las clases medias como eje de una relectura generacional de la transición española." *Kamchatka,* vol. 4, 2014, pp. 63–99.

—. "¿Tan solo una guerra civil? 1936 como conquista colonial civilizadora y Yihad católica moderna" *Bajo Palabra. Revista de Filosofía,* no. 13, 2017, pp. 19–37.

Sánchez-Mazas, Miguel. "The Spanish Miracle". *Ibérica,* vol. 12, no. 10, 1964, pp. 3–5.

Sánchez Recio, Glicerio y Tascón Fernández, Julio, editors, *Los empresarios de Franco. Política y economía en España, 1936–1957.* Crítica, 2003.

Sánchez-Soler, Mariano. *Los banqueros de Franco.* Oberón, 2005.

Santoro Domingo, Pablo. "Science Fiction in Spain: A Sociological Perspective." *Science Fiction Studies,* vol. 33, no. 2, 2006, pp. 313–331.

Santos, Domingo. *Lo mejor de la ciencia-ficción española.* Martínez Roca, 1982.

Works Cited

Saz, Ismael. *España contra España: Los nacionalismos franquistas*. Marcial Pons, 2003.

Scarlett, Elizabeth. *Religion and Spanish Film: Luis Buñuel, the Franco Era, and Contemporary Directors*. The University of Michigan Press, 2014.

Schmitt, Carl. "El orden del mundo después de la segunda guerra mundial." *Revista De estudios políticos*, vol. 122, 1962, pp. 19–36.

Scully, Frank. *Behind the Flying Saucers*. New York, Holt, 1950.

Secretariado de la Junta Nacional de Semanas Sociales. *Crisis de la vivienda*. Secretariado de la Junta Nacional de Semanas Sociales, 1954.

Seed, David. *Science Fiction: A Very Short Introduction*. Oxford UP, 2011.

Segura, Julio. *La industria española y la competitividad*, Espasa-Calpe, 1992.

Semprún, Jorge. "La oposición política en España: 1956–1966." *Horizonte español II*, 1966, pp. 39–55.

Siguán, Miguel. *Del campo al suburbio; un estudio sobre la inmigración interior en España*. CSIC, 1959.

Simak, Clifford Donald. *Spacebred Generations*. Wilside Press, 2009.

Sinova, Justino. *Un siglo en 100 artículos*. La Esfera de los Libros, 2002.

Slobodian, Quinn. *Globalists: The End of Empire and the Birth of Neoliberalism*. Harvard UP, 2018.

Sontag, Susan. *Against Interpretation and Other Essays*. Anchor, 1990.

Sor Citröen. Directed by Pedro Lazaga. Pedro Masó, 1967.

Suárez, Pedro. "La crónica-reportaje sobre los 'platillos volantes'." *Imperio. Diario de Zamora de Falange Española de las J.O.N.S.*, 16 Apr. 1950, p. 4.

Sucedió en mi aldea. Directed by Antonio Santillán. Vértice, 1956.

Sueiro, Daniel. *La verdadera historia del Valle de los Caídos*, Sedmay Ediciones, 1977.

Suvin, Darko. *Metamorphoses of Science Fiction*. Peter Lang AG, 2016.

Tarancón, Vicente. *El pan nuestro de cada día dánosle hoy*. Publicaciones H.O.A.C., 1950.

Tello Lázaro, José Ángel. *Ideología y política: la Iglesia católica española, 1936–1959*. Libros Pórtico, 1984.

Thomas, Maria. *La fe y la furia. Violencia anticlerical popular e iconoclastia en España, 1931–1939*. Comares, 2014.

—. "Twentieth-Century Catholicisms: Religion as Prison, as Haven, as Clamp." *Interrogating Francoism: History and Dictatorship in Twentieth-Century Spain*, edited by Helen Graham, Bloomsbury Academic, 2016, pp. 27–48.

Tiryakian, Edward A. "Dialectics of Modernity: Reenchantment and Dedifferentiation as Counterprocesses." *Social Change and Modernity*, edited by Hans Haferkamp and Neil J. Smelser, University of California Press, 1992, pp. 78–95.

Todo es posible en Granada. Directed by José Luis Sáenz de Heredia. Chapalo Films, 1954.

Tómbola. Directed by Luis Lucia. Guion Producciones Cinematográficas, 1962.

Toscano, Alberto. "Transition Deprogrammed.' *South Atlantic Quarterly*, vol. 113, no. 4, 2014, pp. 659–835.

Trompf, Garry. "UFO Religions and Cargo Cults." *UFO Religions*, edited by Christopher Partridge, Routledge, 2003, pp. 221–238.

"Un coto de uranio se explota en Sierra Morena desde hace año y medio." *Imperio: Diario de Zamora de Falange Española de las J.O.N.S.*, 9 Jan. 1955, p. 1.

"Un platillo con tripulantes rubios." *ABC*, 10 Dec. 1954, p. 36.

"Un platillo volante resulta ser un globo." *ABC*, 17 Dec. 1954, p. 19.

"Un platillo volante sobre nuestra provincia." *Imperio. Diario de Zamora de Falange Española de las J.O.N.S*, 6 Apr. 1950, p. 3.

Valis, Noël. *Sacred Realism: Religion and the Imagination in Modern Spanish Narrative.* Yale UP, 2010.

Vázquez Montalbán, Manuel. *Crónica sentimental de España.* Lumen, 1970.

—. "Medios de comunicación de masas y consumo." *España, ¿una sociedad de consumo?* edited by Alberto Míguez, Guadiana de Publicaciones, 1970.

—. *Diccionario del Franquismo.* Dopesa, 1977.

Vegso, Roland. *The Naked Communist: Cold War Modernism and the Politics of Popular Culture.* Fordham UP, 2013.

Viestenz, William. *By the Grace of God: Francoist Spain and the Sacred Roots of Political Imagination.* University of Toronto Press, 2014.

Vigara Tauste, Ana María. "Sexo, política y subversión. El chiste popular en la época franquista." *Círculo de Lingüística Aplicada a la Comunicación*, vol. 27, no. 7, 2006, pp. 7–25.

Vilarós, Teresa. "Banalidad y biopolítica. La transición española y el nuevo orden del mundo." *Desacuerdos 2. Sobre arte, políticas y esfera pública en el estado español*, edited by Jesús Carrillo, MACBA, 2005, pp. 30–56.

Villacañas, José Luis. *Ramiro de Maeztu y el ideal de la burguesía en España.* Espasa-Calpe, Madrid, 2000.

—. *La revolución pasiva de Franco. Las entrañas del franquismo y de la transición.* Harper Collins Ibérica, 2022.

Viñas, Ángel. *Los pactos secretos de Franco con Estados Unidos: bases, ayuda económica, recortes de soberanía.* Grijalbo, 1981.

—. "Franco's Dream of Autarky Shattered: Foreign Policy Aspects in the Run-up to the 1959 Change in Spanish Economic Strategy." *Spain in an International Context, 1936–1959*, edited by Christian Leitz and David J. Dunthorn, Berghahn Books, 1999, pp. 299–318.

—. *En las garras del águila: los pactos con Estados Unidos, de Francisco Franco a Felipe González (1945–1995).* Crítica, 2003.

Vinyes, Ricard, Montse Armengou y Ricard Belis, *Los niños perdidos del franquismo.* Plaza y Janés, 2002.

Viridiana. Directed by Luis Buñuel. Films 59, Uninci, 1961.

"Visita de la Virgen de Fátima y Santas Misiones." *Imperio. Diario de Zamora de Falange Española de las J.O.N.S*, 6 Apr. 1950, p. 3.

Vogl, Joseph. *The Specter of Capital.* Stanford UP, 2015.

Walsh, Michael. *El Mundo del Opus Dei.* Plaza y Janés, 1990.

Weber, Max. *Essays in Sociology.* Oxford UP, 1946.

Weizman, Eyal. "Control in the Air." *Open Democracy*, May 2002.

Wells, H. G. *The Time Machine.* Penguin Book, 2002.

Wendt, Alexander, and Raymond Duvall. "Sovereignty and the UFO." *Political Theory*, vol. 36, no. 4, 2008, pp. 607–633.

Williams, Raymond. *The Country and the City.* Oxford UP, 1975.

—. "Advertising: The Magic System". *Problems in Materialism and Culture*. Verso, 2005.

Wojcik, Daniel. "Avertive Apocalypticism." *The Oxford Handbook of Millennialism*, edited by Catherine Wessinger, Oxford UP, 2011, pp. 66–88.

Woods Peiró, Eva. *Economy and Society*, edited by G. Roth and C. Wittich, Bedminster Press, 1968.

—. "¡Rehearsing for Modernity in *Bienvenido, Mister Marshall!" Burning Darkness: A Half Century of Spanish Cinema*, edited by Joan Ramón Resina, SUNY Press, 2008, pp. 9–26.

"Ya no son un misterio los platillos volantes." *Imperio: Diario de Zamora de Falange Española de las J.O.N.S.*, 11 Apr. 1950, p. 4.

Zenobi, Laura. *La construcción del mito de Franco: de jefe de la Legión a Caudillo de España*. Cátedra, 2011.

Žižek, Slavoj. *For They Know Not What They Do: Enjoyment as a Political Factor*. Verso, 1991.

Index

25 Years of Peace 184
1959 Stabilization and Liberalization
  Plan 2, 7, 15–16, 61, 173

ABC 1, 42, 49, 62, 69
Acción Católica 151, 153
Acción Española 7, 82
Adorno, Theodor W. 12
advertising 4, 79, 96, 104, 117, 126, 130,
  132, 133–136, 141–143, 149, 168, 174,
  181
Afinoguénova, Eugenia 16
Agamben, Giorgio 10, 59
Agustí, Ignacio 121–122
Aldecoa, Ignacio 116, 159
Aldecoa, Josefina 116
Aldiss, Brian 87
aliens 24, 46, 48, 74–76, 85, 103,
  108–109
Althusser, Louis 4
Álvarez-Buylla, Adolfo 79, 80–83
Ángel Guerra 163–164
angels 53, 59
¡Aquí hay petróleo! 65
Aragó, Ignacio María 145
Areilza, José María 64
Arizmendi, Alfonso 73
Arnold, Kenneth 37
El astronauta 103
atomic bombs 11, 38-9, 40, 42, 45, 54,
  63–64, 67, 110
Atoms for Peace 64
autarchy 2, 3, 4, 6, 10, 13, 14, 15, 24, 37,
  63, 93, 96, 117, 150, 179, 185
Azcona, Rafael 126, 168–169

Balzac, Honoré de 115
Barciela, Carlos 13, 34
Bardem, Juan Antonio 26, 117, 120,
  124–125, 129, 132–133
Barthes, Roland 67, 69, 75, 81
Beltrán, Lucas 7, 119
Benavente, Jacinto 24, 42, 45–46
Benjamin, Walter 10, 118, 128, 179, 180,
  185
¡Bienvenido, Míster Marshall! 43–45, 132, 180
Bloch, Ernst 86
Blue Division 87, 92
La bomba increíble 62
Bravo, Eduardo 49–50
Bretton Woods 21
Buero Vallejo, Antonio 25–26, 74, 77,
  106–111, 124–128
Buñuel, Luis 27, 154, 162–133, 166, 171

Cabeza rapada 159
Cadena SER 79, 131
Caillois, Roger 118, 129, 138
Calabuch 67
Calvo Serer, Rafael 7, 9, 82
Candel, Francisco 16, 153
Cánovas del Castillo, Antonio 13
capital 3, 4, 5, 7, 13, 15, 23, 26, 36–38,
  45, 62, 64, 97, 116–117, 120–122, 125,
  127, 131–135, 137–138, 140–141, 146,
  152, 160, 180–185
capitalism 3, 4, 5, 8, 9, 10, 11, 16–17, 19,
  20–6, 72, 96–98, 117–118, 128, 135,
  138, 150, 152, 180–183
Caritas 40, 151, 174, 177
Cartagena (Murcia) 35, 61

El caso 68–69

Castoriadis, Cornelius 3

Catholic Church 6, 21, 26–27, 52–53, 60, 83, 94, 117, 120, 125, 139, 141, 144–149, 151–159, 161–166, 172–174, 177

La caza 71

Cazorla, Antonio 14, 136, 151, 162

Cela, Camilo José 46

Celaya, Gabriel 24, 59

censorship 9, 69, 77, 79, 84, 86

Cerca de la ciudad 27, 155–157

Certeau, Michel de 133

Cervantes, Miguel de 106–111

chance 3, 5, 25–26, 115–119, 124–129, 133–139, 141–147, 180

charity 3, 8, 23, 27, 119, 120–122, 139, 140, 145–149, 150–159, 161–169, 170–177, 180–181, 185

Christus Dominus (1965) 153

Churchill, Winston 64

El ciervo 120, 145, 149

Cifré, Guillermo 100

Clarasó, Noel 24, 45–46

Clavero, Bartolomé 150

La codorniz 168

Cold War 5, 9, 23–24, 35–36, 38–39, 48, 50, 55, 59, 62, 71, 74, 78, 95, 108, 109, 111, 179, 185

comics 3, 24–25, 36, 41, 72–73, 76, 79, 80, 87, 96–98, 101, 103, 141, 154

Concordat with the Vatican (1953) 27, 78, 81, 154–155, 157, 172

consumption 7, 11, 16–17, 21, 76, 105, 117, 122, 125, 130, 132, 134, 162, 171, 182–184

contest 25–26, 116–117, 128–129, 130–139, 140–149

Conti, Carlos 100

Cornelius, Henry 43

cornucopianism 12, 63

Crumbaugh, Justin 104, 158, 184

CSIC 8

Dan Dare, Pilot of the Future 79, 80

DDT contra las penas 98–99, 100–104

Dean, Jodi 50

Deglané, Bobby 128, 130, 138

Deleuze, Gilles 97–98

Delibes, Miguel 65

Derrida, Jacques 3

development 1–23, 36, 39, 70, 72, 96–97, 111, 152, 159, 162, 165, 173, 176, 179–185

developmentalism 2, 4, 8, 9, 10, 14, 19, 20, 23, 58, 160–161, 179, 182

Devereux, Edward C. 123

Diego Valor 25, 73, 78–79, 80–84

Duvall, Raymond 35

Economic and Social Development Plans (1964–1967, 1968–1971 and 1972–1975) 2, 14, 152, 160

Ediciones Futuro 72

Editorial Bruguera 100

Editorial Valenciana 72

Eisenhower, Dwight 1, 44, 60, 64

Elijo Garay, Leopoldo 156

Enguídanos, Pascual 25, 72, 77, 84, 86

Enrique y Tarancón, Vicente 134

Entreacto 59

Esa pareja feliz 129, 132–136

Escobar, Josep 100, 103

Escrivá de Balaguer, José María 19

Esperando el porvenir 116

Esta cara de la luna 163

Eucken, Walter 7

European Economic Community 9, 84

exile 39, 40, 47, 62, 67, 85, 93

fables 2, 3, 5, 23, 25–26, 107, 120, 133, 136, 147, 185

Falange Española 78, 87, 91–96, 151–154, 177

fascism 10, 20, 39, 78, 85

Feijoo, Benito Jerónimo 51–52, 76

Felices Pascuas 26, 120, 124

Fernán Gómez, Fernando 123

Fernández de la Mora, Gonzalo 7, 22

Fernández Santos, Jesús 159

Fiestas 26, 129, 141, 143–144, 147

First Plan of Economic and Social Development (1963–1967) 61

flying saucer 24, 31–32, 35–38, 40–49, 50–59, 61–62, 70, 75, 84, 103–104, 106–107, 110

Index

Foucault, Michel 10, 104
Fraga, Manuel 21–22, 38, 104–105, 184
Franco, Francisco 1, 2, 3, 4, 5, 6, 7, 9,
    10, 12, 13–19, 20, 23–27, 31, 33, 36,
    40–42, 48, 52–53, 60–63, 72–78, 82,
    94, 96–97, 101, 103, 105, 108, 111,
    115, 117–118, 122–124, 129, 131–132,
    137, 141, 147, 149, 150, 151–152, 154,
    157, 162, 166, 177, 182, 184
Fraser, Benjamin 76
Friedman, Milton 10, 182
Fuertes, Gloria 61

Gagarin, Yuri 58–59
Gajić, Tatjana 6, 93
Galbraith, John Kenneth 17
gambling 5, 23, 25–26, 128, 134–135, 147,
    181, 185
gambling houses 181
game in company 120, 123–126
games of chance 3, 5, 25–26, 117, 122,
    124, 129, 130, 147, 180
García Berlanga, Luis 26–27, 43–44, 54,
    67, 117, 129, 132, 154, 162, 168
García-Donoso, Daniel 6
Garrigues, Antonio 131
Garvía, Roberto 122–123
Gaudium et Spes (1965) 153
Gaulle, Charles de 82
Giménez, Carlos 154
Giner, Eugenio 100
Girón de Velasco, José Antonio 94
Gómez López-Quiñones, Antonio
    117–118
Goya, Francisco de 46
Goytisolo, Juan 26, 117, 129, 141–147,
    159
Graeber, David 10
Gramsci, Antonio 115
Grazia, Victoria de 11

Halma 163–164
Harbou, Thea von 89
Harris, Marvin 44
Hayek, Friedrich von 7, 119, 182
Heinlein, Robert A. 87
Hermandad Obrera de Acción Católica
    (HOAC) 153, 172

Historias de la radio 26, 129, 137–139, 141
Hoy es fiesta 124–128
hunger 40–43, 89, 101, 179

Ibáñez, Francisco 77, 98–99
Ilie, Paul 101
Imperio 31, 32, 35, 55, 56, 104
indicative planning 2, 14
inner exile 25, 77, 101
Instituto de Investigaciones y
    Experiencias Cinematográficas (IIEC)
    132
Instituto Nacional de Industria (INI) 13,
    152
Instituto Nacional de Técnica
    Aeroespacial (INTA) 63
International Eucharistic Congress
    141–142, 147
International Monetary Fund 2
Iris de Paz 54
Irving, Washington 65

Jameson, Fredric 4, 20–21, 73–76
Jarnés, Enrique 78–79, 80–83
Jung, Carl G. 49, 53–54, 106
Junta de Energía Nuclear 63
Junta de Investigaciones Atómicas 63
Los jueves, milagro 54
Jutglar, Antoni 149, 153
Juventud Obrera Católica (JOC) 171–174

Keller, Patricia 6
Kindelán, Alfredo 42
Kojève, Alexandre 82–83

Labanyi, Jo 6, 19, 77, 155–157
Lacan, Jacques 166–167
Lang, Fritz 89
Lazaga, Pedro 27, 159, 162
Lécera (Zaragoza) 49
Ledesma, Ramiro 108
Lenin, Vladimir 85
Lévi-Strauss, Claude 111
Libro de juegos para los niños de otros 159
Lindstrom, Lamont 44
López-Bravo, Gregorio 2
López Rodó, Laureano 2, 14, 18, 93–94
lottery 44, 115, 120–127, 133–134, 181

208 *Fables of Development*

Löwith, Karl 12
Luchadores del espacio 72
Lucia, Luis 154–156
Lukács, George 76
Luxemburg, Rosa 162

Maeztu, Ramiro de 7, 8, 19, 20, 52, 82, 108
Marcelino, pan y vino 27, 154–159
Marsé, Juan 27, 154, 163, 171–177
Marsh, Steven 6, 44, 168
Marshall, George C. 31
Marshall Plan 1, 2, 24, 31, 36, 38, 40, 42, 44–45, 116
Marsuf, vagabundo del espacio 25, 95
Martians 47, 54, 74–75, 98, 101, 103–104, 107
Martín Gaite, Carmen 116, 159
martyrdom 12
Marx, Karl 115
Matute, Ana María 159
Maurras, Charles 82
Metropolis 89
military bases 11, 23, 33–34, 96, 98
Miller, Jacques-Alain 167
Millet, Salvador 119
Ministry of Information and Tourism 98, 183–184
Miracolo a Milano 43
Mito 25, 77, 106–111
modernization theory 11, 77, 183
Moix, Terenci 53, 100, 140
Mont Pèlerin Society 7–9, 119
Moreton, Bethany 8–9, 14, 182
El mundo sigue 123

Naredo, José Manuel 183
National-Catholicism 22, 77–78, 83, 141
NATO 39, 84
Navarra School 7–8, 19
Navarro, Vicenç 152
Navarro Rubio, Mariano 2, 152
La nave 25, 73, 87–89, 90–96
Nazarín 163
Els nens perduts del franquisme 154
neoliberalism 8, 19, 21, 181–184
Nixon, Richard 9
NO-DO 97, 120

oikonomia 10
oil 34–37, 63–69
Opus Dei 2, 7–9, 19, 20–26, 78, 93, 166
ordoliberalism 7–8, 152
Organización Nacional de Ciegos 122
Organization for European Economic Co-operation 2
Ortega y Gasset, José 92
La oscura historia de la prima Montse 27, 154, 171–177
Oteiza, Jorge 58
Otero Navascués, José María 64
outer space 69, 71–79, 85, 96, 101, 103–105, 110–111, 185
Outer Space Treaty 71

Pack, Sasha 104
Pact of Madrid 2, 20, 23, 33–35, 60, 63–64, 78
Palomares 34, 67, 109, 180
Paracuellos 154
Partido Comunista de España (PCE) 95, 175
Paso, Alfonso 124
passive revolution 9
Passport to Pimlico 43
Pavlovi, Tatjana 6–7
Payne, Stanley 2, 184
Peñarroya, José 100–103
Pérez, Dionisio 62
Pérez, Jorge 6, 10, 22, 160
Pérez Embid, Florentino 7, 9, 82
Pérez Galdós, Benito 85, 163
Pitagorín 105
Plácido 27, 154, 162–169, 170
Pope Paul VI 1
Primo de Rivera, José Antonio 91–92
providence 4, 5, 10, 12, 26, 33, 60, 63, 118–119, 120–121, 137–138, 141, 144, 146, 160
providential capitalism 5, 23, 26

quinielas 122–123, 134

radio 25–26, 32, 61, 72–73, 78–79, 83, 104, 129, 130–139, 140–142, 168–169, 170, 180–181
raffles 5, 25–26, 116–119, 120, 136–137, 141, 144–146

Index

Ramírez, Pedro Luis 96
Reagan, Ronald 182
Red Scare 24, 74
remittances 7, 15
Renau, Josep 66–67
La resaca 159
Richards, Michael 14, 152
Ridruejo, Dionisio 91–92
Robledo de Chavela, NASA Space Station 35
Roca, Paco 100
Rodríguez, Braulio "Bayo" 79
Rodríguez, Emmanuel 9
Roglá, Vicente 56
Rojo, Luis Ángel 15
Röpke, Wilhelm 7, 26, 152
Rostow, Walter Whitman 17–18
Ruiz, Jesús 120

Sáenz de Heredia, José Luis 24, 26, 37, 65, 117, 129, 137
La saga de los Aznar 25, 73, 77–79, 84–85
Sales, Pepe 57, 179
Salinas, Pedro 62
Salvador, Tomás 25, 73, 78, 87–89, 90–96, 145
Salvia, Rafael 24, 37, 65
Sampedro, José Luis 15
Sánchez, José María 157
Santas Misiones 55
Santoro, Pablo 72, 76
Sardá, Juan 7, 119
Sástago (Zaragoza) 1
Sastre, Alfonso 116
Saura, Carlos 71
Scarlett, Elizabeth 6, 166
Schmitt, Carl 38–39
Schumpeter, Joseph 7
science fiction 24–25, 71–77, 86–89, 95–97, 106, 111, 180–181
Second Vatican Council 27, 153, 161, 172
secularization 6, 12, 22
Sesma, Fernando 49, 50
Sica, Vittorio de 43
Siguán, Miguel 153
Simak, Clifford D. 87–88
Smith, Adam 5, 9, 119
social imaginaries 3, 4–6, 138, 180

social security 150–152, 176
Sociedad de Amigos del Espacio 49
Solidaridad Obrera 47
Sontag, Susan 73
Sor Citroën 27, 154, 159, 160–162
Spanish Civil War 12–14, 41–42, 49, 52–53, 63, 71, 77, 86–87, 95, 129, 163, 166
Spanish economic miracle 1, 3, 7, 12–16, 23, 43, 143, 160, 182–185
Stackelberg, Heinrich von 7
Strauss, Lewis L. 64
Suanzes, Juan Antonio 96–97
Suvin, Darko 76

technocracy 87, 105
technocrats 2, 7, 8, 9, 14, 17, 19, 21, 61, 78, 94, 179
technology 11, 24–25, 35, 38, 41, 54, 56, 58, 59, 61–64, 70, 88, 95, 97–98, 101, 103, 110, 179
Thatcher, Margaret 182
theodicy 9, 60, 181
El tigre de Chamberí 96
The Time Machine 88
Tío Vivo 100–103
Todo es posible en Granada 24, 35–37, 65, 137
Tómbola 119
tourism 7, 21–23, 98, 103–105, 180–184
Truman, Harry S. 2, 11–12, 39, 80

ufology 41, 49, 50, 58, 106, 109, 110, 111
UFOs 5, 24, 35–37, 46, 49, 50–53, 109
Ullastres, Alberto 2, 7
Últimas tardes con Teresa 174
UMMO 50
UNESCO 94
uneven development 4, 185
United Nations 1, 31, 33, 64, 82
uranium 24, 35–36, 62–65
USA 1, 2, 4, 11, 20–24, 33–39, 41–45, 50–51, 60–69, 80, 82, 85, 137, 180
USSR 16, 38, 61, 72, 75, 87
utopian surplus 86

Vajda, Ladislao 154–158
Val del Omar, José 58

Valis, Noël 6
Valley of the Fallen 9, 122
vanishing mediator 8, 19, 20–22
Vázquez Montalbán, Manuel 17, 38, 101, 116, 118, 129, 130, 135, 182
Viestenz, William 6
Villacañas, José Luis 8, 9, 20
Vinyes, Ricard 154
Viridiana 27, 154, 162–171

Walters, Vernon 9
Weber, Max 12, 16, 19, 20–22
Wells, H. G. 86, 88, 91
Wendt, Alexander 35
Williams, Raymond 130, 162
World Bank 2

Žižek, Slavoj 20–21

Printed and bound by CPI Group (UK) Ltd, Croydon, CR0 4YY
01/04/2024

14477754-0002